A CLUTCH OF CURIOUS CHARACTERS

A Clutch of Curious
CHARACTERS

SELECTED AND INTRODUCED BY
Richard Glyn Jones

Xanadu

British Library Cataloguing in Publication Data

A clutch of curious characters.—(Strange but true; 2)
  1. Biography
  I. Jones, Richard Glyn   II. Series
  920′.02   CT104
  ISBN 0–947761–02–0

First published 1984 by Xanadu Publications Ltd
5 Uplands Road, London N8 9NN

Distributed by WHS Distributors
St John's House, East Street, Leicester LE1 6NE

Typeset by Northumberland Press Ltd

Printed and bound in Great Britain by
Richard Clay (The Chaucer Press), Bungay, Suffolk

Contents

Introduction

In these times, when individuality tends to be stifled by the pressures of job-security and the lures of creditworthiness, when the extremely rich keep a tediously low profile, when rebellion is itself regimented—though I suppose there must have been an original Punk, once—and when an eccentric is a TV performer parading a few carefully-rehearsed mannerisms for the umpteenth time ... in such times as these, it is refreshing to examine the lives of a score or so of people who resolutely refused to fit in.

They are not the usual crowd of eccentrics and loonies whose exploits have filled the pages of so many recent books. There is no Squire Mytton, no Princess Caraboo, no Romeo Coates. Instead, I have looked for less familiar figures, and have tried to do them some justice by allowing a reasonable amount of space for each one; their stories are well worth telling, and they deserve something more than a mere listing of their oddities. The quality of the writing speaks, I hope, for itself.

What these characters have in common is a refusal to accept the status quo. They did not 'know their place' and they all, in their very different ways, tried to do something about it. With Anne Hicks, Benoît, Dan Graham and even Cagliostro it was the relatively straight-forward matter of trying to improve their own situations in life, although they found extraordinary ways in which to do it. Colonel Baker, Antonina Dashwood and The Boy Jones all 'went too far'—beyond the permitted limits of behaviour into what was for all of them a very dangerous hinterland. For Ludovic Muggleton, Canon Townsend and Miss Nightingale the problem was to try and change the whole world, and it is interesting to note that out of all the adventures described in the book theirs had the happiest, if not the most successful, outcomes.

Indeed, as the collection grew it began to resemble a series of moral or cautionary tales. Many of the characters typify a particular characteristic that exists to a greater or lesser extent in all of us: Christopher Sykes exemplifies the Snob, Dan Graham the Bully, James Cook the Hypocrite and Canon Townsend the Optimist, while The Boy Jones seems to be nothing but Curiosity, de Montesquiou all Conceit, Florence Nightingale the very spirit of Determination. The moral must remain unpointed, however, for although most of them suffered appallingly and many came to terrible ends, they all acted from some odd inner impulse and could not have done otherwise than they did. This is, in essence, what makes them 'characters' rather than eccentrics, mere schemers or out-and-out lunatics; the term denotes something of strength as well as strangeness.

The parabolic nature of the book was unintentional. I did make some efforts, however, to include as many *female* characters as I could, as they are usually left out of such collections, either through sheer neglect or on the grounds that in the past a woman's subservient role left her little scope for the expression of individuality. There is something in the latter view, and the women who do figure in the book tend to be ones who fought against this very thing, but even so, they are outnumbered by the men by approximately two to one, and the only consolation I can offer is that this proportion is considerably lower than in most other collections of this sort. Florence Nightingale is scarcely unknown to history, of course, but I have included her because for many people the legend of the gentle 'lady with the lamp' still prevails over the much stranger truth about her, even despite the celebrity of Strachey's account. But a character she was, and her story is fascinating for those who may not know it.

The collection as a whole contains a wealth of out-of-the-way social history, psychological oddity and some perfect examples of the biographer's craft, and if these add to its appeal, so much the better— but they are incidental. I compiled it, and I hope that you may be tempted to look further into it, for no better reason than that it is amusing to read of such things.

THE EDITOR

DEREK HUDSON

The Duke of Wellington's Miss J.

The reader may well ask 'Who was Miss J.?' If we are to consider one of the oddest but most fascinating episodes in the nineteenth century, we may as well begin at the beginning.

Until the year 1889 the public had no idea whatever that Miss J. played any part in the life of the great Duke of Wellington, or indeed that she ever existed. In that year there appeared in New York a book entitled '*The Letters of the Duke of Wellington to Miss J., 1834–1851*. Edited, with extracts from the diary of the latter, by Christine Terhune Herrick.' At the outset, Mrs Herrick explained that the book was based on the Duke's original letters and on the diary of Miss J., which had 'lain for years in a trunk in the attic of a country-house within thirty miles of New York city'. Little notice seems to have been taken of the volume in America, but when T. Fisher Unwin published it in England in 1890 it precipitated a vigorous controversy.

On the face of it, it seemed almost incredible that the Duke should have been able to keep up an acquaintance with a lady over a period of seventeen years, during which he wrote her nearly 400 letters, without any whisper of the fact reaching his biographers or the general public until thirty-eight years after his death. Wellington's old friend Lady de Ros thought the first few letters might be authentic, but on the whole plumped for a forgery. Even the name 'Christine Terhune Herrick' was alleged to have 'an air of unreality' (though actually she was an established American author who wrote under the name of Marion Harland).

Others contended that the Duke's style as a letter-writer was un-mistakable—and asked who would go to the pains of concocting such an elaborate forgery anyway? In the end they were fully justified, for after about ten years Sir Herbert Maxwell had an opportunity of inspecting the letters and the diary, and in the second edition of his Life of Wellington established, once and for all, that they were perfectly genuine. He also revealed that Miss J. was really Miss A. M. Jenkins, and that most of the letters had been addressed to her at 42 Charlotte Street, Portland Place, 'a few having been sent to the care of a tradesman in the same street'.

History was therefore enriched beyond doubt by 390 letters of the Duke of Wellington. Fisher Unwin brought out another edition of the letters in 1924, with a valuable introduction by W. H. R. Trowbridge, and in *The Duke*, published in 1931, Philip Guedalla paid due heed to them, summarizing the long correspondence in eight carefully written pages. But neither Trowbridge nor Guedalla, nor anyone else, has been able to answer quite all the questions we should like to ask about this historical and psychological curiosity.

The early stages of Wellington's and Miss J.'s acquaintance can perhaps be rationally explained by what is known of the occasional romantic inclinations of gentlemen in their sixties. The Duke was then a widower of sixty-five, while in 1834 Miss J. was a very beautiful girl of about twenty, deeply religious and convinced of an evangelical mission. Having succeeded in converting a condemned criminal,[1] she turned to higher things and decided 'to write to the Duke upon the necessity of a new birth unto righteousness'. To her first letter, dated January 15, 1834, she received an acknowledgement by return of post, and on April 24 she handed in a Bible at the Duke's London house.

The Duke failed to acknowledge the Bible, and Miss J. heard nothing from him for several months, until she received a letter dated August 27 expressing a wish to meet her. (It is pertinent to point out—and Guedalla does so—that the Duke's great friend Mrs Arbuthnot died in the first week of August.) The suggestion was accepted by Miss J., and Wellington's next letter has the sentence: 'Although the Duke is not in the habit of visiting young unmarried ladies with whom he is not acquainted, he will not decline to attend Miss J.' The meeting took place on November 12, and was sufficiently extraordinary.

Before seeing the Duke Miss J. prayed earnestly for guidance, and declared that she was directed to put on her 'old *turned* dark green merino gown, *daily* worn' and 'not to be decorated in any way likely to attract notice'. On entering the room in which the Duke was waiting she was pleasantly surprised to see that he had 'a beautiful, silver head' such as she had 'always from childhood admired'. 'This is very kind of

---

[1] Evidently a common pursuit amongst young ladies of this period; see 'The Converted Murderer'—Ed.

your Grace!' said Miss Jenkins. The Duke received her hand 'graciously and respectfully—but spoke not a word'.

The pair sat down in chairs on each side of the fireplace and, taking up a large Bible, Miss J. read to the Duke the opening verses of the third chapter of St John's Gospel. When she reached the words 'Ye must be born again', she pointed emphatically at her visitor. To her astonishment, she found her hand seized by the Duke, who exclaimed, '"Oh, *how* I *love* you! *how* I *love* you!' repeating the same over and over and over again with increasing energy.' This was his first remark. Miss Jenkins commented in her diary that God seemed to have struck the Duke dumb on beholding her. 'He must have influenced the Duke of Wellington to love me above every other lady upon earth from the first moment he beheld me.'

They did not meet again for several weeks. Miss J. promised to write to the Duke, but found when she attempted to put pen to paper that 'such was not the will of God'. The Duke himself was exceptionally busy, for the Whig Government had been defeated and he was acting temporarily as Prime Minister and three Secretaries of State, while a courier dashed to Italy to retrieve Sir Robert Peel. Nevertheless he found time to write to Miss J. and tell her he would call upon her on December 23. The following is Miss Jenkins' account of this interview:

'During the next visit from the Duke he exclaimed, speaking of his feeling for me, 'This must be for life!' twice over successively. He then asked me if I felt sufficient for him to be with him a whole life, to which I replied: "*If it be the will of God*". I observed much excitement about him, and he in a very hurried manner told me that he was going on a visit to the King. This led me to reply, "I wish you were going on a visit to *The King*," which he evidently interpreted to mean The King of kings. He left me hastily, saying he purposed returning in a short time. In the interim I locked my door and knelt down, beseeching God to be with me and protect me, showing me what he would have me do under such marvellous circumstances. Forgetting that the door was fastened, I was obliged on the Duke's return to explain wherefore, stating that it is written, 'When thou hast shut thy door, pray to thy Father which is in secret, and thy Father which seeth in secret shall reward thee openly'; adding, "*Therefore* I locked the door when you were gone, Your Grace, to kneel down and ask God to take care of me." On hearing this his eyes dropped, but he said nothing. On his asking me why I had not written to him during his absence from town, I replied, "Because *God* would not let me"; when his eyes again fell, and he was silent.'

Clearly the affair was not now proceeding as the Duke had hoped. No one would be surprised to hear that—having discovered that he had to deal with someone who, however beautiful, suffered from a form of religious mania—the Duke had decided for the future to leave Miss J.'s letters unanswered. But this is just what he did not do. It is obvious that from the first he had conceived for Miss J. a strong affection which enabled him for many years (though not quite for ever) to tolerate a degree of eccentricity and tediousness which most people could not have put up with for a fortnight.

It is also perfectly clear that Miss Jenkins was in love with the Duke and hoped to become the Duchess of Wellington. When the Duke told her 'This must be for life!' she presumed that he spoke of marriage. As for herself, she felt she 'should confer as high an honor on a Prince in bestowing my hand on him as he could on me in receiving it'. But the Duke had different ideas. When he asked her 'What would be said, if I, a man of seventy years of age, nearly, were to take in marriage a lady young enough to be my Granddaughter?' she commented sadly in her diary:

> '*Alas! Alas!* how deceitful is the human heart! For I am convinced that although the Duke *wrote* thus, there was not a moment during our acquaintance when if I had *not* been *by the Grace of God* what I was and am that he would have thought I was too young to bow down before me with the most sinful adulation.'

Was it, perhaps, a mild feeling of remorse towards this beautiful, pious, well-meaning—but oh how wearisome!—creature that induced the Duke to keep up a correspondence with her for the next sixteen years? Flattering though the attentions of a pretty girl must have been to him, it is astonishing that the great man of the Realm, the hero of Waterloo, could have found time in his exceptionally busy public life to answer these interminable screeds written, as he once complained, 'with much celerity, in light coloured ink'. But probably behind the iron exterior there was loneliness, and it was something to have the interest of a fellow being in his health, his family bereavements, even his eternal welfare. Although Miss J. continually and endlessly rebuked him— once she wrote 'nineteen sides of paper under three covers'—he bore it all with wonderful patience. Wisely, he never committed his affection to paper in very striking terms, but many of his letters show a tender side of his character not revealed elsewhere.

He wrote her seventy-eight letters in 1835 and fifty-six in 1836. Then his output dropped, and three years, 1841 to 1843, were entirely unproductive. But somehow or other Miss J. got him started again, and in 1844 he wrote her fifty-five letters and in 1845 thirty-two. He even called on her several times, and gave her his portrait in wax on a visiting card.

In 1846 Miss J. upbraided him once too often for an 'unkind silence'. 'If you could have attended to anything so trifling as what you might read in the Newspapers about Me!' wrote the Duke, now seventy-seven, 'You might have seen that in the last week I was occupied at a distance from London during five days out of the seven and that in that space of time I have travelled and rode little short of 800 miles.' And then he made a solemn pronouncement: 'You shall not again have reason to complain of disappointment. I announce to you that I will write no more.'

Despite this resolution, the Duke was writing again in a few weeks' time in reply to a letter about a financial transaction of Miss J.'s, written in so involved a style that the Duke concluded she was asking him for a loan. Impersonal and dignified, he declared: 'I will give her any reasonable assistance she can require from me; when she will let me know in clear distinct Terms what is the Sum she requires. But I announce again: that I never will write upon any other Subject.' Miss J. took this very hardly, for, to do her justice, she had not intended to ask for a loan. 'O my God,' she wrote in her diary, 'wherefore hast Thou thought proper to let Satan try and distress me in this unanticipated manner?'

But it would be unprofitable to examine further the out-pourings of the unfortunate Miss J., unless indeed for their psychological significance. It was probably largely from motives of pity that the Duke, even after 1846, still intermittently continued the correspondence—though for the last eighteen months of his life he was silent. Miss J., of course, went on writing. When she heard the 'awful blow' of the Duke's death she was 'riveted to her seat and speechless'.

Soon afterwards she departed to America to stay with her sister; but her peculiarities made it impossible for them to live peacefully together. She died in New York in 1862—leaving her only claim to fame, her diary, and the Duke's letters, to await the attentions of Mrs Christine Terhune Herrick.

We are told that Miss Jenkins was very beautiful, but it seems that no portrait of her has come down to us. If we had one, probably we should see in it the most convincing explanation of those 390 letters.

CHRISTOPHER SYKES

Behind the Tablet

'So, Uncle, there you are.'
—Hamlet.

I like to reflect that my name may be immortal; that though it may be forgotten before Shakespeare's sonnets are, it will live as long as certain monuments of Princes. It is inscribed on a tablet over the portal of a renowned royal chapel. If you read the legend, you may learn that a man bearing the same Christian and surnames as myself was for many years the friend of the Prince with whose name the chapel is so intimately connected; that he often worshipped God in this same temple in company with this Prince; that the Prince in memory of his greatly valued friend erected this tablet; and so on. It runs for about eight lines. Well, that is not an immortality to run very far against powerful rhyme, but it is better than nothing, and I am sure that my uncle, Christopher Sykes, would have been very touched and grateful. It is his reward. He liked fame, and fame in this form would have suited his taste very well. I am glad that he did get something out of his long career of painful, of agonizing devotion. Many hundreds of visitors to the chapel must see the tablet every year, and I suppose a few score of them trouble to read the legend over the rich Gothic porch, and of these last a few may pause at a dim evocation of some noble companionship of yore. None of them, I feel sure, guess at the appalling story which lies behind the simple words.

The story begins a long way away both in place and time from the holy vulgarities of the royal chapel. It begins, roughly speaking, in the latter half of the eighteenth century on the chill wolds of East Yorkshire, in the house of Christopher's father.

It is a weakness of our imagination, a constant falsification of understanding by the artistry of memory, that we so easily think of the past in terms of its most exquisite masterpieces. Fielding showed us of what

14

raw savage stuff eighteenth-century life in England was made, but we persist in imagining that ferocious epoch as one enormous picture by Sir Joshua Reynolds, a limitless minuet, a dream of colonnades, porticoes, and classical palaces. I doubt whether its most probable virtues, its stability and harmony, the 'sweetness of life' extolled (in old age) by Talleyrand, existed at all noticeably outside small choice circles. In the person of my hero's father the eighteenth century lived long into the nineteenth on those then remote uplands, and the last glimpse of the age of reason which men had through him did not recall Lord Chesterfield so forcibly as Squire Western.

He was famous in his day. In such centres of sporting culture as Yorkshire, Melton Mowbray, and Newmarket, he is not quite forgotten even now. He was called Sir Tatton Sykes. Frequent references to this baronet occur in the novels of Surtees, in which he figures generally as 'old Tat', also as 'Sir Tat', and 'Tatters'; and I have noticed that it is often difficult to determine whether he is treated as a figure of fun or veneration in those splendid romances. Possibly as both. He lived to extreme old age, being born before the Duke of Wellington and not dying till the eighteen sixties. From youth to death he never weakened in an almost insane passion for fox-hunting, racing, and the very companionship of horses. It formed the whole basis of his life and character. He never sold a horse if he could avoid doing so, and yet, oddly enough, he parted at a cheap price with the best and most famous of his breed. Taking Surtees as my authority once more, I find myself in doubt as to whether he was looked on as an astute or a poor judge of the animal he so madly worshipped.

As might be expected, he was an eccentric. Until his death in the age of peg-top trousers he wore the long high-collared coat of the regency, chokers, frills, and mahogany topped boots. Although he had received the education of a gentleman, at Westminster and Brasenose College, Oxford, he spoke in the dialect of Yorkshire throughout his life, using extreme modes of that extreme variation of English speech. This affectation was very typical of the English eighteenth century. He was very vain, he exploited the then meagre arts of publicity with shrewdness. His engraved picture and later his daguerreotype, taken in the act of patting or, as portrayed by Sir Francis Grant, riding one of his numerous favourite horses, or reposing in his boots after hunting, with a smile on his countenance fairly bursting with benevolence and cunning, these likenesses were widely circulated among sportsmen of the time. Ludicrous and yet respected, a charlatan in some ways, and yet a homely, comforting, familiar figure, a symbol and a caricature of England, I dare say he was revered and mocked in equal degrees. He was much loved too. To the credit of our humanity, the last departing tenants of an age received an affectionate farewell as a rule. 'Tat' was almost the last human being of the eighteenth century to leave the world, and his fellowmen honoured him greatly for it. But they would have honoured him a little less, I feel, if they had known how he preserved to the last the more revolting vices of the brutal age which produced him.

His pleasant Adamesque house was a barbaric hell. He ruled over his family with the vicious rage of a stone-age tyrant. That fierce and obscure revival of parental oppression which, according to its historian, Samuel Butler, first became noticeable in the mid-eighteenth century and did not decline till some eighty or ninety years later, this extraordinary relapse found absolute personification in the home life of the old sportsman. He begot a large family: two sons and six daughters. On them he imposed simple and intolerable rules of life: that the virtues resided in rising at dawn in Winter and Summer, on no hot water, on no creature comforts (the girls slept in one small room), and on submission to frequent applications of the paternal whip. An enigmatical portrait survives of his wife, painted by Sir Francis Grant. Resignation and hardness are oddly combined in her features; one wonders whether she made this bestial manner of life less unbearable for her children. There are traditions that in Yorkshire she was of no account in the house, but that in London, where she was a hostess of fashion, Tatton went in considerable awe of her. As the children spent most of their life in Yorkshire, it may be taken as fairly certain that, even if she possessed a kind heart, which I doubt, their sufferings were little mitigated; and with increasing age the old tyrant relinquished none of his heavy rule.

When his sons returned from the squalor of school they were often greeted with flagellations which must have made them sigh for the birches of Harrow; on one occasion the discipline was administered because, on unpacking, the unmanly frippery of tooth-brushes was discovered among the effects. The elder boy, being the weaker of the two, was treated with a special concern. The heroic old father was once seen armed with a whip driving the child barefoot and screaming down the drive. It is not surprising that normal growth was contorted on this poisonous ground. That the two boys should have grown up to detest their father was natural and even proper. What I find interesting is the extraordinary divergence in character, divergence both in protest from the paternal type and from one another, which their later history manifested. The elder son, Tatton, turned into a sensitive, bitter, eccentric, loveless man. What the younger son Christopher became it is my purpose to show.

One thing only did the two brothers have in common. The forms of escape which they chose were in both cases profoundly romantic. The second Tatton put himself at the greatest possible distance from the world; he sought consolation in Oriental travel, in building quantities of Gothic churches, in solitude. His strange character was strangest in the conjunction of a harsh aptitude for business and this enthralling preoccupation with a dim and imaginary past. Christopher, on the other hand, sought refuge in the glitter of life. He was a true Quixote; he was one of the few beings to whom the term can be applied accurately. Into the loud vulgarity of rich society he stepped all innocently, in the spirit and indeed with the air and appearance of a paladin of old; his one abiding fault, grave as it was, was essentially a fault of blindness.

I may as well blurt it out at the beginning, for there is, I fear, no avoiding the painful truth: that Christopher was a shocking snob and his tragedy another moral lesson. It furnishes a sermon which is rarely out of season in class-conscious England, but among the causes why I have hesitated before delivering the homily is my consciousness of what great talents have gone before me in this particular pulpit. Sir Max Beerbohm and Mr Desmond MacCarthy have already overwhelmed congregations with this theme, and I only down pulpit-fright by the recognition of a clear distinction in kind between the calamities of Maltby, Braxton, and Monsieur Bouret,[1] and the fate of Christopher. For whereas my predecessors have dwelt on the woe and ruin attending frustrated snobbism, Christopher illustrates a cruder and older moral: the chastisement which Mammon inflicts on his favourites, the hell to which men can be led by way of the great plush paradises of this world. The story which follows is not new, but neglect may have made it unfamiliar.

At the age of twenty Christopher appears before the world. There is a crayon sketch of him, by Sir Francis Grant as usual, made when he was an undergraduate at Cambridge University around 1850. Very tall, very slender, noble in countenance, the melancholy of the eyes is

[1] See 'Maltby and Braxton' in *Seven Men* by Sir Max Beerbohm, and 'Snobbishness', an essay by Desmond MacCarthy which includes a description of the sufferings experienced by Monsieur Bouret in his attempts to become the intimate friend of Louis XV of France. Mr MacCarthy's essay is published in a volume entitled *Experience*.

as yet empty and the classical features lacking in strength. A pale, charming face, slightly epicene in its unusual beauty.

When his second son came of age, old Tatton provided him with comfortable circumstances. He was given a pleasant Jacobean manor-house not far from Beverley, in Yorkshire, which, for the sake of economy, he was commanded to share with a maternal uncle, Sir Henry Foulis. It was the hope of old Tatton that at this house, Branting-ham Thorpe, Christopher would become another hero of the hunting field in the country of Holderness, Sir Henry Foulis being his artful though not subtle choice for the furtherance of the plan. This baronet was another, though less volcanic, survival of the former century. His portrait shows him in early middle age, before our period, with ginger curls clustering about his forehead, his hearty countryman's features twisted into an expression of Roman majesty, his immense muscular hands clutching a book and doing what they can to look languid and refined. Tatton felt that such a guardian, knowing nothing of the vanities of London life, would soon wean Christopher from the glitter of his mother's drawing-room (in which he had already achieved some youthful success) and confirm him in the virile ambitions of the chase. But the flexibility of Christopher's nature probably made his father overestimate its weakness. Years of withstanding the Tattonian oppres-sion had taught Christopher much, and he found Sir Henry Foulis easy game. He loaded him with the tedious side of life at Brantingham Thorpe, and thus gave himself more leisure for his major task: the conquest of London.

During the 'fifties his progress in conquest was gradual. There were reasons for this; Tatton's disapproval was to be avoided, and the oligarchy of fashion was in a mood of fierce exclusion. At that time the 'rule of the Dandies', as club historians have termed it, was rapidly declining but was by no means ended. They were fighting their last rearguard action. We think of the dandies to-day with sentimental affection, as being, one and all, men of the stamp of d'Orsay or Bulwer Lytton, but contemporary records tell a very different story. They are described as sitting grouped in the clubs, in the theatres, wherever fashion congregated, sunk in dull silence, broken only by loud insults hurled at any one whose chance appearance or manner happened to displease them. They had taken the art of offensive snobbism to a pitch hardly attempted before. Their spiritual descendants are easily recog-nized to-day, but in those days such people possessed, or had recently possessed, a very important degree of power. They had ruled the clubs, and from the clubs they had influenced not only the great families but in large measure the House of Commons, for even after the Reform Bill there existed an intimate connection between such places as Boodles, Whites, Brooks, and Parliament, which has since almost wholly disappeared. The clubs were in many ways the equivalents of the modern 'Party Machines', and indeed it is far from impossible or even improbable that in their extreme old age the bright efficient party machines of to-day may yield some such high irrationality as 'the rule of the Dandies'.

The 'fifties were an age of final transition. The dandies were old or ageing men, slowly and with bitter tenacity giving way before the new titans of fashion, the 'heavy swells' as they were called by the populace. But these were different from their predecessors in a most important respect: they had no wish to 'rule'. In large part the dandies had been an extreme, a fantastical assertion of an aristocratic will to yield nothing to rising powers, and one can imagine how that will had been weakened, by alarm at the narrow escape of the 'thirties and 'forties, and by the prospect, vivid to men of the time, that civilization in Macaulay's words, might have been destroyed by the barbarism it had engendered. It had been weakened, too, perhaps, by a sly gratitude at having got off so cheaply. The 'heavy swells', no matter how portentous their bearing, entertained slighter ambitions. Pleasure, not power, was their aim. In the slow, semiconscious way of human societies men were forming themselves into an order more adaptable for defence against the contemporary threat, and, surprising effect, the clubs and the world of fashion were becoming less of an industry and more of a complicated game. Unlike the dandies, the 'swells' were more purely frivolous.

Gently, imperceptibly, Christopher joined their number.

The family circle in London provided a useful base for his patient campaign. The house had acquired high fashionability as the scene of receptions which were attended by the Duke of Wellington. Christopher learned there the complex art of paying desired attentions to the great, to the rising great, and the setting great. He learned other important lessons too. Once or twice it occurred that in the midst of his mother's entertainments there would burst in the old monster from Yorkshire in his boots and spurs (for like his contemporary, Colonel Sibthorpe of Lincoln, he had an aversion to railways, and even to coaches), and on these rare occasions Christopher observed the deftness with which his mother stowed the old man away out of sight. Old Tatton, recognizing his limitations, suffered himself to be controlled thus in London, but it is interesting to note that the brief glimpses he obtained of his younger son in the hated smart world even impressed that gross old man. 'Aye,' he confided to a fellow-centaur in Yorkshire, 'ee's a clever lud is Chris. Ee kona's oo t'hond leadies in curriage. Ee's a regular Broomel is Chris.'

This phase in Christopher's career of conquest lasted for a little more than ten years. In 1861 his mother died. And then in 1863 old Tatton died too, an event which was mourned throughout sporting England. He had been a very remarkable man. In this story it is not possible to do him justice because, watching him from the point of view of his children, we see only the dark side of his character. To those children his death must have come as a relief, particularly to Christopher, who by this time had made himself into a well-known man of fashion.

To a casual observer it might have seemed for a moment that he now resolved to quit Vanity Fair in order to direct his footsteps along the stony path of public toil, for in 1865, when he was thirty-four years of age, he entered the House of Commons as the member for Beverley. But a careful observer, such as the author of *Punch*'s 'Essence of Parliament', might have perceived that the deliberations of the State were never likely to excite his serious concern. Christopher is described in the act of taking his seat, standing with drooping eyelids and head slightly tilted to the side, as the ancient ceremonies were enacted at the bar. He took the oath. As he was leaving, he noticed the Speaker leaning towards him. He peered at him in curiosity, noticed his outstretched hand, and after touching the tips of his fingers strolled out into the lobby. That, with a wealth of ponderous sarcasm, is the description of *Punch*. Though the implied arrogance is probably a libel, it gives a vivid if distorted picture of Christopher's high antique grace. He was a popular and even conscientious member, but he displayed no vestige, or, to be accurate, only one vestige, of serious interest. He sat in the House of Commons from 1865 to 1892, and in that long interval he made in all six speeches and asked three questions. Disraeli's career was a gradual abandonment of dandyism. Christopher was more faithful to his first avocation.

We may now fairly consider Christopher as he approaches the eminence to which he aspired, in the first radiance of his magnificence.

We look back from the slaughter-house of to-day to that calm noon of high Victorianism with nostalgia and envy. Its solid furniture, its teeming wealth, 'its objects', as a later recorder, Henry James, noted them, 'massive and lumpish in silver and gold, in the forms to which precious stones contribute, or in leather, steel, brass, applied to a hundred different uses or abuses', together with the triumphant parade of domestic virtue, seem to us to assemble in a stupendous panorama of contentment; coarse, unimaginative, unintelligent, perhaps, but contentment authentic and unexampled none the less. The error has been corrected many times. It has been pointed out that the sense of precariousness which haunted the first half of the century persisted, that the great cult of 'respectability' was not a mode of self-expression, but an anodyne adopted by people who pictured disaster as imminent. Our forebears, we are assured, were as inwardly tormented as ourselves. Well, that may be so, but I have a suspicion that in their excitement at having uncovered the hidden impulses of that age, modern critics underestimate the importance of the obvious surface. Any doubts which I have experienced that the later nineteenth century was in truth an age of grave and sincere tranquility are dispelled by the image of Christopher, that age's greatest fop and dandy.

Where the fops of other ages took the butterfly as their model, he found inspiration in heavier matter. Dignity, majesty, and beautiful gloom, rather than brilliant skimming coloured parabolas, provide the keynote of his style. There is a remarkable half-length portrait of him by Pellegrini made about this time. He has changed much in appearance since his first upward footsteps in the 'fifties. The epicene beauty of youth has given way to a formidable grandeur of mien. The melancholy eyes are set at a downward angle from the fine thin nose, the whole face gives an impression of angularity and length, terminating in a drooping moustache and a long, golden beard. The lofty forehead is surmounted by gloriously well-brushed hair. From his abnormal height he has developed a stoop, not of one loaded with burdens, but such as would not have ill-befitted a Roman Emperor—indeed, his visage bears a certain resemblance to the bust of Antoninus Pius. It is difficult to reconcile this massive appearance, this face which might have done service for the wisest of mankind, with the uncontrollable frivolity which was in fact the principle of his nature, and which led him to founder in coarse and frightful tragedy.

There is a second picture by Pellegrini made some five years later. The grandeur, the stoop, the noble condescension are all there wholly unchanged, but the artist has given redoubled attention to the clothes. One sees what an impressive thing the old white top-hat could be, and how the later dreary version of the frock-coat could assume the proportions of a work of art, following the figure in exquisite rhythm and disciplined variation; but the point which is instantly apprehended as the difference between the dandy and the well-dressed man is that the former literally shines. His tie, his boots, his tall white hat send out gleam upon gleam. He is a work of art. One glance at this fine caricature makes it easy for me to believe what I have been told by elderly people who knew him: his carriage and grace made those about him seem common.

The second caricature bears a legend, at first sight out of harmony with the figure it portrays: 'The Gull's Friend.' This nickname derived from his Parliamentary career. Contemporary members may smile at his six speeches and three questions, but he achieved what few of them do to-day. In 1869 he introduced a private members' bill for the preservation of sea-birds, and it passed into law. From this he obtained the nickname. It clung to him for life. The double meaning was intended.

But the House of Commons plays no part in the story. The tragedy was not acted on that humdrum workaday stage. The attention should be diverted from the Palace of Westminster to the northerly side of St James's Park. That is where Christopher wrought his wonders. The splendours and follies depicted by Thackeray were increasing, both in momentum and in the corpulence of vulgarity; the hideous glories of flunkeydom were setting amid violent glows of ostentation; and to add design to the whirligig of fashion, the insane proceedings of society had found a president in the young lately wed Prince. There he stood, the Lord of London, with his inscrutable German eyes, his Tudor face, his gross pleasures, and more and more frequently there appeared by his side the huge, beautiful mournful form of Christopher.

While the explanation of all deep friendships lies ultimately in the inexplorable depths of the human heart, there are several guesses which, taken together, seem to solve much of the riddle of this once famous attachment, an attachment which, though it destroyed Christopher utterly, yet also opened for him such depths of childish delight. Christopher was ten years older than the Prince, they had certain important psychological conditions in common: both had felt in childhood an unusual weight of parental authority, and from the resulting complex had found in the romance of fashion an escape and anodyne. To the younger man Christopher appeared in the deliciously combined rôles of a sage worldly counsellor and of an irresistible minister of pleasure. To Christopher—well, though everyone who knew him testifies to the sweetness and gentleness of his character, there is no avoiding the fact, as I have already warned my readers, that he had an overriding weakness for which I regret that there is no inoffensive word in existence. He was an unredeemed snob; a snob, I fear, even by the standards of those intolerably snobbish days.

The Prince, of course, was not wholly a creature of romance. He found Christopher extraordinarily useful. To begin with, there was the Prince's taste for horse-racing, in the indulgence of which he liked to be entertained not only with the maximum of comfort and splendour but in strict accordance with his idiosyncrasies: he was fastidious in his vulgarity. For the great Doncaster meeting in September, the meeting for the last classic of the season, the St Leger Stakes, he found exactly what he wanted at Brantingham Thorpe. The distance to Doncaster by rail was convenient, and Christopher had carriages in attendance at either end. The entertainment was lavish throughout, the guests were perfectly suggested, and disposed about the table with admirable tact, imagination, and correctitude; nor was there any whim of the Prince which was not immediately and abundantly translated into fact. Did he wish to gamble, there were the very newest and best counters, cards, tables, and whatnots; did he wish to dance, there was the best of orchestras; and did he wish for some innocent royal horseplay, that was also to hand, as will appear more clearly later. There is in existence a photograph taken on the first of these occasions. The Prince and his beautiful Princess stand in the centre of the picture. Nestling close to the Princess is a foreign queen, a royal duke is artistically placed in the left middle distance. On the other side, enormous, droops the slender figure of Christopher, his beard the least bit stirred by a passing breeze. In the background is what appears to be a midget luggage-van, with the Prince's emblems on it. Scrutiny with a magnifying glass discovers this to be the photographer's technical transport. The year is 1869, and the day must have been one of the happiest in Christopher's life, happy with delicious thrills, doubts, and reliefs, every harassing moment bright with the promise of fame.

The house, fashionable since ten years, was hereafter hallowed, and there begins a succession of sumptuous entertainments, now for hunting, now for shooting, now once again for the St Leger, while the scene is crowded to capacity with great names. Among the few Christopherean relics which have survived are tomes filled with photographs of these assemblies and others in the great houses of England where, it is testified, so great was Christopher's triumphant fashionability, that the absence of his signature in the visitor's book was to be accounted as some dowdiness. The great melancholy man looms in the background, the head always at the slight characteristic tilt, the clothes always a little more beautiful than the imagination would evoke, the supreme dandy, and yet always with a curious uneasy look in the eyes, suggesting perhaps that the pleasures of snobbism depend in part on a continuance of that stimulating nervousness which accompanies first footsteps in the brilliant mocking world. It is a fine assortment of smartness and history. The tomes contain a considerable collection of snob masterpieces.

As one appraises them, one is left with the impression that few indeed are the great house parties which can vie in choice majesty with those held at Brantingham Thorpe. The house itself, from being a pleasant, modest Jacobean manor, was enlarged to the dimensions of a stately seat in the revived Jacobean style, but the painful vulgarities attending this familiar experiment were avoided; the furniture, for example, was not Jacobean or revived Jacobean, but eighteenth century, and in the finest taste. In spite of the enlargements the house was never immense, the parties were small by the large standards of the time; Christopher was refined in an age of heavy bigness. The choice of the guests displays the exquisite sense of fashionable values for which he was so justly admired. There is always a solid groundwork of historic peerages in which a few famously 'fast men' are cunningly included. Taking the latter as a fresh starting-point, a few of the new vulgarians, those loud, extremely rich men for whom the Prince had an abiding taste, are harmoniously worked into the structure. Eminent politicians of the worldly kind and a famous journalist, or other piece of decoration, are firmly built in, while, in almost every case, the pyramidal point is supplied by the rapidly fattening figure of the Prince himself. He is the inspiration though not the rule. Sometimes a party is assembled about other royalty: that uniquely uninteresting man, the Duke of Cambridge; a massive German couple, the Duke and Duchess of Saxe-Weimar; the Crown Prince of Hanover; and I have wondered sometimes whether, as a man always ready to oblige in the feasting of kings, Christopher was not used in an unscrupulous way by Government officials, for amid these trophies of great English and German princes there survives an unexplained photograph of a negro potentate.

But other beings in whom flowed the royal blood were as bye-day sport compared to the Prince. He it was and he alone who had conferred hallows on Holderness, and the achievement was the work of Christopher. In the transmogrification of Brantingham Thorpe into a temple of kingliness my uncle had successfully reached the limits of his ambition—he had done what he set out to do. However . . . perhaps he overlooked the fact, perhaps he rashly gambled against it, that the great guest was as tyrannical as he was affable, that the lord of fashion, for all his great girth, was a hurtling Will o' the Wisp. Perhaps as the beautiful bearded man looked down his monstrously laden table, where the coiffures, tiaras, and necklaces alternated with the white cravats, precious studs, whiskers and beards, a thrill of premonition sometimes transfixed his sensitive mind as his eye lighted on the robust groomed face of Lord Hardwicke. That unfortunate earl (who deserves a place in history as the inventor of the polished silk hat) had followed a similar career to Christopher's some ten years before, in the course of which he accompanied the Prince on his tour of India. He also became involved in the same fatal game, first of competitive and then of commanded entertainment, but (Christopher may have reflected with some comfort) with the disadvantage of having to vie with Oriental despots in splendour and to use elephants among the pieces on the board. The dreadful fact remained that, as a result, Lord Hardwicke lost a large part of his fortune. He was fated to lose the home of his ancestors also. Christopher was not unintelligent. He must have seen that he was playing a dangerous game.

Has someone been forgotten? What had become of Uncle Foulis? He was all right. He was upstairs enjoying a capital dinner in his room. He was happy and invisible. In the first days of the magnificence the good man had seen plain that he was not made for this kind of thing. Christopher agreed. He had foreseen this. It has been noted that he absorbed a useful lesson from the stowing of the elder Tatton in the early 'fifties, and without the suspicion of an unkind word or a hint at anything but the worthy baronet's convenience, he coaxed him into solitary recreation at such times. Uncle Foulis lived happily to the end of his days.

Christopher's troubles began in earnest early on in the 'seventies. He made the error of taking a handsome house in Hill Street, quite large enough for the purposes of royal entertainment. The Prince took careful note. Mightily satisfied with his experiences at Brantingham Thorpe, always anxious, the mischievous said, to save a little money, always glad of an agreeably appointed drawing-room in which gambling 'within the reasonable and harmless limits which he always insisted upon' might go forward, the Prince saw no reason why he should not honour his friend freely in London. And, having taken this decision, he not only stuck to it for many years, but was amazed at its success. The Prince often said that there was no host in London or the country who could compare with 'dear old Christopher'. He was impressed not only by the polish and sobriety of these occasions, their cheer and their respectfulness, their dash and their smoothness, but by the almost incredible speed with which ambitious dinners could be put together without any stray sign in the result of hurried composition. All manner of strange, wild millionaires were wandering round London then, and the Prince, perhaps recognizing natural soul-mates, yearned to make these men his friends. All sorts of precedents and inhibitions stood in the way, but Christopher could produce the unique, the flawless occasion for the encounter. He knew how to mix the traditional guardians and companions of the throne with the new raucous offspring of Mammon, and to mix them to such a nicety that not only was discord dispelled but a most pleasing novel harmony brought to charm. The Prince found Christopher invaluable, and in the myopic way of the fortunate he began to overplay his great new toy. Commands would arrive from his house giving Christopher only a week's notice. Commands having been met, the next ones to arrive gave a couple of days. Before very long the Prince would send round a note to Hill Street in the morning requesting a dinner the same evening. And these commands were met too. Christopher's large income began to show signs of contracting rapidly.

This, worry enough, was by no means all. By no means! The note of horror has been wanting hitherto. Sometime in those gorgeous days in the 'seventies this note was introduced by a very dreadful episode. Shortly before, the Prince, moved with impatience at the excessive conservatism of Whites, had founded the Marlborough Club, of which Christopher was a foundation member. It was at the Marlborough that the dreadful episode occurred. A supper was in progress after a late sitting of the House of Commons. Christopher was sitting next to the Prince, when the latter, moved by heaven knows what joyous whim, emptied a glass of brandy over his friend's head.

It may be recalled that Boswell tells of a similar royal assault on General Oglethorpe.

> The General told us that when he was a very young man ... He was sitting in a company with a Prince of Wirtemberg. The Prince took up a glass of wine, and by a fillip, made some of it fly in Oglethorpe's face. Here was a nice dilemma. To have challenged him instantly might have fixed a quarrelsome character on the young soldier; to have taken no notice of it, might have been considered as cowardice. Oglethorpe, therefore, keeping his eye upon the Prince, and smiling all the time, said: 'Mon Prince, that's a good joke: but we do it much better in England'; and threw a whole glass of wine in the Prince's face.

If only Christopher had followed that excellent man's example! Perhaps he would not have carried the whole company with him as Oglethorpe did; it might have meant the end of the great attachment; but how much more desirable, even that privation, than what in fact followed.

When the brandy landed on his hair and trickled down his face to the golden beard, Christopher showed a rare thing: an excess of presence of mind. Not a muscle moved. Then, after a pause, he inclined to the Prince and said without any discernible trace of annoyance or amusement: 'As Your Royal Highness pleases.' The effect of this is recorded as being quite indescribably funny. The whole room burst into violent paroxysms of laughter, and no one laughed more heartily, and certainly not more loudly, than the Prince. Laughter begat laughter, and the jest was prolonged till the very act of mirth was unbearable. Christopher dripped. Without a smile on his face he made no effort to mop up the tiny rivulets of spirit. The brandy had been poured by a royal hand. It was sacred. I would give much to know just how much conscious humour there was in Christopher's performance. I believe there was none.

The Prince flattered himself that he had made a discovery. Always an enthusiast for comedy, he had lighted on the greatest comic act of his time: to heap farce and buffoonery upon the Antonine figure of his friend and enjoy the contrast between clowning and persistent dignity, here was an absolutely infallible formula. One of the Prince's weaknesses has already been remarked in this story—namely, that with the secret of eternal youth he retained the child's pure enthusiasm which no amount of repetition can dim, and having enjoyed the great game of sousing Christopher once, he wanted to have it, in the touching way of infancy, 'again'. Well, royalty can command, and he had it again, he had it unnumbered times, he had it to the very end.

The Marlborough was the usual scene, but Brantingham Thorpe also was allowed to become a royal playground, as were a few of the brighter great houses. The Prince's simple taste liked enlargement. In place of the glass a full bottle was substituted, and another royal discovery was that even funnier effects could be conjured by pouring the precious liquid not on to his hair, but down his friend's neck. Amid screams of sycophantic laughter the Prince invented an entirely new diversion. Christopher was hurled underneath the billiard-table while the Prince and his faithful courtiers prevented his escape by spearing at him with billiard-cues. And there were further elaborations of the sousing theme.

Watering cans were introduced into Christopher's bedroom and his couch sprinkled by the royal hand. New parlour games were evolved from the Prince's simple but inventive mind: while smoking a cigar he would invite Christopher to gaze into his eyes in order to see the smoke coming out of them, and while Christopher was thus obediently engaged, the Prince would thrust the burning end on to his friend's unguarded hand. And the basis of the joke never weakened. To pour brandy down the neck of some roaring drunken sot of a courtier was one thing; but Christopher remained the statuesque figure he had been on the great night of the brandy glass. He never failed his audience. Never. His hat would be knocked off, the cigar would be applied, the soda-water pumped over his head, and he would incline, and murmur: 'As Your Royal Highness pleases.'

On one occasion the Prince attended a fancy-dress ball. Christopher accompanied him, dressed in complete steel. As they approached the house, the Prince declared that to avoid making a public appearance in his costume he had arranged for the party to be let in by the back door. It was a plot and it succeeded. As the party entered, Christopher found himself last, and, at the moment when he was about to walk in, the door was slammed and locked. He knocked. He knocked many times. He knocked in vain. As the minutes went by, the unusual spectacle began to attract a crowd of curious people. The house into which he so passionately wished to go was one of those immense built-round family palazzos whose back door was in a part of London not distant from, perhaps, but not sharing life with, the region in which the front door was situated, so much so, in fact, that the inhabitants of the back-door area had not become involved in the excitement in front. They had not heard about it. What they saw was a knight fully armed standing in a street. Christopher saw that there was nothing for it: he must walk down the street, turn left up the next street, second right, and then left down to the main street, and so left again to the front door. Normally five minutes, six in armour. It is said that, when he arrived, the vociferous crowd which he brought with him was large enough to add a good third to the numbers already assembled about the front door. Six minutes in armour can be a very long time.

Among the Prince's many practical jokes, this episode of the armour appears to be the only one in which his unflagging cruelty is redeemed by wit. He had much to put up with in Paradise, had the Gull's Friend.

Is it possible that he enjoyed these practical jokes—these hideous outbursts of high spirits among men far past their youth? The answer is that he detested every moment of them. He was not one of those unhappy beings who derive pleasurable excitement from humiliation and pain. He was a normal man afflicted with one excessive abnormality: the complex of ill-balanced predilections which we may classify as snobbism. It must not be forgotten that his snobbism was not the ordinary vulgar kind allied to the enjoyment of any or every kind of ostentation: it was deeply romantic. The Prince was an object of unstinted veneration; through a mist of ancient associations of chivalry the Prince to him was Charlemagne and he one of the paladins surrounding him—yes, he was as blind as all that, and of course—this is where the story is ugliest—it was precisely this blindness which informed the Prince's pranks with such inexhaustible comedy.

It must not be supposed, however, that Christopher sunk into a state of total degradation. He was not quite unmanned by his weakness. He did not suffer his martyrdom without protest, nor without protest of an effective sort. He had a certain wit, not the kind which survives in collections of aphorisms, but, rather, the short-range and sometimes highly formidable kind which depends on allusion and innuendo. The Prince would sometimes find Hanoverian broadsides met by a thrust which went right home and left him momentarily 'out', not so much as a shadow of disrespect having passed. On one occasion Christopher used a more direct method. Following some unusually ferocious outburst, the Prince shouted at him in cacophonous good-fellowship: 'What d'ye take yerself for, Christopher, hey!' Christopher fixed upon him a stern look. 'For,' he replied, 'Your Royal Highness's obedient, loyal, and most tried servant.' It is said that the unexpected and awful solemnity of his tone reduced the Prince to silence for the moment, and to civilized behaviour for some weeks.

But there could be no turning back. Having committed his capital error, this gentle loyal man found himself in Macbeth's predicament: stepped in so far, that should he wade no more, returning were as tedious. Mature chronic snobbism, as Dr Ponde would be the first to admit, allows of no remedy, and it is at this point in the sermon that the preacher's voice must rise to its highest monitory bellow echoing in the dim heights of the upper arches and the hollow lantern. For the fearful truth is that whereas grosser evils can be wiped off a human record, snobbism never can be on account of a terrible peculiarity. It is not the unforgivable sin—far from it—but it *is* the unrepentable sin. The disillusioned snob may often cry out in bitterness, 'All is vanity,' and again, 'Put not thy trust in princes,' but he can never keep wholly away from the objects of his baseless, even his consciously baseless, adoration. No love and no drug exerts a more blasting spell. But to return to the story.

The 'eighties dawned and the routine went on; the photographers turned up to perpetuate a little the hunting, the shooting, the St Leger Stakes entertainments; their long record remains in the tomes. His family, his agent, his bankers united in supplication that he would abandon his ruinous career of pleasure. He was fifty, he would gladly have agreed to their wishes, if—if he might entertain the Prince for the St Leger, and perhaps one shooting-party, and perhaps one or possibly two tremendous dinner-parties in London, no more. The thing would be kept within modest limits. Agreement was reached, but in vain. There was a magic in the gay, gruff royal voice outside the bounds of economic calculation; there were joys unknown to bankers in the act of inclining to a request for the tenth dinner in the season and murmuring the words: 'As Your Royal Highness pleases.' Everything went on, including most of the horse-play, just as it had been done in the 'seventies. But the moments of stark sobriety were more frequent. The photographs turn to a sadder key.

Christopher's beard is beginning to turn grey. He is no longer the heaviest of the heavy swells. Beside his younger guests, dashing young men with short curly hair and neat though large moustaches, he begins to strike a note of survival. His dress, in the manner of ageing men, becomes fixed in a rigid style. For the St Leger, which in those days shared the honour of compulsory formal dress with all the major race meetings, Christopher cannot only compete with but can absolutely outshine the younger men in smartness. His silk hat, lapels, boots, tie, shine as only a great dandy's can shine. But on less imposing occasions he begins to appear slightly quaint. The young men wear the newest varieties of bowler hat, while Christopher sticks throughout to that high-domed compromise between the bowler and top hats whose life Mr Churchill has prolonged to our own time. Later they all wear the Homburg hat. But not Christopher; he sticks in his grey hairs to that hat which was an innovation in his youth. The clothes suggest the same predicament as the hat: they are faintly ''sixtyish'; more impressive, certainly, than the others, not quite so fashionable. But the major difference between this Christopher of the 'eighties and the great golden figure of the 'seventies appears in the deepening gloom of the face. The affected melancholy gives way to a sincere, helpless regret. Doom is near.

The ever-fresh appetite of the Prince and the weakness of his friend kept the mechanism in operation until early in the 'nineties. Then came the crash. It came inevitably. It happened simply thus: Christopher was approaching old age, the possibility of marriage with an heiress had passed, his income was less than half its original figure, his debts were enormous. So the creditors closed in. They found insolvency, they proposed bankruptcy. 'What a thoroughly bad business!' exclaimed the Prince when he heard of it.

The stricken paladin was far too noble-mannered to appeal for aid, but surely he had the right to hope that his Charlemagne would hear the winding of a horn from the deep forest of despair; that he would remember the long, patient fidelity, the reckless generosity, the luxury and the loyalty that had never been withheld. Well, if he hoped, he hoped in vain. The Prince had his own very considerable troubles. The years succeeding that dreadful business at Tranby Croft[1] were not easy ones in which to tap the royal bounty, especially on behalf of one of the guests at that notorious affair. 'What a thoroughly bad business!' he cried, and (so he supposed) was obliged to let it go at that. But here he made a curious miscalculation. The winding of the horn was indeed heard and help did come, but from an unexpected quarter.

Christopher had a sister-in-law with whom he had never been on very intimate terms. She appears only once in the accumulation of the Brantingham photographs. She was a woman of Napoleonic energy, with a passion for life as deep as Christopher's, but, unlike his, a hearty and unrestrained passion. Her eccentric and violent temperament had proved a considerable anxiety to her friends, and her scorn of all conventions kept the excessively conventional Christopher in a state of steady disapproving alarm. On her side she had not given any sign of being very fond of her brother-in-law. She regarded him as a fool and said so frequently. She had a gift for satire and mimicry which she used without much charity. She was the last person from whom the poor man would have expected aid, but her very being was made up of contradictions: there was a heavenly generosity in her spirit which, like so much about her, was intense and even terrible. In a great rage she came down to London bent on rescue.

There was no doubt in her mind from what source rescue was to be

---

[1] Tranby Croft, the home of the Prince's friend Mr Wilson. This house was the scene of a gambling party at which accusations were made against a guest of cheating. These allegations led subsequently to a law-suit in which the Prince, though only indirectly concerned, was obliged to give evidence.

drawn. It waa the Prince's fault, she said simply, so the Prince must pay. The Prince did not know her very well, but, accurately informed as always, he knew not only of her disorders but of her unforgivable remarks about himself and some of his friends. However, she was not easy to withstand. No barriers solid enough had yet been contrived to keep this impossible woman from where she happened to want to go. She could be irresistibly feminine or unbearably domineering, not only by turns, but, what was so disconcerting, simultaneously. Her smile and engaging lisp were sometimes accompanied by eyes blazing forth in fire; hammering logic mingled with screaming farce; thunder with sunshine. What happened at her interview with the Prince is not known. The stories about it are too contradictory or too melodramatic to command belief, while the two people who knew the truth left no record. What is known is that, shortly after the crash, she went in high fury and by appointment to the Prince's great house in London, was closeted with him for a short time and then left. The main part of Christopher's debts was paid.

He was saved from the awful disgrace of bankruptcy, but he was left, for all that, wounded and horseless indeed. Most of his capital had to go; and not only the house in Hill Street, but the hallowed fane at Brantingham Thorpe left his possession for ever. Not much remained. The great dandy was now a poor man, not only by the elevated standards of those days, but by our own.

People sneered that the great attachment was only another case of cupboard love; wait and watch it dissolve, they sniggered. In this they were wrong. Evil nature was not in the Prince. The friendship went on, in much the same uproarious manner as before, not, mercifully, in a turmoil of practical jokes, but with roars of coarse rallying, back-slapping, and broadsides. And the old broken courtier still had the spirit to send back keen respectful arrows into the bowels of the attacking craft. Nevertheless nothing could hide the grim fact of the fall; the 'nineties were a long process of deepening twilight. The great host was now an eternal guest. Wearily, mournfully, from habit as much as anything else, the melancholy man journeyed from house to house, from comital to ducal pile, from dukeries to royalty, and back again, to and fro. He had left the House of Commons in 1892, and he now had very little with which to occupy his mind. He who had spent so recklessly now had to count every coin; his visits to the great houses began to become noticeably protracted. Nor was he now preeminent in the glory of dress and dandyism. As he declined, a new sun was rising, outshining him as he had outshone thirty years before. In the later photographs the first figure to seize the attention is that of Lord Chesterfield— immaculate, beautiful, whether in formal, ordinary, or sporting dress. He stands forth from pampered crowds magnificent and erect, while Christopher's once impressive studied stoop is the bent attitude of an old and tired man. It was a fall indeed.

It would be better if the story ended here, but Christopher had a little farther to go, nor were his woes quite terminated. Among the miseries which thickened about his last years ill health took a place. He was a delicate man, years of sumptuous eating had put a strain on his innards the effects of which were becoming serious. An important part of his small income was devoted to a yearly cure at Homburg; and it was during one of these necessary periods of retirement that he met his end under extraordinary and yet appallingly appropriate circumstances. One day in the July of 1898, while Christopher was undergoing the most drastic cure yet attempted upon him, an event occurred at Waddesdon Manor, the house of Baron Ferdinand de Rothschild, which was destined to have wider consequences than at first appeared. The Prince, while descending the marble staircase of Waddesdon in the course of a week-end visit, slipped, lost balance, and then fell down so heavily that his left knee-cap was fractured. Suffering great pain, he was conveyed the next day to his house in London, whereupon there rose up around him one of those voluptuous outbursts of sympathy which appear to be a kind of psychological necessity to the English people. Every day the newspapers published lengthy articles describing the circumstances of the agony in close detail; flocks of noblemen and noblewomen called at the Prince's house to enquire as to the hopes or progress of his recovery, sometimes making long journeys from the country for this purpose; great crowds of people lingered round the street entrance, and it was noticed that many of the women were unable to withhold their tears; clergymen preached on the subject for several Sundays. England was enjoying herself very much in her own dignified way.

As the anguish subsided, the danger of permanent lameness, acute in the early stages, was gradually dispelled, but it became clear that the Prince must spend some weeks in prostration. To him the pleasures of illness were a closed book, as were most books when they lay in his plump hands. Ingenious efforts were made to amuse him, including the fitting of an electropohone in his room connected by telephonic wire with the chief music halls of London, but none of these measures were of much avail; he was defenceless against the pains of boredom. He began to grow restless and exasperated. Then a member of his circle, or perhaps the Prince himself, had a bright idea. His favourite recreation, the Cowes Regatta, was drawing near, and it was pointed out that if the great patient could be moved to his yacht without risking any further damage to his injured knee, he would be able to watch the sport while inhaling sea air. The plan was approved by his doctors, and on the 30th of July the Prince travelled to the south and was placed on his yacht, the 'Osborne'. Then, after a week or so, happier now but with the dark angel of boredom still there at that bookless berthside, another idea came to him. Where was Christopher? What! At Homburg! Good Gracious, send him a telegram immediately! See that arrangements are made for him to be met at Ostend! See that he's here by tomorrow! See that a cabin is got ready for him!

A reply came from Homburg. Christopher presented his duty; he asked leave to sympathize with His Royal Highness in his mishap, which he was deeply relieved to learn was not as grave as might have been anticipated at first. He begged to be allowed to express a hope for His Royal Highness's swift recovery. With submission he must with great regret ask His Royal Highness to excuse him from accepting the very gracious invitation to attend His Royal Highness on board. He had consulted his medical man, who had assured him that any break in the cure he was undergoing might have grave and incalculable consequences. His Royal Highness would appreciate the very sincere regret and disappointment which he felt at being obliged to send such a reply.

The Prince was roused to anger. Never once in the many years he had known him had Christopher failed him. He had asked him to do preposterously difficult things and he had done them, now he asked him to do an easy thing and he refused. In a moment of impatience he dictated a second telegram ...

In Brussels Christopher had a few hours between trains. He spent part of them sitting in the sun in those pleasant gardens which lie like a miniature Tuileries in front of the palace. There he met, by chance, a stout young man, a guest of former days, by name Lord Vaux of Harrowden. To him he confided that he felt the end of his life drawing on quickly, and he seemed disturbed as to how he could support the strain of his impending visit. 'I have tried to explain,' he said. Valiantly he went on. He stayed on board for a little more than a week. He looked very old and very ill. The Prince noted the change and did not press him to stay on when he asked permission to go home. Soon after his arrival in London he suffered a stroke from which he never wholly recovered. He died at the end of that year.

When he heard the news the Prince was seized with remorse. He realized what he had done. For the first time, perhaps, he realized how much blame he incurred for the whole ghastly episode, and he was smitten by a gust of grief such as was rare with him. Selfish as he was, there is no doubt that the affection he felt for Christopher was in essence warm and generous.

I should like that to be the end of the story, but Christopher's adventures continued a little farther than death. For his besetting fault Fate was hard on this mild sweet-natured man.

The Prince, moved by a good-hearted wish to make amends, decided to travel to Yorkshire for the funeral at Brantingham Thorpe, and he was accompanied by an immense concourse of fashionable mourners. It was to be such a funeral as Christopher might have wished for—as sumptuous and as distinguished as any frolic for the St Leger had been. The ceremony went forward impressively, with never a hitch or flaw. Until the final scene at the grave. The diggers had not calculated the abnormal length of the coffin. The grave was of ordinary size. When the pathetic moment arrived for the coffin to be lowered it remained on the surface. It did not fit the grave. Attempts were made to lower it crookedly, feet foremost, then head foremost. And then someone remembered the brandy glass. One or two suddenly turned away. Then the Prince got out his handkerchief. The officiating ecclesiastic signed to the undertakers to leave the coffin where it was. The ceremony went on, and the reading of the great and inspired words was interrupted by gulps, artificial coughings, and the use of more handkerchiefs than tears. Would it were not so, but The Gull's Friend, even in death, could not escape from the comedy which pursued him like a harpy, which pursued him literally to the grave.

The epilogue is brief. A year or so later a subscription for a memorial to Christopher was raised by his friends, the money being entrusted to the Prince for disposal. 'A memorial to dear old Christopher!' he exclaimed. 'Well, now, what about a clock over the stables?' It is said, how truly I do not know, that Lord Rosebery recommended that a tablet would be more fitting. At all events the tablet was erected, and still testifies to the friendship of those two very different men.

Two years later, in 1901, the Victorian reign came to an end. Henry James wrote from London to a friend living in Paris, 'We all feel motherless to-day. We are to have no more of little mysterious Victoria, but instead fat vulgar dreadful Edward.' One wonders whether the old Queen had ever heard of the awful saga of Brantingham Thorpe and Hill Street. Probably it was carefully kept from her, but she had sharp eyes and ears. If she did hear, I feel that she was not amused.

Is there anything to add to the end of Christopher's story? The moral is so plain, the wheel of folly and chastisement comes full circle so perfectly that only a dunce could miss the lesson. And yet ... I wonder sometimes whether there is not something esoteric in the story, something of great and once obvious importance now invisible in the confusion of decay. To be loved long after death is not the lot of many impoverished old bachelors, but Christopher's name was honoured with that rare and lovely tribute. I am thinking in particular of a strangely moving homage which was paid to his memory. One of his nephews was Admiral Sir William Pakenham, whose name may now be little remembered, though he was well known as a distinguished and fearless naval commander at the time of the First World War. He was a man of severe and beautiful character. In his youth he knew Christopher well. Every year, on the anniversary of Christopher's death, he journeyed to Yorkshire to visit his uncle's tomb at Brantingham Thorpe. Not once when he was in England did he neglect this pious act, from 1898 to the year preceding his death in 1935. I cannot believe that such a man would have made such an offering to mere hollow foolishness, and the recollection of it is a salutary check to pompous sententiousness. The past is often as much distorted as clarified by the distance of time. Much has been said of the artistry of memory, but it is too facile an interpreter for the ultimate purposes of History; it preserves garish highlights but neglects the deeper shades.

Who, in this generation, knows anything about THE BOY JONES? Yet his escapades were very daring and his story is very true—but so strange is it that, in order to be believed, I must, at least, in part, give the chapter and verse for it:

The Times, 15 Dec., 1838:
QUEEN SQUARE.—Yesterday, a lad about 15 years of age, who gave his name as Edward Cotton, whose dress was that of a sweep, but who was stated to be the son of a respectable tradesman in Hertfordshire, was charged with being found in the Marble hall of Buckingham Palace, under circumstances of an extraordinary nature. It should be stated that Buckingham Palace, even during the absence of the Queen, is guarded by the gentlemen porters of the establishment, two

inspectors of the A division of police, and sentries from the Foot Guards. In spite of this, a number of cases have lately occurred at this office, where persons have been found in the interior of the Palace under unaccountable circumstances.

George Cox, one of the porters, having been sworn, said, that at five o'clock yesterday morning he saw the prisoner in the Marble hall. The latter endeavoured to make his escape into the lobby, but he pursued him, and he then took a contrary direction, across the lawn at the back of the Palace. Witness called for the sentry at the gate, and a policeman of the B Division who was on duty in James Street, caught the lad, after a long chase over the lawn. Mr Cox added, that he found, in the lobby, a regimental sword, a quantity of linen, and other articles, all of which had been purloined from the Palace. The sword was the property of the Hon. Augustus Murray, a gentleman attached to the Queen's establishment. Witness went into that gentleman's bedroom, and the bedding was covered with soot. The prisoner had, evidently, endeavoured to get up the chimney, in order to effect his escape; there was a valuable likeness of Her Majesty, in the Marble hall, which was broken, and covered with soot; and it was supposed that the lad, in the first instance, had descended from the top of the building, and had endeavoured to make his way back again in the same manner.

James Stone, 31 B, deposed that he was called upon by the last witness to secure the prisoner. There were marks of soot in several of the bedchambers, as well as in one of the corridors of the Palace, and the Grand (or Marble) hall. He found upon him two letters, one addressed to Her Majesty, and the other to the Hon. Mr Murray. These letters had been placed underneath Her Majesty's portrait, and had, no doubt, been taken by the prisoner at the time the picture was destroyed. Part of the scabbard of the sword was discovered in one of the beds, and a quantity of bear's grease, part of which he had placed upon his flesh, was taken from him—it belonged to one of the servants of the Palace. Upon being taken to the station house, he said he came from Hertfordshire, and that his father was a respectable man.

Mr White, the sitting magistrate, observed that it was a most extraordinary thing that persons could get into the Palace under such circumstances.

Several persons belonging to the Palace said that every inquiry had been made, but it could not be accounted for.

Mr White (to the prisoner): Where do you come from?

Prisoner: I came from Hertfordshire 12 months ago, and I met with a man in a fustian jacket, who asked me to go with him to Buckingham House. I went, and have been there ever since. I got my victuals in the kitchen, and I thought myself very well off, because I came to London to better myself.

Mr White: Well, you could not go to a higher place.

Prisoner: I declare it to be the case, and I lived very well. To be sure, I was obliged to wash my shirt now and then.

Mr White: You fared, then, altogether, pretty well?

Prisoner: Very well indeed, Sir, and I was always placed, when the Queen had a meeting with the Ministers, behind a piece of furniture in the room; but I, certainly, did live well.

Mr White: Indeed! And which was your favourite apartment?

Prisoner: The room in front of the gardens; but I was always in the secret when the Ministers came.

Mr White: Do you mean to tell me that you have lived in the Palace upwards of 11 months, and been concealed when Her Majesty held a Council?

Prisoner: I do.

Mr White: Were you hid behind a chair?

Prisoner: No. But the tables and other furniture concealed me.

Mr White: Then you could hear all Her Majesty said?

Prisoner: Oh, yes! and her Ministers too.

The prisoner's answers to the questions of the magistrate were given in the most shrewd manner possible, and he evidently appeared to be a lad of some education, but nothing further could be elicited from him.

Mr White said it was a most singular affair, and that it should be strictly inquired into. For the present, he should remand the prisoner until Wednesday next.

The magistrate also told Cox that, as he should be sitting there every day, he should be glad to receive any information upon the subject.

The letters found upon the prisoner were directed to be sent to the Palace, under seal of the Office, the prisoner having broken them open.

The case excited great interest, and, in the first instance, was sent to Bow Street; but Sir Frederick Roe being out of town, it was ordered to be heard at this office.

The Times, 20 Dec.—Yesterday, the lad found in Buckingham Palace, who had given his name as Edward Cotton, and described himself as the son of a respectable tradesman living in the town of Hertford, was brought before Messrs. White and Gregorie for final examination. It will be recollected that he had purloined, amongst other articles, two letters, which were immediately sealed up, and sent back to the Palace. The prisoner turns out to be the son of an industrious tailor, named Jones, residing in York Street, Westminster; and, it appears, had frequently expressed his intention to enter the Palace, under any circumstances. He had often stated that he wished to see the grand staircase, in order to take a sketch of it, and had often expressed his determination to see the Queen, and to hear her sentiments when Her Majesty and her Ministers were assembled in Council.

Frederick Blume now deposed that he was valet to the Hon. Mr Murray, and that a sword, a quantity of linen and other articles, had been stolen from that gentleman's apartments in the Palace.

Mr White: When were they stolen?

Witness: I can't recollect.

Mr White: Was it a week, a month, or three or four months ago?

Witness: I cannot say.

Mr White: Where was your master's sword at the time you saw it last?

Witness: When I went to Windsor.

Mr White: When was that?

Witness: I cannot exactly recollect, and then he added, that about a week since, he had sent from Windsor to the Palace, a portmanteau containing his linen, and three pairs of trousers, four of stockings, and three cravats were missing. The padlock of the portmanteau had been forced by the sword having been applied to it. The sword had broken in the attempt. He had also lost five 10 sous pieces, which had been found upon the prisoner.

Mr White: What is the value of the articles you have lost?

Witness: I don't know; but I should like to give three guineas to get them back.

Mr White: Can you swear to the French coin found upon the prisoner as being yours?

The witness was then shown the coin, and he said that he certainly could. They had been taken from his bedroom.

Mr White: Can any information be given as to the manner in which the prisoner gained access to the Palace? Cox, one of the porters to the Palace, said that the principal entrance door was always locked, and the key in his possession. At 5 o'clock on Saturday morning, just as he was about to get out of bed, the prisoner opened the door of his room, as witness considered, to obtain the key; his face and hand were disguised with soot and bear's grease, and he was asked whether he came to sweep a chimney: he did not make any answer, but endeavoured to escape.

Inspector Steed, A division, said that upon examining the gates of the principal entrance of the Palace, he found that, at the Marble Arch, there was a vacuum sufficient to admit a boy into the Palace, without any inconvenience.

Mr White: And is there no sentry at this gate?

Witness: There are two.

The inspector said that he had examined the boy's boots, and the gravel upon them corresponded with that lately laid down close to the Marble Arch. The boots had been taken off by the prisoner, and left in one of the apartments appropriated to the use of the porters of the Palace.

Mr Griffiths, builder, Coventry Street, said that the lad had been in his employment for a few months; he had always expressed his intention to get into the interior of the Palace by some means or other; he was a clever lad, and had made a sketch of the exterior, and a view of the enclosure fronting the Palace. He had left his service two days since, and witness was very much distressed, as were his parents, to know what had become of him. Upon reading the accounts in the newspapers, he immediately went to Tothill Fields, and identified him, much to the gratification of his father, who supposed that he had drowned himself, the latter having, on account of his son's bad conduct, turned him out of doors.

The Magistrate, after telling the boy that he would, most likely, be committed for trial, asked him what he could say in his defence.

Prisoner: I wished to see the Palace, and I went in with a man in a fustian jacket. I had the whole range of the Palace for a day or two, but the money found upon me I picked up in one of the rooms.

Mr White: Tell me the truth, for I am about to send you for trial.

Prisoner: Oh, very well; with all my heart.

He was fully committed to the Westminster Sessions, and all parties bound over to prosecute.

He was tried on 28 Dec., and was most ably defended by his Counsel, Mr Prendergast, who turned everything to ridicule, and the jury returned a verdict of Not Guilty, regarding the escapade in the light of a youthful folly, and being, also, mindful of the fact that the boy did not enter the Palace for the purpose of theft.

But we shall hear of THE BOY JONES again.

—John Ashton, *Gossip*

PATRICK CAMPBELL

Mr Smyllie, Sir

When, in these trying times, it's possible to work on the lower slopes of a national newspaper for several weeks without discovering which of the scurrying executives is the Editor, I count myself fortunate to have served under one who wore a green sombrero, weighed eighteen stone, sang parts of his leading articles in operatic recitative, and grew the nail on his little finger into the shape of a pen nib, like Keats.

Even the disordered band of unemployed cooks, squabbling like crows over the Situations Vacant columns in the front office files, knew that he was Robert Maire Smyllie, Editor of the *Irish Times*, and fell silent as he made his swift rush up the stairs.

He was a classical scholar, at home among the Greek philosophers. He was the incorruptible champion of the fading Protestant cause in holy Ireland. His political and humanitarian views won international respect, and he spent most of his time on the run from the importunities of such characters as Chloral O'Kelly and Twitchy Doyle.

They lay in wait for him every evening in their chosen lairs in the front office and threw themselves in his path, as though to halt a rushing locomotive, as soon as he appeared at the door.

Chloral O'Kelly was a deeply melancholic youth who drank disinfectant, and was in constant need of 3s. 9d. for another bottle. Twitchy Doyle was a little old man with a straggly, jumping moustache who lived by reviewing reprints of Zane Grey. The moment the Editor burst through the front door they closed on him with urgent appeals, battling for position with Deirdre of the Sorrows, an elderly woman who believed for twelve years that she was being underpaid for her contributions to the Woman's Page. The Editor shot through them, weaving and jinking, crying: 'No—not tonight—tomorrow—good-bye'—and put on an extra burst of speed which carried him up the stairs to the safety of his own room, there to deliver his unforgettable cry: 'Pismires! Warlocks! Stand aside!'

41

I looked up 'pismire' once in the dictionary and found it meant an ant. It pictured, vividly, the unrelenting tenacity of his hangers-on.

For four years, six nights a week, I worked beside this enormous, shy, aggressive, musical, childlike, cultured and entirely unpredictable human being, separated from him by only a wooden partition, in a monastic life cut off almost completely from the world.

We worked in a high, dusty room topped by an opaque glass dome. There were no outside windows, so that the light burned day and night. Alec Newman, the Assistant Editor, and Bill Fleming, the theatre critic, shared the outside part. Then came the Editor's office, partitioned off by battered wooden panelling. I had a tiny box jammed between him and the wall, with a sliding hatch between us for the purposes of communication. When it was open I got a portrait view of the great head, hair brushed smoothly back, brick-red face, snub nose supporting glasses and a ginger moustache enclosing the stem of a curved pipe the size of a flower-pot. 'Mr Campbell, we do not wish to be observed,' was the signal for the hatch to be closed.

Alec, Bill and I got in about nine-thirty every night and started to scratch around for leader subjects in the English papers. At ten o'clock the Editor burst in like a charging rhino, denounced pismires and warlocks, and went to ground in his own room.

At ten-thirty came the inevitable inquiry: 'Well, gentlemen—?'

Alec assumed the responsibility of answering for all of us. 'Nothing, Mr Smyllie, sir. All is sterility and inertia.'

The reply was automatic. 'Ten-thirty, and not a strumpet in the house painted! Art is long, gentlemen, but life is shuddering shorter than you think.' 'Shuddering' and 'shudder' were favourite words of complaint.

Alec made his set protest. 'You're hard, Mr Smyllie, sir. Hard!'

'Mr Newman?'

'Sir?'

'Take your King Charles's head outside and suck it.'

I never discovered the origin of this extraordinary injunction, but it meant that some disagreement had taken place between them during the afternoon and that Alec had better be careful from now on. My own orders came floating over the partition.

'Mr Campbell?'

'Sir?'

'Prehensilize some Bosnian peasants.'

'Immediately, sir.'

The cryptic order had a simple origin. The Editor, seeking once to commend a piece of writing that clung closely, without irrelevant deviation, to its theme, had hit upon the word prehensile, which passed immediately into the language of our private, nocturnal life. Somerset Maugham, for instance, was a prehensile writer, Henry James unprehensile in the extreme. From here it was a short step to prehensilizing an untidily written contribution. Reprehensilization covered a second re-write. We didn't even notice we were saying it after a week or two.

The Bosnian peasant came from a discovery of mine on the back of the *Manchester Guardian*—an exceedingly improbable story about a Balkan shepherd who'd tripped over a railway line and derailed a train with his wooden leg. The shepherd, in addition, had only one eye, and was carrying a live salmon in his arms. I cannot imagine, now, how even a short fourth leader could have been written on such a theme, but for months I was dependent on the *Guardian*'s Balkan correspondent for my ideas. Acceptance of this *argot* led me once to frighten the life out of the Bishop—I think—of Meath.

I'd come in very late and burst straight into the Editor's room. 'I'm sorry I got held up, Mr Smyllie, sir!' I cried. 'I can always reprehensilize some one-eyed Bosnian bastards!' It was only then that I saw the Bishop sitting in the visitor's chair with his top-hat on his knee. I've never seen a man so profoundly affected by a sentence containing only eight words.

If pursuing his personal, King Charles's head war with Alec, the Editor would suddenly give him the first, interminable leader to write on some political theme, while doing the second and shorter one himself.

Silence settled in for about an hour, with the four typewriters rattling away.

Sometimes, then, we got: 'Cold—cold—cold—'

Almost anything could start it off, from the mere weather conditions to some philosophic reflection that had entered the Editor's mind.

His typewriter stopped. The rest of us paused, too, expectant in our boxes. The voice rose, high and ghostly, from the Editor's compartment:

'Cold—cold—cold—'

We echoed it, still higher and thinner:

'Cold—cold—cold—'

The Editor's voice took on a deeper, tragically declamatory note:

> 'Cold as a frog in an ice-bound pool,
> Cold as the tip of an Eskimo's tool,
> Colder than charity—'

There was a long pause, while we stuffed our handkerchiefs into our mouths, struggling to remain silent. The next line came out with rasping cynicism:

'And that's pretty chilly—'

He allowed this to sink in, then returned to the dramatic narrative form:

'But it isn't as cold as poor Brother Billy—'

We all joined in, vying with one another to achieve the maximum in greasy self-satisfaction, on the last line:

''Cause *he's DAID!*'

There was another pause, while we savoured the dying echoes. 'Get on with it, gentlemen,' said the Editor, and the four typewriters started again. But now that his appetite for music had been aroused—and he was a profoundly musical man, with a fine baritone voice—he would give us an encore, singing the words of his leader in a long recitative, like a chant:

'O, the Dublin Corporation has decided

In its wis-*dum*—'

We joined in, like a Greek chorus, in the background:

'In its wis-*dum* ... its wis-*dum* ...'

'To sign the death warrant

Of the traam-*ways*—'

'Traam-*ways* ... traam-*ways* ...'

'A measure with which we find ourselves

In agree-ment—'

'In agree-ment ... agree-ment ...'

There'd be a sudden break in the mood. The voice came out with a snap. 'Thank you, gentlemen, and give my regards to your poor father.'

When he was writing the words poured out of him in a flood, without correction, and at times, indeed, without much thought. He'd been doing it too long. But there were occasions when he bent the whole of his courageous and intelligent mind to denouncing the rising tide of parochial Irish republicanism—notably on the death of George V.

This long-drawn-out decline was being charted much more thoroughly by the *Irish Times*, with its Unionist sympathies, than by the other newspapers. Night after night Smyllie put a new touch to his obituary leader, after the routine inquiry, 'Has the poor old shudderer passed on?' Finally, the King died and the leader was sent out for setting. We were all in the Editor's room when the first edition came off the machines. He tore open the leader page to see how it looked, and gave a scream like a wounded bull when he saw that the second half of it, possibly inadvertently, had been printed upside down. Pismires and warlocks that morning were relegated to the ends of hell.

This concern for the English King got us into scattered forays with the IRA, leading once to the windows of the office in Cork being broken by a shower of stones. When the news reached the Editor he made, taking as his framework, 'They cannot intimidate me by shooting my lieutenants,' one of the most carefully formulated battle-cries I've ever heard in my life.

We were in the office at the time. He instructed me to give him the noggin of brandy, filed under B in his correspondence cabinet, and took a steady pull. 'These shudderers,' said Robert Maire Smyllie, 'cannot intimidate me by throwing half-bricks through the windows of the branch office while my lieutenants are taking a posset of stout in the shebeen next door.'

When we left, round about two o'clock the following morning, however, he was in a noticeable hurry to mount his bicycle. As he swung his massive weight into the saddle one of the pedals snapped off clean. He fell off, sprang up again, shouted, 'Mr Campbell, as your superior officer I order you to give me your velocipede!'—snatched it out of my hand, leaped aboard and sped off into the darkness. I limped after him on the broken one. When we got back to his house we drank Slivovitz until breakfast, in further defiance of 'the porter-slopping shudderers from Ballydehob'.

In the office there was indeed at this time the feeling of a beleaguered garrison, one which prompted all of us to remain in the place until daylight, rather than face the dark streets on our bicycles. Those were the great nights of the domino games that kept us locked in combat over the Editor's desk until the charwoman came in the morning.

'A little pimping, Mr Smyllie, sir?' Alec would suggest, after the paper had gone to bed.

'A little pimping, Mr Newman, would be acceptable.'

No one could ever remember how it came to be called pimping, with the additional refinement of 'hooring', to describe the act of blocking the game with a blank at both ends, but because of Smyllie's complete purity of mind these technicalities added a notable spice to the game.

I can see him now, his green, wide-brimmed hat set square on his head, the great pipe fuming and a glass of brandy by his side, delicately picking up his tiles with the pen-nib fingernail raised in the air.

The unspoken purpose of the three of us was to do him down by a concerted onslaught, all playing into one another's hands to present him with a blank, when his turn came to play, on both ends.

'Pimp, Mr Newman, pimp,' I would urge Alec, sitting on my right. We always used these formal titles when in play.

Alec would close one end. 'Hoor, Mr Campbell, hoor!'

If, happily, I had a suitable blank I would lose no time in playing it, then we all burst into a triumphant cry:

'Hoored, Mr Smyllie, sir—hoored! Take a little snatch from the bucket!'

With an expressionless face, and the dainty fingernail raised in the air, the great man would draw some more tiles from the middle, on occasion being lucky enough to find a seven, and then play it with an elegant flick of the wrist, like an eighteenth-century gallant. 'That, gentlemen,' he would say, 'should wipe the shuddering grins off your kissers. *Nemo me impune lacessit*—and best wishes to all at home.'

I left the *Irish Times* under rather dubious circumstances, intending, in fact, only to take a week's holiday in London, but I was also writing a column for the Irish edition of the *Sunday Dispatch* at this time, and thought it might be interesting to call at headquarters. As a result of this I wrote a piece about the English scene which they used in all the editions, and paid me a little more than five times what I was getting for a whole week's work at home. I sent Smyllie a telegram, saying I'd been held up, and hoped to be back soon. He countered with a letter saying he would be delighted to see the last of me if I'd send him a year's salary, in lieu of notice. I replied that I'd see my bank manager about it. I remained on in London, and the correspondence came to an end.

In the next three years I returned fairly frequently to Dublin without daring to go and call on him, until one day I opened the *Irish Times* and saw a paragraph in his Saturday diary column, which he wrote under the name of Nichevo.

It was very short. 'My spies tell me,' it read, 'that Paddy Campbell is back again in Dublin, after a long safari looking for tsetse fly in the bush. He is now preparing a definitive biography of Schopenhauer, and is doing a lot of field research on the subject in the back bar of Jammet's, and the Dolphin Hotel.'

It was an intimation that peace had been declared. But he was dead before I could say, 'Good evening, Mr Smyllie, sir,' again.

GILES PLAYFAIR

Indecent Assault by a Colonel

I

When the London-bound train from Portsmouth passed through Walton Station at about 4.45 in the afternoon of June 17th, 1875, William Burrowes, a bricklayer employed by the London and South Western Railway, saw something to make him rub his eyes in astonishment. A young lady was standing with one foot on the step and the other on the footboard of a first-class compartment. With her left hand she was clinging to the outside door handle, while someone inside the compartment was supporting her by her right arm. In fact, she had been travelling for several miles in this unconventional and precarious position, for she had preferred to risk death rather than face the worse fate that, right or wrongly, she believed was intended for her by the strange gentleman with whom she had found herself sharing the compartment. William Burrowes alerted the station-master, who signalled ahead to Esher; and before the train reached the platform at Esher, it was brought to a screeching stop.

Engine-driver, guard, and a number of passengers who had heard the young lady screaming but had been unable to do anything to assist her since the train was not equipped with a communication cord, now rushed up to find out what the trouble was. She was helped down on to the gravel. Her hat had blown off (it was subsequently discovered, five hundred yards from Walton station, by a plate-layer on the line), and she was in a great mental agitation, though she did not appear to be physically any the worse for her ordeal. She pointed out her fellow occupant of the compartment, who by this time had joined the group on the gravel. She said that he had 'insulted' her and would not 'let her alone'.

Three days later, on June 20th, the British public learned that Colonel Valentine Baker had been arrested on a warrant issued in

47

Guildford, though he had subsequently been released on bail. He was charged with indecent assault. The complainant was Miss Rebecca Kate Dickinson, a 21-year-old girl, who lived with her widowed mother and two unmarried sisters at Midhurst.

This was sensational news, and it was prominently reported under such headlines as *Extraordinary Charge Against A Colonel*. Not that there was anything extraordinary about the charge itself. Indecent assaults (and worse) were common occurrences, which the courts, try as they might, could not stamp out. But they were supposedly offences that, as one newspaper put it, 'only men of the lowest type would be deemed capable of contemplating'. To accuse a Colonel of this sort of 'outrage', was, therefore, extraordinary, particularly a Colonel of such high social standing as Valentine Baker.

He was nearing 50 at this time, though he probably looked younger since he was neither bald nor grey, and kept himself in excellent physical shape. Less than a year before, he had been appointed Assistant Quartermaster-General at Aldershot following his compulsory retirement under the seniority rules as commanding officer of the 10th Hussars. By birth, he was not an aristocrat nor even, according to the strict contemporary definition of the word, a gentleman. He was a merchant's son; his father had done most of his business in the West Indies, and he himself, after a somewhat sketchy education, had joined the army as an ensign in the Ceylon Rifles at the age of 21.

But by adoption, so to speak, Colonel Baker was rather more than a gentleman. The paradox, as well as the strength, of the British class system during the Victorian era was that while everybody was supposedly still born to know and keep his 'place', it was never impossible for a person of sufficient will and talent to rise above it. Queen Victoria had given the principle of birthright a new and acceptable rationale, through personifying the idea that inherited privileges were a fair return for a heavy burden of inherited duties, notably a duty to exemplify the ideals of family life and sexual virtue. But a purified monarchy would not have been enough to keep the class structure intact, if the aristocracy had made the mistake of isolating itself or of representing itself as a rigidly closed circle, for in that event an ambitious and increasingly powerful bourgeoisie would have been eager to challenge the equation of high birth with natural moral righteousness and hence with natural fitness to rule. It was only because of its flexibility and adaptability, its ever-readiness to welcome newcomers to its ranks, that the aristocracy was able to command the sycophantic support from below which it needed if the myth of its exceptional rectitude was to be convincingly enough maintained.

Both Valentine Baker and his devoted eldest brother, Samuel (the Bakers were a large and closely-knit family), were men of courage and ambition; both had brains and brawn; both were fervent patriots; both were apparently excellent mixers, and both renounced the prospect of a secure and opulent life 'in trade' for more adventurous pursuits in their country's service. Samuel had already achieved fame, a knighthood and royal favour as an Empire-building explorer. Valentine had not only won national acclaim as a regimental commander—he was said to be fearless in battle and, though a remarkably strict disciplinarian, to be adored by his men—but had established a considerable reputation for himself as a military theorist. By 1860, the year in which he became officer in command of the 10th Hussars, he had already published several books, which revealed him as an expert on cavalry tactics. In short, his career, like his brother's, was of a distinguished enough kind to make social advancement likely, and socially he had progressed far. He was an intimate of both the Prince of Wales and of H.R.H. The Commander-in-Chief, the Duke of Cambridge, who only recently had called him 'one of the best officers in the British army'. He mixed in the most fashionable circles, and if he still couldn't properly claim to be an aristocrat in his own right, he had undoubtedly been raised to the position of an associate member of the aristocracy. It was for this reason that newspaper reporters came swarming to Guildford on June 24th, when he was due to answer the 'extraordinary' charge that had been brought against him before the local bench of magistrates.

II

The reporters found Miss Dickinson to be an exceedingly pretty girl, and most 'ladylike' and 'self-possessed', though becomingly 'modest'. The story she told from the witness box likewise impressed them. It possessed the simple and elementally appealing qualities of a Victorian melodrama.

The villain had come upon his innocent prey when he caught the train at Liphook and entered the compartment where the heroine was already seated. He did not give her any immediate cause to suspect his evil intentions; on the contrary, he was bound to conceal them, for until the train reached Woking (a full 50 minutes away) it made frequent stops—at every little station. But, in the most kindly, charming and avuncular way he lured her into conversation.

Didn't she feel a draught? No? Then he would leave the window open. Wasn't the country pretty? Yes, and she thought the country between Midhurst and Petersfield the prettiest on the branch. She lived at Midhurst. Indeed? He had often stayed there; it was very convenient for Goodwood. And had she ever been to Aldershot? Yes, she had a brother stationed there—in the Engineers—and she'd been to the steeple-chase ball not long ago. Her brother was away now—camping out. Pontooning? Something of the sort, she supposed.

What regiment did *he* belong to? None. He was on the staff at Aldershot. He noticed that her luggage was labelled 'Dr Bagshawe, Dover'. Was she going to Dover, then? Yes. Alone? No, her brother-in-law, Dr Bagshawe, was meeting her in London, and tomorrow morning she'd be leaving from Dover with her sister for a holiday in Switzerland. She wouldn't be spending long in London, then? Only a couple of hours. Not nearly enough time to see the sights, he said. Oh, but, she told him, she had spent a whole fortnight in London a little while ago. And been to all the theatres? No, only Hamlet. Did she know that there was a new Italian actor coming out, named Rossi, who was supposed to be even better than Salvini? He doubted himself whether there were any good English actors left. But didn't he even admire Mrs Kemble? Was she a believer in mesmerism? (Laughter in court.)

So they continued to talk about this and that until the train pulled out of Woking, from where it was due to travel non-stop to Vauxhall, twenty miles and a full hour away, as they both knew. The moment for villainy to unmask itself had come, and Colonel Baker, so Miss Dickinson was now testifying, began to insult her.

'I suppose you don't often travel alone?'

'No.'

'Can you fix a time to be on the line again?'

'Never.'

'You mean you won't.'

'No, thank you.'

'Tell me your name.'

'I shan't.'

'Tell me, so that I may know it when I hear it again.'

'I shan't.'

'Why not?'

'Because I don't choose to. I don't see any reason why I should.'

'What is your Christian name, then?' She didn't reply.

'May I write?'

She still didn't reply. He got up from his corner seat opposite her, and without asking her leave, closed the window. Then he sat down next to her. He took her hand in his.

'Get away,' she said. 'I won't have you so near.'

'You are cross—don't be cross.' He put his left arm round her waist. He kissed her on the cheek. 'You must kiss me, darling.'

She pushed him away, got up, and tried to ring the bell or dial for the guard, which was on the other side of the compartment; but it wasn't working. 'Don't ring, don't call the guard,' he said. He forced her back into her seat, and this time held her powerless while he kissed her repeatedly on the lips. 'If I give you my name,' she said as soon as he allowed her breath enough to speak, 'will you get off?'

If he made any answer, she didn't hear it. He sank down in front of her. She felt one of his hands under her dress—on her stocking above her boot. He didn't touch her with his other hand. She wasn't sure what he was doing with it, though she had an impression ...

She struggled to her feet again. She tried without success to smash the window glass with her elbow, then managed to lower the window, and, leaning on it with her elbows, put her head out and screamed.

Colonel Baker pulled her back—and she 'felt quite strangled'. She screamed again, but she was afraid it was the last time she would be able to scream, so in desperation she twisted the door handle, and got out backwards. Colonel Baker caught hold of her arm. 'Get in, dear, get in, dear,' he said. 'You get in, and I'll get out of the other door.' But she knew that the other door was locked. She had seen it locked at Guildford. 'If you leave go, I shall fall,' was all she said.

She saw two gentlemen leaning out of the window of the next-door compartment. She asked them how long it would be before the train stopped, but she could not hear what they answered. Just before the train was finally brought to a stop, Colonel Baker said to her: 'Don't say anything. You don't know what trouble you will get me into; say you were frightened. I will give you my name, or anything.'

She was too exhausted at that point to say more than she did—that the gentleman had insulted her and would not let her alone. Colonel Baker was put into another compartment. She got back into the same compartment, but she said she felt unable, in her upset state, to travel by herself, and one of the passengers who had come to her assistance, the Rev. Baldwin Brown, volunteered his company.

At Waterloo Station, she and the Rev. Baldwin Brown were conducted to the Inspector's office; Colonel Baker was brought there, too. She declined to go into the details of her complaint, but she gave the interviewing police sergeant her name and address. 'I know your brother very well, indeed,' Colonel Baker said, referring to her soldier brother who she had already told him was stationed at Aldershot. 'Give me his address, and I will write to him.' 'You may do what you choose,' she replied. But she did not give him the address.

She went straight from Waterloo, still accompanied by the Rev. Baldwin Brown, to the house of another of her brothers—a physician living in Chesterfield Street—and she told him the whole story. Next morning she and her brother, Dr Dickinson, caught an early train for Guildford; several of the railway officials went with them. They called at the police station to apply for a warrant for Colonel Baker's arrest.

III

That concluded Miss Dickinson's evidence before the Guildford magistrates. She had made a convincing witness, and it was clear that if her story were left unchallenged, Colonel Baker would find himself in a very unenviable position. The magistrates would be bound to commit him for trial, while every newspaper reader in the country, and every potential juror, would be convinced of his guilt in advance. Significantly, however, Henry Hawking. Q.C., Colonel Baker's leading counsel, waived his right of cross-examination. He informed the Chairman of the Bench that since he would eventually be obliged to question Miss Dickinson in 'another tribunal', he did not wish to subject her to the same ordeal twice over. Further, he foreswore any intention of impugning her word or her honour. When he did come to cross-examine her, he said, it would merely be for the purpose of seeking elucidation of certain points in her testimony.

Henry Hawkins was to announce at the trial that in adopting this course he acted under strict instructions from Colonel Baker himself, though he was also to say that if he had received different instructions he would have refused the case. Both these assertions were presumably true—at least they must have had a basis of truth to them. Nevertheless, in the magistrates' court Colonel Baker betrayed impatience with such rigid gallantry.

Perhaps, he was more provoked by Miss Dickinson's evidence than he had anticipated he would be, and if so, he must have felt increasingly frustrated at having to suffer her accusations in silence, when testimony

followed from two other witnesses, which seemed to provide circumstantial corroboration of her story. Henry Bailey, the guard, told the
magistrates that he had taken matters in hand after the train was
brought to a stop. When Miss Dickinson made her complaint, so his
story ran, he asked Colonel Baker what 'he had done to the young
lady'. Colonel Baker said 'nothing', and added that he 'knew her
brother at Aldershot'. But Henry Bailey noticed that Colonel Baker's
trouser buttons were 'three parts undone'. He put him in another
compartment, and, after asking for his name and address, locked the
door.

William Hatter, the police sergeant who interviewed the parties at
Waterloo, confirmed in his evidence that Miss Dickinson had been
unwilling to specify the details of her complaint, but he also alleged that
Colonel Baker had admitted 'insulting' her. 'I asked him his name,'
Hatter testified, 'and he said, "Colonel Valentine Baker, Army and
Navy Club, and Aldershot." At my request, he gave me his card. I said,
"it is very unfortunate," and he replied, "I am sorry I did it. I do not
know what possessed me, I being a married man."'

If this was an exercise in 'putting in the verbal'—and it sounds very
like it today—it none the less tied a neat bow on the prosecution's
undisputed case. But there was a worse shock in store for Colonel Baker.
Though he was allowed bail—his brother, Sir Samuel, and Lord
Valentia came forward as sureties, each in the sum of £1,000—the
magistrates decided to send him for trial, not only on the charges of
common assault and indecent assault that Miss Dickinson had preferred, but on the much graver additional charge of 'assault with intent
to ravish'—attempted rape.

Colonel Baker could not contain himself. Against the advice of the
Bench, and the more urgent advice, one may assume, of his counsel, he
insisted on making a personal statement: 'I am placed here,' he said,
'in the most delicate position. If any act of mine on the occasion referred
to could have given any annoyance to the complainant, I beg to express
to her my most unqualified regret. At the same time, I solemnly declare
on my honour that the case was not as it has been presented today by
her under the influence of exaggerated fear and unnecessary alarm.
To the evidence of the police-sergeant Hatter I give a most unqualified
denial.'

That, for a man of Colonel Baker's profession and training, was an
outburst. But it was the first and only attempt he made to vindicate
himself. Thereafter he stuck to the code of his class. Throughout the rest

of his life and his shattered career, he was never to say a word in his own defence.

IV

The trial took place at the Croydon Assizes on Monday, August 2nd, a Bank Holiday, and it provided the masses with a special sort of Bank Holiday treat. In spite of the unusually warm weather, many Londoners renounced the opportunity of more healthful pursuits in favour of getting on a packed train to Croydon, though few of them had any hope of actually seeing the show when they arrived.

The curtain was not due to rise until 10.30 a.m., but, to quote one newspaper report, 'the doors were besieged for at least an hour and a half previously by an excited multitude, amongst whom were many well-dressed women, who stood the pressure with an endurance and persistency which proved they must have been not only strong-minded, but tolerably stout in mind and body'. This same report told how two 'ladies'—the inverted commas presumably implied that no female, however well-dressed, would have dreamed of attending such a show, had she really been a lady—were hoisted up to a window-sill, about seven feet from the ground level, and then 'pulled in by friends from above, amidst the jeers and shouts of the mob'. The police thereupon barred this 'irregular mode of ingress', but they obligingly admitted people by way of the cells and the dock as well as the doors, until every inch of space for the public to sit or stand in was taken. In fact, when learned counsel entered the courtroom, they found they could only reach their places at the bar by passing through the dock. The sight of them doing so raised a big laugh, which was doubtless a delighted comment on the humiliation shortly awaiting Colonel Baker. Meanwhile, distinguished visitors had arrived to occupy the bench: among them the Earl of Lucan, General Sir Thomas Steele, General Airey, Sir William Fraser, M.P., the Hon. Grantley Berkeley, Viscount Halifax, the Marquis of Tavistock, and Lord Valentia. Some had come to lend moral support to a beleaguered friend; but not all of them. Others were there to demonstrate that, horrifying though the show might be, the class they represented knew it to be necessary, and could watch it without fear, or a guilty conscience.

Not that the 'mob' was entirely convinced of this. Various stories of 'influence' at work had begun to circulate as soon as the Guildford magistrates committed Colonel Baker to the Croydon Assizes for trial.

One such rumour said that when the Prince of Wales left for his projected tour of India, he would conveniently arrange to take the Colonel with him; another that a 'high personage' had been in communication with Miss Dickinson's family, and had offered her soldier brother promotion if she would drop the case.

On July 7th, an application had been made to a Judge in Chambers seeking to have the case removed, by a writ of certiorari, from the Croydon Assizes to the Court of Queen's Bench, where it might be heard by a special jury. The grounds for this application were that so much prejudice had been aroused against the defendant, notably as the result of a street-corner pamphlet entitled 'Alleged Indecent Outrage by Col. Baker in a Railway Carriage—Courageous Conduct of Miss Dickinson', that a common jury could no longer be relied on to consider the evidence fairly and impartially. Though the application was refused, it led to intensified rumours that a way was being sought, and would somehow be found, to halt or interfere with the course of justice.

Nor were these rumours finally stilled until a Grand Jury at the Croydon Assizes found a True Bill, and Mr Justice Brett refused an application for a postponement of the trial to enable the defendant to apply again in November for the removal of his case to the Court of Queen's Bench. The law, said Mr Jusice Brett, did not allow the rank or social position of a defendant to be accepted as a reason for selecting a jury from a class superior to that from which jurors were ordinarily summoned for duty, and there was no other sufficient reason to justify Colonel Baker's application.

This was a decision to be logically welcomed rather than resented among the highest-born in the land, and one may feel morally certain that 'influence' was never exerted, in any organized sense, to protect Colonel Baker from 'justice'. Undoubtedly, he had individual friends who deeply sympathized with him, and would have liked to rescue him from his predicament, but the hard fact was that whether due to recklessness, folly or mere misfortune he had committed the unforgivable error of being caught, and class interests had nothing to gain, and everything to lose, from an attempt to spare him the consequences.

It is clear, moreover, that in the social climate of the times the truth or falsity of Miss Dickinson's story was an irrelevance. Had she herself belonged to the aristocracy, her family would have needed no persuading that silence was preferable to scandal. Had she belonged to the working class, her evidence before the Guildford magistrates, however truthful, might still have been so discredited that the case would have been thrown out of court. For working-class girls who tangled with gentlemen were *prima facie* considered no better than they should be, and Henry Hawkins, Q.C. was known as one of the most skilled and ruthless cross-examiners at the Bar. As *The Spectator* remarked, he would not have hesitated to exercise his talents on a milliner.

But unfortunately for Colonel Baker, Miss Dickinson belonged to a class which was at once too low to be privately tolerant (or forgiving) of sexual transgression and too high to be publicly represented as anything but irreproachably moral, upright and well-balanced—the backbone of the nation. Presumably, Colonel Baker had meant to imply in his statement to the magistrates that she was an hysteric, but it would have been worse than useless for him to persist in this charge; it would have been a betrayal of caste.

So now, as he was placed in the dock, though he 'bore the painful ordeal to which he was submitted with a certain nonchalant air', and pleaded 'Not Guilty in a firm and distinct tone to all the counts of the indictment', he knew that he faced certain conviction except on the charge of attempted rape. 'He stands before you,' Mr Sergeant Parry, Q.C. said, in opening the case for the prosecution, 'charged with a cowardly, unmanly attack upon a young lady ...' Colonel Baker, like most of the spectators, may not have heard this remark, for there was too much noise coming from the disappointed mob left in the street outside the courtroom. 'Turn out the women,' the men had begun to chant in unison. 'Turn out the women.'

'We cannot administer justice,' Mr Justice Brett eventually expostulated, 'while this disturbance continues. I must have the street cleared.' There was a ten-minute recess while the police did their best to oblige, though not with complete success. 'I wish you to hear also,' Mr Seargeant Parry said before calling Miss Dickinson, 'that Mr Hawkins, who appeared for the defendant at the examination before the magistrates, took a course which reflects upon him the highest honour. He declined to torment the young lady with a single question; and in the presence of his client he said that he would not cast the shade of an imputation upon her, and that any question he might have to put to her would only be by way of explanation.'

Mr Hawkins in no way appeared to violate this undertaking when his turn now came to cross-examine. He wanted to hear more, first of all, about the harmless conversation Miss Dickinson had had with Colonel Baker during their fifty minutes together before the train reached Woking. What, for example, had been said on the subject of

mesmerism? Well, Colonel Baker had asked her whether she had seen
Maskeleyne and Cook. 'Yes,' she had told him. 'You believe in
mesmerism?' he had asked her. 'No,' she had said. 'But I suppose there
is something in it.' Then he had told her he had a friend who believed
in mesmerism, and could make young ladies, who had never seen him
before, follow him about. She had said that she didn't think it easy
to believe that. 'I think you could be mesmerized,' Colonel Baker had
said. 'Why?' she had inquired, and he had answered something which
she didn't hear, so she had begged him to repeat it. 'I don't know,' he
had said, 'But you have a look about you.' There had been nothing
more said on the subject of mesmerism.

Could she recollect anything else they'd discussed? Yes, the
Academy, the theatres, and Mr Walker's murder. Mr Hawkins wasn't
interested in these parts of their conversation, but hadn't there been
some mention of where she had stayed on her visit to London? Yes,
Colonel Baker had asked her, and she had told him at Mr Logan's Hotel
in Clifford Street. 'How very odd you should mention that,' he had said.
'I was sleeping there last night.' And he had added that it was a very
quiet hotel.

She had found the frequent stoppages very tedious, had she not? Mr
Hawkins continued. Yes, but she didn't remember remarking on the
fact, though she might have done so. Hadn't Colonel Baker replied to
her complaint about the slowness of the journey, 'We do not stop any
more after leaving Woking?' She didn't think that he had, though she
couldn't be sure that he had not. At any rate, Mr Hawkins went on,
she had had no cause to complain of Colonel Baker's conduct up to the
time the train left Woking? No—not until then. Nor had she for her part
said or done anything she regretted? No, nothing.

The line of the defence was already becoming clear. It was to admit
the indecent assault, but to deny an attempt to ravish. Mr Hawkins did
not mean to imply by his questions to Miss Dickinson (so he was to
assure the jury in his closing speech) that there was any 'levity in her
character which induced or led up to the assault'. On the contrary, he
wished to show that before the train left Woking her conversation with
his client had been of such a transparently innocent kind—they had,
after all, exchanged information about one another, even though they
hadn't told each other their names—that the idea of attacking the
young lady could not conceivably have entered Colonel Baker's mind.

This was a plainly absurd argument in the light of what it was
admitted Colonel Baker had done as soon as he supposed he safely

could, and it seems probable, therefore, that Mr Hawkins hoped the jury would infer Miss Dickinson's answers to his questions precisely what he disclaimed any idea of suggesting: namely, that here was an exceedingly pretty, rather pert-looking girl, unusually free and easy in her manner, who, wittingly or unwittingly, had encouraged Colonel Baker to believe that she was virtueless or was at least prepared to lose her virtue. The cross-examination otherwise appeared to get nowhere, and Mr Hawkins might not, perhaps, have bothered with it, if he hadn't thought it necessary to do everything possible to counteract prejudice.

For the prosecution had such an intrinsically weak case to support the charge of attempted rape that prejudice was really all that the defence had to fear. The question was not whether Colonel Baker had meant to seduce Miss Dickinson; nor even whether he had at any moment—before or after the train left Woking—formed an intention of overcoming her resistance by force. Miss Dickinson's testimony provided no proof that he had done so. It showed that the furthest he had gone towards 'ravishing' her was to put one hand under her dress, 'on her stocking above her boot'. She had no more than an 'impression' of what he was doing at the time with his other hand.

But this 'impression' was relevant, of course, to the evidence about Colonel Baker's unbuttoned trousers; which Henry Bailey, the guard, duly repeated, though he became hopelessly rattled under cross-examination:

Q. Did you notice Colonel Baker's dress was undone when you first saw him?

A. Directly I saw him on the gravel.

Q. Did you call his attention to it?

A. I did not.

Q. Why not?

A. Because it slipped my memory.

Q. Do you mean by that you did think of telling him, but forgot to do so?

A. I never thought to tell the gentleman of it.

Q. Remarkable. You have told my learned friend that the buttons of Colonel Baker's trousers were unfastened except for the top one?

A. To the best of my recollection they were.

Q. Is your recollection good enough to swear that they were?

A. To the best of my recollection.

Q. Did you give evidence before the magistrates on this matter?

A. I did.

Q. Did you then say that the trousers were three parts unbuttoned?

A. I cannot say.

Q. Did you say so?

A. I may have said so.

Q. If you did say so, did you mean that every button was undone except the top?

A. They looked to me nearly all unbuttoned.

Q. Upon reflection, do you mean to say that they were three parts unbuttoned?

A. Yes. Three parts unbuttoned. That is what they looked to me.

Q. Which will you stick to now?

A. Three parts unbuttoned.

Q. And you will give up, 'All the buttons except the top one?'

A. That is it, sir. (Laughter.)

This was pretty certainly an instance of the law's having its educated fun at the expense of a perfectly honest but uneducated witness. In fact, it wasn't in the least remarkable that a guard, conscious of his 'place', should have failed to inform an 'officer and gentleman' that his fly buttons were undone; it was more remarkable that he should have taken as decisive an action as he did. Nevertheless, Henry Bailey's evidence would undoubtedly have been laughed out of court, been 'worth nothing', as the Judge was to put it, if it hadn't been substantially corroborated by two new witnesses. They were Messrs Pike and Burnett, businessmen both of them, and they had been occupants of the compartment which Colonel Baker was put into by the guard.

According to their testimony, Colonel Baker had immediately shown himself anxious to assure them of his innocence. He had remarked that there was always the risk that a lady would become alarmed if she found herself alone in a compartment with a strange gentleman, and that this was an occurrence which the railway companies ought to take steps to prevent. His observations met with a chilling response. 'No wonder, the lady was frightened,' Pike said, with a meaningful glance at Burnett, 'considering the state of your dress.' For Pike had noticed that several of Colonel Baker's trouser buttons were undone; he could see a portion of white under-garment through the gap. Colonel Baker didn't answer him, but shortly afterwards both Pike and Burnett saw that he was apparently re-fastening his trouser buttons under cover of his coat.

Pike said in cross-examination that the trousers were neither completely undone nor three parts undone, but 'opened in the same way as would have been the case had there been an accidental omission to fasten the buttons'. This enabled Mr Hawkins to suggest that there might, indeed, have been just such an 'accidental omission' on his client's part, and though he couldn't have seriously expected anyone to believe this, the rest of the evidence relating to the charge of intent to ravish was heavily weighted on the side of the defence.

The prosecution alleged that Colonel Baker had put up the window after the train left Woking to prevent Miss Dickinson's screams from being heard. But, by her own account, she had not, in fact, screamed while the window was closed, and it was obviously more than possible that Colonel Baker had simply wanted some extra privacy for his intended love-making. He had put an arm round her waist, but she had none the less been able to get free of him to try to ring for the guard; and though it was true, according to her testimony, that he had held her down while he kissed her, she had subsequently got up and opened the window and then the door—actions which a man of his physical strength could and would surely have stopped her from taking if he had been determined to use force to attain his ends. Finally, all the witnesses who saw Miss Dickinson after the train was stopped outside Esher agreed that, apart from the loss of her hat, there had been nothing disordered about the state of her own dress.

The Judge reiterated these points in a summing-up which, granted that Colonel Baker had offered no defence against the secondary charge of indecent assault, was as favourable to him as it could have possibly been. Mr Justice Brett drew the jury's attention to the fact that whatever the defendant's intention might have been before Miss Dickinson got out of the carriage, 'his only efforts afterwards were devoted to saving her from the terrible danger of her position'. He said that the 'character and mercy of the law of England were, in the interpretation of the law, to give to every doubtful act the most merciful interpretation'. He advised the jury that if they concluded that Colonel Baker had planned to win, 'not an absolute, but a reluctant consent', from Miss Dickinson, 'partly by force and partly by exciting her passions', they would still have to acquit him of an 'intent to ravish'. Before they could convict him on that count, they would have to decide on the evidence, guided 'solely by reason and intelligence', that he had been determined to 'offer any amount of brutality against any resistance she might make'.

The jury would have had to be blinded by prejudice to ignore so clear an expression of judicial wishes and expectations. In fact, they took only ten minutes to reach their verdict. They found the defendant Not Guilty of Intent to Ravish; Guilty of Indecent Assault and Common Assault. His fate was now in the hands of the Judge.

At this tense moment, apparently, several of Colonel Baker's fellow officers either entered the dock or stood up by the dock to demonstrate their undiminished loyalty to him. According to one or two of the newspaper accounts, General Sir Thomas Steele was among them, but this was later denied in Parliament by Sir William Fraser who spoke from first-hand knowledge. What Sir Thomas did do was to follow General Sir Richard Airey into the box as a character witness. Both generals testified to Colonel Baker's hitherto unblemished record as a 'man of honour'.

Mr Justice Brett had more than a few words to say in passing sentence. 'Prisoner at the Bar, when this story was first told a thrill of dishonour passed through the whole country. When it was told that a young and innocent girl, travelling by the ordinary conveyance of this country, had been obliged to risk her life in order to save herself from a gross outrage, every household in England felt a sense of personal injury. And when it was heard that the assailant was a soldier, an officer of high rank, a gentleman, the news was received with astonishment, and, I may say, with disgust.'

The Judge went on to eulogize Miss Dickinson: 'It may be suggested that this abominable outrage on this lady has defiled her, but I pronounce that she leaves this court as pure, as innocent, and as undefiled as she ever was in her life—nay, more, the courage she has displayed has added a glory to her youth and her innocence and her beauty.'

He addressed the prisoner again: 'Of all the people who travelled in that train that day you were the most bound to stand by and defend a defenceless woman. There was nothing in her conduct to justify the course you took ... Your crime is as bad as it could be ...'

Thus far Mr Justice Brett appeared to be uninfluenced by the evidence he had heard from the two generals and by the sight of solidarity among 'officers and gentlemen' still before his eyes. But suddenly he switched course. He would not, after all, he implied, be 'failing in his duty, were he not to pass the maximum sentence that the law allowed'. On the contrary, his 'duty' obliged him to take certain mitigating factors into consideration: that the jury had rightly acquitted the prisoner of the 'graver charge'; that the prisoner's high position was not owed to 'accident of birth', but had been won by his own 'individual exertions and brilliant services'; that the prisoner had previously 'borne a character' of so unsullied a kind that the outrage of which he now stood convicted could only be explained as a 'sudden outbreak of wickedness'. These mitigating factors, the Judge said, led him to believe that he was dealing with a prisoner who was not beyond hope of rehabilitation.

'Therefore,' he told Colonel Baker, 'I shall not pass upon you a sentence which will carry with it all the personal and all the physical degradations which would follow an ordinary sentence for this offence. If I passed such a sentence, I feel that it would subject you to a penalty far greater than it might really be to persons differently situated who might be found guilty of such an offence. If that sentence were passed upon you, I am aware you would be subjected to a continuous torture which would possibly prevent you from the result which I hope will follow for you, that after a period of long repentance you may be reinstated in the eyes of your fellows in some position somewhat like that you now enjoy. I shall, therefore, spare you those physical degradations, hoping, as I have said, after a long repentance, you may by some brilliant service, of which your past life shows that you are no doubt capable, wipe out the injury you have done to your country ...'

'But,' the Judge continued, 'the sentence I must pass on you will be a severe one. It is that you be imprisoned in the common gaol of this county, without subjecting you to the physical degradation to which I have alluded, for Twelve Calendar Months; that you pay a fine of £500 ...'

Inside the courtroom, there was only a 'subdued murmur of approval'. But a big cheer went up from the crowd outside as soon as the news reached them. Pretty certainly, all they realized was that Colonel Baker had 'got a year'—a stiff sentence by comparison with the penalties ordinarily imposed for indecent assault.[1] If they understood yet that it was to be served without 'physical degradations', they hadn't more than the haziest notion of what that meant.

Colonel Baker, for his part, 'did not move a muscle or display the least sign of emotion. He stooped for his umbrella and hat and descended by the stairs within the dock' to the cells below. Miss Dickinson and her family left the courthouse immediately, and received a royal ovation from the crowd as they drove off in a hired carriage to their hotel. Mrs Dickinson, the mother, appeared to be 'much affected'. But the crowd had to wait for nearly two hours to catch a sight of Colonel Baker in

[1] For example, just ten years later, John Watkins, commercial traveller, was given three months, though with hard labour, for an exactly similar offence in a railway carriage. His alleged victim was a governess.

captivity. There was evidently difficulty experienced on this Bank Holiday afternoon in procuring a suitable means of conveyance to transport him to the Surrey county gaol in Horsemonger Lane. Ironically, when he did leave at last, it was in the same hired carriage that the Dickinsons had used. He was accompanied by a warder and by the governor of the gaol in person.

Meanwhile, the London newsboys were crying 'verdicansentence' all in one word. Verdict alone would have had much less sales appeal; it might even have aroused sales resistance. 'Verdicansentence'—found guilty and punished—was the story people had been waiting and hoping for. It offered a most festive climax to a festive day. Or, so people thought.

V

The Press next morning was virtually unanimous in believing that justice had been done. *The Times* found 'every reason to be satisfied with the conduct and result of the trial'. It called Colonel Baker's offence 'a brutal assault inpired by animal passion', and noted that the 'prejudices of the class from which jurymen in criminal cases are taken' had not, in the event, provided the defendant with any reasonable grounds of complaint. *The Morning Post* was of a similar opinion; after all, it said, Colonel Baker's act 'was not one of mere libertinism; it was, in plain language, an act of ruffianism'. *The Standard* believed that an example had rightly been made of an 'officer and gentleman' for 'sinning against his lights, superior advantages, and all the social and moral conditions which should have held him back'.

Most of the weekly papers, when their turn came to speak, were equally approving of both verdict and sentence. 'We have indeed heard Colonel Baker's conduct ascribed to "a moment of impulsive gallantry",' wrote *The Saturday Review*. 'That is language which might have been intelligible and in season in one of the grossly licentious and cynical comedies of Wycherley and Vanbrugh.'

The Spectator implied that the law had squarely met a vital challenge to the country's social stability. 'We suspect', it wrote, 'that there was a deeper cause for the interest of the populace in this case than the passion for prurient detail which exists, no doubt, in great strength under all our English respectability, and which would make another trial like that of Queen Caroline as hurtful a nuisance as that one was. The lower orders of this country have shown that a feeling of caste-jealousy has been diffused here, and may yet produce consequences of the utmost gravity.'

However, there were two dissenting voices among the weeklies. *Vanity Fair* said that Colonel Baker had been punished for 'making a mistake'—and much too severely punished. 'As a matter of course,' it continued, 'his trial and sentence have called forth all the virtue which slumbers in the British breast in readiness to blaze up whenever any man is brought into a public conviction of being worse than his fellows will make public confession of being.'

If those words reflected the attitude of Colonel Baker's supporters in 'Society', which presumably they did, they failed to say what *Vanity Fair* really meant. Colonel Baker still had many loyal friends, including members of the Army and Navy Club, who were insisting that his resignation should not be automatically accepted by the club committee but should be a matter for a general meeting to decide. But whatever moral lapses these friends of his may have been guilty of in their time, they were not standing by Valentine Baker now out of a willingness to brand themselves as libertines and sexual 'ruffians'. They were standing by him because they believed (and logically had to believe, if they were to maintain that the word of a gentleman meant anything) that when he had sworn on his honour in the Guildford Police Court that the case was 'not as Miss Dickinson presented it', he had not lied.

This, for obvious reasons, could not be said openly, and *Vanity Fair*'s dissent, honest and courageous though it may have been as a protest against the Press 'chorus of offended modesty', had little or no relevance to the reality of the situation. But the other dissent was much more pertinent. This was voiced by *Reynolds's Newspaper*, a Sunday journal that spoke for extreme radical opinion.

Colonel Baker, *Reynolds's Newspaper* argued, had only escaped being convicted of attempted rape because of the prosecution's failure to press the charge against him with sufficient determination. Yet, even so, he had been found guilty of the most aggravated kind of indecent assault imaginable. Why, then, the paper asked, shouldn't he have received the maximum sentence (two years with hard labour)? It answered its own question by lambasting Mr Justice Brett: 'He was looking on one of the most cowardly ruffians that ever stood in a place where a vast number of ruffians had already appeared before him, and only saw in the atrocious criminal in the dock the highly-favoured Colonel of Hussars, the intimate friend of the Prince of Wales, the Duke of Cambridge, etc.—and he regulated his sentence accordingly. Shame—shame upon the head of the judge who spared from that 'physical degradation' he so richly merited a miscreant who strove to plunge a pure, an innocent, a defenceless girl into the lowest depths of "physical degradation" to which one of her sex can fall! So flagrant, so shameful, a miscarriage of justice as that witnessed on Monday at Croydon, is sufficient to arouse the indignation of every honest-hearted Englishman who has ever been brought up to believe that English justice really knows no distinction of person ...'

This, of course, was raucous stuff and its overstated point could easily be disregarded for as long as people remained ignorant of what Mr Justice Brett had meant by imprisonment without 'personal and physical degradations'—or what he had intended it to mean in Colonel Baker's case. But a few days later, *The Morning Post* reported without comment: 'He (Baker) is allowed to wear his own clothing, to buy his own food, to furnish his rooms—he has had two allotted to him—with what is reasonable, necessary, and not extravagant; to have wine at his own cost, not exceeding one pint, or malt liquor not exceeding one quart, per day. He is not required to do any work, to clean his apartment, make his bed, or perform any menial office, all these being done for him by an officer of the prison. He may have any unobjectionable books or newspapers which he chooses. He may write or receive letters or papers, but these must in the first instance be examined or read by the Governor. Lastly, he may see friends in his apartment from 9.0 a.m. to 6.0 p.m.'

In other words, imprisonment for Colonel Baker had apparently turned out to be nothing harsher than a period of honourable detention, and this made expressions of horror at his crime seem manifestly incompatible with an uncritical acceptance of the sentence imposed on him. It looked as though the public had been cheated of its prey, as though 'influence' had, after all, defeated 'justice'. Wild stories began to circulate of the drinking parties Colonel Baker was holding in gaol, and of visits he was receiving from his royal patrons as well as from selected ladies of the town.

In the House of Commons, the notorious Dr Keneally tried to raise a storm over the issue, and might have succeeded, if he had been a less unpopular and more trusted figure. As it was, Mr Cross, the Home Secretary, could not deny the accuracy of *The Morning Post*'s report, but he disclaimed responsibility. He was powerless, he said, and properly powerless, to interfere with a judicial decision. Colonel Baker had been sentenced as a first-class misdemeanant, and was simply being dealt with according to the rules laid down for the treatment of prisoners of the first division.

Since this explanation put Dr Keneally in his place, it was received with loud applause from both sides of the House. But it was not necessarily watertight. *The Standard* subsequently printed a letter from an anonymous prison governor, who called Colonel Baker's imprisonment a 'farce', and said it was nonsense to pretend that all prisoners of the first division (the great majority of them were people convicted of contempt of court) had to be treated alike. In his own gaol, he said, a first-class misdemeanant would certainly not be given two 'rooms' to himself; nor would he be excused such menial tasks as cleaning out his cell.

Moreover, the fact that the House of Commons refused to respond to Dr Keneally's outburst did not mean that it felt no cause for concern. One member stooped very low in an apparent effort to confuse the issue. He recalled that, twenty years ago, Dr Keneally had himself been sent to prison as a first-class misdemeanant for an assault on one of his own children, and that, therefore, he should be appreciative, rather than disapproving, of this form of judicial mercy.

More significantly, another member, Sir William Fraser, who had been present at Colonel Baker's trial, found it opportune to try to correct the impression that the case had anything to do with the duties, responsibilities or morals of the governing class. 'It has been stated by the Member for Stoke (Dr Keneally) that Colonel Baker was a member of fashionable or aristocratic circles. I have had no means of judging whether Colonel Baker was a man of fashion—I never saw him before the other day when he was in court; but as regards aristocratic connections, neither of the parties in this regrettable affair is connected, I think, with what are conventionally called the upper classes. As to the heroine of this unpleasant romance—I do not mean to use that phrase offensively—she certainly does not belong to the upper classes; and as to the prisoner I think no one can accuse him of being in any way connected with the aristocracy.'

This, of course, was a naïve attempt to undo the damage caused by Mr Justice Brett's indulgence. In the public's mind, the mind of the 'populace', Colonel Baker was more than connected with the aristocracy; he was identified with it. Otherwise, as *The Spectator* perceived, his trial might have attracted little, if any, attention; no more, possibly, than the case, a month later, of a 13-year-old boy who was sentenced at the Croydon Assizes to six months hard labour, to be followed by five years in a reformatory, for *attempting* an indecent assault on a girl playmate in a field.

'However grateful Sir W. Fraser's aristocratic constituents may be for his advocacy,' wrote *Reynolds's Newspaper*, 'there can be no doubt that the classes of society which do not need Sir W. Fraser's services in the House will feel that whether the blue in Colonel Baker's veins does or does not exist in sufficient quantity to make his blood thoroughly aristocratic, his proclivities, and his conduct eminently qualify him to be put forward as a fair representative of the upper ten thousand.'

More 'respectable' organs of the Press than *Reynolds's Newspaper*— those that had the best interests of the governing class and hence of the nation at heart—did not attempt to conceal their alarm. Belatedly, they awoke to the fact that the sentence passed on Colonel Baker wouldn't do as an expression of moral outrage at his 'extraordinary' crime. *The Daily Telegraph* pointed out that even unconvicted (legally innocent) prisoners were kept in solitary confinement, forbidden to smoke and forced to perform menial tasks, and it remarked that Colonel Baker had only escaped this fate because, unlike men of humbler position charged with a similar offence, he had been allowed bail.

The World referred to the sentence as Mr Justice Brett's 'indiscretion', and explained: 'It may well be considered intolerable and even incredible that the lower orders in England should lend an ear to the blatant balderdash, seditious trash, etc., of *Reynolds's*. Just the same, if all indecent assaulters are to be sentenced as first-class misdemeanants, if will look uncommonly like a legal palliation of one of the most brutal and detestable crimes which a man can commit.'

The paper went on to praise Sir Baliol Brett as 'an excellent and wisely severe judge when the offences of people of inferior station come under his consideration', and it noted with approval his recent sentence of two years with hard labour passed on the leaders of the gas stoker's strike. But it added, 'Sir Baliol is one occupant of the Bench who is, in a singular degree, open to what are called "influences of society".'

In short, the scandal of an officer and gentleman being exposed as a 'sexual ruffian' was threatening to grow up into a bigger scandal; the revelation that officers and gentlemen could be sexual ruffians with impunity. It needed the intervention of a very powerful personage to put matters right.

There was always a worse punishment facing Colonel Baker than any the law could impose on him—lasting social disgrace and the ruin of his career. Immediately after the trial, he wrote to the War Office offering to resign his commission. The reply, which did not come until a fortnight later, exploded the assurance Mr Justice Brett had given him about his future. He was not to be allowed to *resign* his commission. Instead, he was to be cashiered—'removed from the Army, Her Majesty having no further occasion for his services'.

For Colonel Baker this must have been a bitter shock, but it was balm for an aroused public opinion; and it also showed that there was someone in the land who knew better than Mr Justice Brett what the true interests of society demanded, when the social system needed to be defended against the sort of attack to which Colonel Baker's folly had exposed it.

That someone was the sovereign herself. 'If as is believed,' wrote *The Daily News* on August 14th, 'the decision is due to the intervention of the Queen, we can say it is another proof of that firm good sense and clear perception of duty which we associate with Her Majesty ... Something like this was due to the moral feeling of the country that had been a little puzzled and scandalized by the exceptional lenience shown to Colonel Baker.'

And at least one member of the lower orders who ordinarily 'lent an ear to seditious trash' now felt reassured. 'The Queen,' an anonymous wife and mother wrote to *Reynolds's Newspaper*, '... by cashiering the rascal who disgraced her uniform, has shown a far keener sense of the atrocity and outrage committed than her judge did. Nearly every mother in England will shudder at the mention of his name. To Miss Dickinson be every attribute of praise given for proving herself worthy of the name given her by her creator—a woman, a true woman—a nobler title than lady, or any other Society can bestow.'

So the day was saved. Members of the side were rarely caught breaking the rules, but when one of them was, the only logical thing to do was to order him off the field forever. Queen Victoria knew that.

VI

To claim that English justice recognizes no distinction of person has always been a hollow pretence. If men have occasionally fared better at the hands of the criminal law by virtue of being 'someones' rather than 'no ones', they have probably more often fared worse. For the whole theory of deterrence depends on the practice of making 'examples' of people; and if a person accused of a crime has an identity which attracts an unusual amount of publicity, he is an obvious candidate to be made an example of. In this respect, Colonel Baker was fortunate. He would, almost certainly, be less fortunate today.

But it is just as hollow a pretence to claim that there is now, or can ever be, such a thing as equality of punishment. On the contrary, the more uniform punishment may be made in theory, the greater its inequality in practice. A fixed fine for a given offence manifestly discriminates against the poor. By contrast, standardized imprisonment discriminates, broadly speaking, against the rich, in the sense that conditions, which the least favoured members of society may find tolerable, will for the most favoured members of society be torture.

Imprisonment, when Colonel Baker was sentenced, was not quite such a standardized method of punishment as it has since become, and one may, perhaps, credit Mr Justice Brett with a sort of selfish, class-bound humaneness for taking advantage of this fact. One may at least doubt whether he yielded as much to the 'influences of society' as he did to the influences of his own background, which was not dissimilar from Colonel Baker's. Here was an offender with whom he could identify. He may, like too many judges in our own time, have been brutally ignorant and careless of what prison might do to the great majority of offenders whom it was his 'duty' to send there. But evidently he did have an awareness, knowing himself, of what its ordinary cruelties and indignities might do to a man of Colonel Baker's standing.

Those cruelties and indignities were, of course, a good deal worse in 1875 than they are now, and it is unlikely that Colonel Baker could have survived an experience similar to the one that awaited Oscar Wilde without irreparable damage being done to his personality. Yet although he was, in fact, more considerately treated than any convicted or even unconvicted prisoner could hope to be treated today, there is still some reason to believe that he suffered greatly in body, if not in mind.

After he had been in the Horsemonger Lane gaol for little more than three months, *The Times* reported that he was critically ill. A few days later, *The Times* published a letter from his wife, who must presumably have forgiven him—assuming she ever believed he had anything to be forgiven for. She wanted to assure 'her dear husband's many friends' that he was no longer in immediate danger of losing his life. 'I am thankful to state,' she wrote, 'that the most serious symptoms, which recently caused so much alarm both to myself and his whole family, have yielded to medical treatment. I cannot, however, hide from myself the terrible fact that such continued and trying confinement, after his active and useful life, has rendered him thoroughly out of health, and his condition causes me the most constant and distressing anxiety.'

Very possibly, Colonel Baker was hoping to secure an early release for her husband on medical grounds, but the outcry, if she had succeeded, might have been of a magnitude to bring down the Government, and, in fact, he served his full term. Almost immediately afterwards, he and his family (he had two daughters) left England, where his services were no longer required and where he was never to make his home again. He did not rot in exile. The cashiered British Colonel became a Lieutenant-General in the Ottoman army, and during the Russo-Turkish war fought a glorious rearguard action at Tashkessan. Later he accepted an appointment from the Khedive as commander of the Egyptian gendarmerie; during the Sudan war he made a gallant, though disastrous, attempt to relieve Tokar at the head of an ill-trained, ill-disciplined Egyptian force, which was cut to pieces, and in a later action he himself was seriously wounded. In short, the twelve years of life that remained to him after he left prison were richer in incident and achievement, in triumph and failure, than those that had gone before. If the end of his career as Colonel Baker had not heralded the beginning of his career as Baker Pasha, his name might never have reached the history books.

But this is not the place for a detailed account of his story in exile. It is enough to say that he was always the patriot who fought for the Ottoman Empire out of a passionate conviction that its security was inseparable from British interests, and, as commandant of the Egyptian gendarmerie, was a servant of Britain in all but name. Yet he waited in vain for a signal from his homeland that he had earned forgiveness. This, the one reward that he wanted and strove for, he was denied until it was too late for him to know that it had arrived.

England did not forget him, though. When he returned to London for a period of convalescence after he had been wounded, a large crowd gathered at Victoria station to welcome him with cheers. By then, his friends had begun actively campaigning for his reinstatement in the British army, and there appears to be little or no doubt that they would have had their way, but for the Queen's obduracy. Whether or not her subjects, or most of them, were willing to forgive him, she was not. Not, that is, until the very end.

On November 12th, 1887, Valentine Baker died at Tel-el-Kebir. The cause of death was a heart attack following a bout of typhoid fever—the same scourge that, a few years earlier, had killed the younger of his two daughters. The British pro-Consul in Egypt, Sir Evelyn Baring, sent a cabled despatch to the Prime Minister, the Marquis of Salisbury, saying that though the death of Baker Pasha was a deep loss to him personally, it was one that he believed to be a greater loss to Britain. In reply, the Marquis of Salisbury assured Sir Evelyn that Her Majesty's Government shared his view. At the same time, H.R.H. the Commander-in-Chief cabled orders from the War Office for Baker Pasha, cashiered British officer, to be buried in Cairo with full military honours.

These orders, which must have had the Queen's approval, were duly carried out. The coffin, on its gun carriage, was wrapped in a Union Jack, and crowned with garlands. Four British generals, as well as Sir Evelyn Baring and a representative of the Khedive, were among those who marched beside it in the procession. Mounted Police, an Egyptian regiment, and the English Rifle Brigade formed the cortege.

Back in Britain, the Press, with the notable exception of *Reynolds's Newspaper*, voiced no disapproval of this posthumous rehabilitation, while *Vanity Fair* remained true to the spirit of its original dissent from the general line. 'The death of Baker Pasha, better known as Valentine Baker,' it wrote, 'is a loss to England of one of the best, the bravest, and the worst-treated of her sons. No truer gentleman, no abler General, no more gallant soldier, no man of better manners or more promising abilities, ever stepped on English earth, or was ever more cruelly cast out to exile by an English Sovereign ... When Her Majesty reflects upon the very lenient way in which errors proceeding from the same source as that of Valentine Baker have always been treated in the Royal Family, and when she thinks of this able and gallant man driven out of the country he loved and had served so well, to die in a foreign land, she will feel glad that, although too late, she at last relented. For the saddest part of this sad history is that ... had General Baker lived but a few weeks longer, he would have been reinstated in the British army.'

Did *Vanity Fair* KNOW that the Queen had relented? Or was this merely a deduction from the fact that she had consented to the funeral arrangements? In the latter case, one may doubt if *Vanity Fair* was necessarily right. It seems more likely that the only way Valentine Baker could ever have earned his sovereign's forgiveness was through dying. And, if this was so, it may be that, once again, Queen Victoria knew best.

VII

Organized hypocrisy in England has always been concerned with the living. If it has never been able to command the loyalty of posterity, neither has it had any need to do so. Once the concealed purpose for which a man may be victimized in the name of sexual morality has been fulfilled, the apparent reason for it can safely be rejected as grossly hypocritical or insufficient.

Thus it is unlikely, to say the least, that any Member of Parliament or editorial writer alive today would attempt to defend the treatment of Oscar Wilde or deny that this disgraced the administration of English justice. Yet, in theory, there is nothing to prevent an exactly similar persecution taking place tomorrow—and, ironically enough, as a result of precisely the same sort of criminal charge. It is true that the ill-judged Labouchere provision in the Criminal Law Amendment Act of 1885, which trapped Wilde, was finally reformed in 1966, but the homosexuality laws were not thereby restored to the *status quo ante*. Parliament still insists that 'youth' must be protected against homosexual corruption, youth being defined for this special purpose as any male, *not* female, under the age of 21. Wilde, therefore, would be as guilty of an offence against the law today as he was in 1895. Whether a reason to punish him as severely for it would be needed or found is another matter.

The persecution of Oscar Wilde is frequently explained as a manifestation of the prejudice in Victorian England against writers and artists. 'If he [Wilde] had been a general or a so-called empire builder,' Frank Harris wrote, '*The Times* might have affronted public opinion and called attention to his virtues, and argued that they should be taken in extenuation of his offences; but as he was only a writer no one seemed to owe him anything or to care what became of him.' But twenty years earlier, as we have seen, *The Times* was not, in fact, prepared to affront public opinion with a plea of extenuating circumstances on behalf of Colonel Valentine Baker, who *was* an empire builder. Nor can there be much doubt that if Colonel Baker had been convicted of an 'unnatural' crime, the Press onslaught on him would have been even more virulent than it was and the loyalty of his friends correspondingly less in evidence. Admittedly, the fact that Oscar Wilde was an artist, and one who had delighted in shocking the bourgeoisie, may have made a philistine judiciary, press and public especially zestful in seizing an opportunity to show how cruel they could be. But Wilde was not victimized *because* he was an artist, any more than Colonel Baker was victimized because he was a soldier. Both of them paid the penalty for being identified with a governing class and committing offences against the adopted morality of that class which could not be concealed. This penalty was social banishment. Imprisonment was never more that an incidental part of it, which Wilde certainly, and possibly Baker, too, could have avoided by going into exile before the law had time (or inclination) enough to strike.

What was actually done to Wilde was, of course, far more brutal than anything done to Baker. It also left an uglier stain on English civilization in the sense that its effect was to destroy a genius, whereas Baker, whatever he may have suffered, was neither a genius nor was he destroyed. On the other hand, one may at least be sure in Wilde's case that under the law he was guilty as charged, and to this extent had himself to blame for what happened to him. But one has no certainty that Colonel Baker was fairly convicted. Even if he had been offered an opportunity to defend himself under oath (which he was not, for in 1875 accused persons did not have the right to enter the witness box), it seems most unlikely that he would have accepted it. Yet the fact remains that, in the police court, he swore on his honour that Miss Dickinson had given a distorted account of what happened between them. Can one believe that this was a mere lie, coming from a man who was trained to set a high value on his word of honour and who knew very well (assuming that his counsel told the truth at his trial) that he could not hope to save himself by speaking out?

One thing is certain. If Miss Dickinson's story was the whole truth, Colonel Baker must have given way to an uncontrollable sexual impulse. This was the explanation of his behaviour that he himself eventually came to accept. At least, in the only public reference he ever made to the case after his release from prison—it occurred when he had an emotional shipboard reunion with his old British regiment, the 10th Hussars, following the Tokar defeat—he spoke of a 'moment of madness' of which he was 'ashamed' and which he 'deeply and bitterly deplored'. 'I shall strive,' he told his former comrades-in-arms, 'to show my countrymen that I am worthy of their forgiveness.'

But if he was mad enough on one occasion to disregard the almost certain consequences of assaulting a respectable young girl from the middle classes, who had offered him no encouragement and was plainly determined to resist his advances, why, one wonders, wasn't he mad enough to run similar risks on other occasions?

Maybe, Mr Justice Brett seriously believed in the idea of a 'sudden outbreak of wickedness'. But 'outbreaks of wickedness', if that is what one chooses to call them, do not come without forewarning or only once in a lifetime. Either Colonel Baker was some kind of sexual lunatic—or he wasn't. If he was, it is remarkable that he avoided trouble before he met Miss Dickinson, and little less remarkable that he avoided it afterwards. If he wasn't sexually unbalanced, there is more than his own word of honour to suggest that Miss Dickinson must have twisted the facts.

It is clear from the conversation he had with her, when he learned, among other things, about one of her brothers being an officer stationed at Aldershot, that he could not have mistaken her social station or imagined her to be the class of girl whose word would automatically be disbelieved and whom a 'gentleman' could, therefore, ordinarily 'insult' with impunity. She was obvious scandal bait.

Yet if, as she testified that he did, he implored her not to say anything when the train was brought to a stop, he did not afterwards behave as though he felt any great cause for alarm. He made no attempt to deceive either the guard or the police sergeant at Waterloo station about his name and address, though the latter suspected that this was just what a gentleman in his predicament would try to do, and, in order to check, sent a plainclothes detective along with him to the Army and Navy Club. Colonel Baker raised no objection to this. He evidently regarded it as a pure formality. If he had supposed himself to be in serious danger of arrest, he would presumably have sought immediate legal advice. But he took no action at all.

Nor was his apparent confidence that he had heard the last of the matter entirely misplaced, for the police would not have moved against him on their own initiative, and Miss Dickinson herself only decided to charge him after her family insisted on her doing so. When he *was* arrested, he was taken completely by surprise. This happened on June 19th, two days after the assault, at Guildford station, where the train on which he was travelling in his ordinary way of business was met by a Police Inspector with the warrant Miss Dickinson had applied for. He asked the arresting officer to tell him who had made the charge, and when he learned it was the 'young lady herself', he wanted to know whether the charge would be dropped if he 'arranged the matter'. Plainly, he believed even then that the matter could be 'arranged'.

But how, if he were really guilty as charged? What sort of explanation would he then have offered Miss Dickinson's brother, given the chance to speak or write to him? Would he have admitted to undoing his trouser buttons in his attempt at seduction or hope of possession? If he knew all along that the story which Miss Dickinson eventually told from the witness box was the unvarnished truth—a story which contained nothing in it to shame her or make her afraid of confiding it to her family—what possible grounds could he have had for supposing that any explanation he might offer the girl's brother would suffice?

And why—to revert to the original point—when he first heard her tell this story under oath should he have been provoked into challenging it, in defiance of legal advice and of his own previous instructions to his legal advisers?

'Provoked' is surely the right word, for if his statement had been a calculated effort to deceive, how could he have hoped to reconcile the assertion that Miss Dickinson had been 'under the influence of exaggerated fear' with the fact of his unbuttoned trousers?

Assuming he was a man neither plagued by uncontrollable sexual impulses nor stupid enough to imagine that it would serve him to lie on his word of honour, the only plausible conclusion is that Miss Dickinson was not as innocent as she represented herself to be—that she must have done something to encourage the assault. This was the story whispered among Colonel Baker's apologists, though it was never, of course, publicly stated. It seems possible, and it would certainly fit the facts, that he found her receptive to his advances until she sensed that he intended to go beyond kissing, when she took fright and, despite assurances from him that he meant her no harm, beat her melodramatic retreat out of fear of herself, perhaps, as much as of him. If this was the case, then he did not lie in calling her, in effect, an hysteric. Equally, it would account for his seeming lack of concern before his arrest and his conviction that he could still 'arrange the matter' when he *was* arrested. For if he rightly supposed that she would never dare tell the whole story, he may have assumed that as soon as she recovered her mental equilibrium she would realize that it was in her own interest to accept any disclaimer he might make of dishonourable designs on her person. What he could not have bargained for, if this theory is correct, was the highly circumstantial story which she did tell and which left her invulnerable and him defenceless.

But whatever the truth may have been, it became buried under so many layers of pretence that it can never be properly exhumed. Conservative opinion gladly accepted Mr Justice Brett's view of the assault as an 'outbreak of wickedness', utterly untypical of the class to which Colonel Baker belonged or of his own previous record as a 'man of honour', which was to say a man who had never veered from the path of strict sexual rectitude. Radical opinion, by contrast, chose to treat the case as an instance of appalling vice in high places, which was seldom exposed and never visited with its just deserts. Thus Dr Keneally's papers, *The Englishman*, joyfully pounced on a report carried by the Overland Ceylon Observer to the effect that as a young subaltern in the Ceylon Rifles Valentine Baker had been sentenced to a month's imprisonment for 'being found at night on private premises for an unlawful purpose' (copulation), but that at the intervention of the 'army' the sentence had been remitted by the Governor.

Conservative and radical opinion, however, were at one in their moralistic posturing, and neither side admitted, or anyhow publicly admitted, to a scintilla of doubt that the story which emerged from the trail could be anything but the total truth. No one thought to question the likelihood of this in the light of the fact that the defendant was gagged, not only by the rules of legal procedure, but, even more effectively, by social convention.

Nor did anyone pause to wonder why Miss Dickinson had considered it necessary to charge Colonel Baker, and hence to instigate a national scandal, when she wasn't under the slightest pressure from the police to do so. 'No plaintiff . . .' wrote *The Spectator*, 'ever stood in a case of this kind so thoroughly and so justly acquitted by the public as Miss Dickinson.' But what accusation was made against her that she needed to be acquitted of? The 'public', certainly, would never have heard of her existence if she hadn't been persuaded by her family to apply for a warrant for Colonel Baker's arrest. Only a few strangers, whom she was most unlikely to meet again, would have known that she had complained of being 'insulted' by a gentleman in a railway carriage; and not one of them (as they testified) suspected for a moment that she had been 'defiled', or considered her reputation to be compromised.

In sum, the case was a pointless scandal. Miss Dickinson may have been a courageous girl—she was undoubtedly a self-assured and articulate witness—but it was pretence to picture her as fighting and winning a battle for her good name, when, under the influence of her family, she and she alone, was responsible for putting her good name in issue.

Even the idea, still much cherished, that a sensationalized criminal trial serves a useful deterrent purpose turned out to be palpable pretence on this occasion. For the case was followed by a veritable outbreak of indecent assaults in railway carriages. Colonel Baker's lasting monument in the corridor.

JONAH BARRINGTON

Dr Achmet Borumborad

Until England dragged the sister kingdom with herself into the ruinous expenses of the American War, Ireland owed no public debt. There were no taxes, save local ones: the Parliament, being composed of resident gentlemen, interested in the prosperity and welfare of their country, was profuse in promoting all useful schemes; and no projector, who could show any reasonable grounds for seeking assistance, had difficulty in finding a patron. On these points, indeed, the gentlemen who possessed influence, were often unguarded, and sometimes extravagant.

Amongst other projectors, whose ingenuity was excited by this liberal conduct, was one of a very singular description—a Turk who had come over, or (as the *on-dit* went), had *fled* from Constantinople. He proposed to establish, what was greatly wanted at that time in the Irish metropolis, 'Hot and Cold Sea-water Baths;' and by way of advancing his pretensions to public encouragement, offered to open free baths for the poor, on an extensive plan—giving them, as a Doctor, attendance and advice gratis, every day in the year. He spoke English very intelligibly; his person was extremely remarkable; and the more so, as he was the first *Turk* who had ever walked the streets of Dublin in his native costume. He was in height considerably above six feet, rather pompous in his gait, and apparently powerful; an immense black beard covering his chin and upper lip. There was, at the same time, something cheerful and cordial in the man's address; and, altogether, he cut a very imposing figure. Everybody liked Doctor Achmet Borumborad: his Turkish dress, being extremely handsome without any approach to the tawdry, and crowned with an immense turban, drew the eyes of every passer-by; and I must say that I have never myself seen a more stately-looking Turk since that period.

The eccentricity of the Doctor's appearance was, indeed, as will readily be imagined, the occasion of much idle observation and conjecture. At first, whenever he went abroad, a crowd of people, chiefly boys, was sure to attend him—but at a respectful distance; and if he turned to look behind him, the gaping boobies fled, as if they conceived even his looks to be mortal. These fears, however, gradually wore away, and were entirely shaken off, on the fact being made public, that he meant to attend the poor; which undertaking was, in the usual spirit of exaggeration, soon construed into an engagement, on the part of the Doctor, to cure *all disorders whatever!* and hence he quickly became as much admired and respected as he had previously been dreaded.

My fair readers will perhaps smile, when I assure them that the persons who seemed to have the least apprehension of Doctor Borumborad, or rather to think him 'a very *nice* Turk!' were the ladies of the metropolis. Many a smart, snug little husband, who had been heretofore considered 'quite the thing',—despotic in his own house, and peremptory commandant of his own family, was now regarded as a wretched, contemptible, close-shaven pigmy, in comparison with the immensity of the Doctor's figure and whiskers; and, what is more extraordinary, his good humour and engaging manners gained him many friends even among the husbands themselves! he thus becoming, in a shorter period than could be imagined, a particular favourite with the entire city, male and female.

Doctor Achmet Borumborad, having obtained footing thus far, next succeeded surprisingly in making his way amongst the Members of Parliament. He was full of conversation, yet knew his proper distance; pregnant with anecdote, but discreet in its expenditure; and he had the peculiar talent of being humble without the *appearance* of humility. A submissive Turk would have been out of character, and a haughty one excluded from society: the Doctor was aware of this, and regulated his demeanour with remarkable skill upon every occasion (and they were numerous) whereon (as a *lion*) he was invited to the tables of the great. By this line of conduct, he managed to warm those who patronized him into becoming violent partizans; and accordingly little or no difficulty was experienced in getting a grant from Parliament for a sufficient fund to commence his great metropolitan undertaking.

Baths were now planned after Turkish models. The money voted was most faithfully appropriated; and a more ingenious or useful establishment could not be formed in any metropolis. But the cash, it was soon discovered, ran too short to enable the Doctor to complete

his scheme; and, on the ensuing Session, a further vote became necessary, which was by no means opposed, as the institution was good,
fairly executed, and charitably applied. The worthy Doctor kept his
ground: session after session he petitioned for fresh assistance, and
never met with refusal: his profits were good, and he lived well; whilst
the baths proved of the utmost benefit, and the poor received attention
and service from his establishment, without cost. An immense cold
bath was constructed, to communicate with the river: it was large
and deep, and entirely renewed every tide. The neatest lodging rooms,
for those patients who chose to remain during a course of bathing,
were added to the establishment, and always occupied. In short, the
whole affair became so popular, and Dr Achmet acquired so many
friends, that the annual grants of Parliament were considered nearly
as matters of course.

But alas! fortune is treacherous, and prosperity unstable. Whilst
the ingenious Borumborad was thus rapidly flourishing, an unlucky
though most ludicrous incident threw the poor fellow completely
a-back; and, without any fault on his part, nearly ruined both himself
and his institution.

Preparatory to every Session, it was the Doctor's invariable custom
to give a grand dinner, at the baths, to a large number of his patrons,
Members of Parliament, who were in the habit of proposing and
supporting his grants. He always, on these occasions, procured some
professional singers, as well as the finest wines in Ireland; endeavour-
ring to render the parties as joyous and convivial as possible. Some
nobleman, or commoner of note, always acted for him as chairman,
the Doctor himself being quite unassuming.

At the last commencement of a Session, whereupon he anticipated
this patronage, it was intended to increase his grant, in order to meet
the expenses of certain new works, &c. which he had executed on the
strength of the ensuing supply; and the Doctor had invited nearly
thirty of the leading members to a grand dinner in his spacious saloon.
The singers were of the first order; the claret and champagne excellent;
and never was the Turk's hospitality shown off to better advantage,
or the appetites of his guests administered to with greater success.
The effects of the wine, as usual on all such meetings in Ireland,
began to grow obvious. The elder and more discreet members were
for adjourning; whilst the juveniles declared they would stay for
another dozen! and Doctor Borumborad accordingly went down
himself to his cellar, to select and send up a choice dozen by way

of *bonne bouche* for *finishing* the refractory Members of Parliament.

In his absence, Sir John S. Hamilton, though a very *dry* Member, took it into his head that he had taken enough, and rose to go away, as is customary in these days of freedom when people are so circumstanced: but at that period men were not always their own masters on such occasions, and a general cry arose of—'Stop, Sir John!—stop him!—the bonne bouche!—the bonne bouche!'—The carousers were on the alert instantly: Sir John opened the door and rushed out; the anti-chamber was not lighted; some one or two-and-twenty staunch Members stuck to his skirts; when *splash* at once comes Sir John, not into the street, but into the great *cold bath*, the door of which he had retreated by, in mistake! The other Parliament-men were too close upon the baronet to stop short (like the horse of a Cossack): in they went, by fours and fives; and one or two, who, on hearing the splashing of the water, cunningly threw themselves down on the brink to avoid popping in, operated directly as stumbling blocks to those behind, who thus obtained their full share of a *bonne bouche* none of the parties had bargained for.

When Doctor Borumborad re-entered, ushering a couple of servants laden with a dozen of his best wine, and missed all his company, he thought some devil had carried them off; but perceiving the door of his noble, deep, cold salt-water bath open, he with dismay rushed thither, and espied eighteen or nineteen Irish Parliamentmen either floating like so many corks upon the surface, or scrambling to get out like mice who had fallen into a bason! The Doctor's *posse* of attendants were immediately set at work, and every one of the Honorable Members extricated: the quantity of salt-water, however, which had made its way into their stomachs, was not so easily removed, and most of them carried the beverage home to their own bed-chambers.

It was unlucky, also, that as the Doctor was a Turk, he had no Christian wardrobe to substitute for the well-soaked garments of the Honorable Members. Such dresses, however, as he had, were speedily put into requisition; the bathing attendants furnished their quota of dry apparel; and all was speedily distributed amongst the swimmers, some of whom exhibited in Turkish costume, others in bathing shifts; and when the clothes failed, blankets were pinned around the rest. Large fires were made in every room; brandy and mulled wine liberally resorted to; and as fast as sedan-chairs could be procured, the Irish Commoners were sent home, cursing all Turks and infidels, and denouncing a crusade against anything coming from the same quarter of the globe as Constantinople.

Poor Doctor Achmet Borumborad was distracted and quite inconsolable! Next day he duly visited every suffering Member, and though well received, was acute enough to see that the ridicule with which they had covered themselves was likely to work out eventually his ruin. His anticipations were well-founded: though the Members sought to hush up the ridiculous parts of the story, they became, from the very attempt, still more celebrated. In fact, it was too good a joke to escape the embellishments of Irish humour; and the statement universally circulated was—that 'Doctor Borumborad had nearly drowned nineteen Members of Parliament, because they would not promise to vote for him!'

The poor Doctor was now assailed in every way. Among other things, it was asserted that he was the Turk who had strangled the Christians in the Seven Towers at Constantinople!—Though everybody laughed at *their own* inventions, they believed those of *other people*; and the conclusion was, that no more grants could be proposed, since not a single Member was stout enough to mention the name of Borumborad! the laugh, indeed, would have overwhelmed the best speech ever delivered in the Irish Parliament.

Still, the new works must be paid for, although no convenient vote came to make the necessary provision: the poor Doctor was therefore cramped a little; but notwithstanding his embarrassment, he kept his ground well, and lost no private friends except such as the wearing-off of novelty estranged. He continued to get on; and at length a new circumstance intervened to restore his happiness, in a way as little to be anticipated by the reader as was his previous discomfiture.

Love had actually seized upon the Turk above two years before the accident we have been recording. A respectable surgeon of Dublin, of the name of Hartigan, had what might be termed a very 'neat' sister; and this lady had made a lasting impression on the heart of Borumborad, who had no reason to complain of his suit being treated with disdain, or even indifference. On the contrary, Miss H. liked the Doctor vastly! and praised the Turks in general, both for their dashing spirit and their beautiful whiskers. It was not, however, consistent either with her own or her brother's Christianity, to submit to the Doctor's tremendous beard, or think of matrimony, till—'he had shaved the chin at least, and got a parson to turn him into a Christian, or something of that kind'. Upon those terms only would she surrender her charms and her money—for some she had—to Doctor Achmet Borumborad, however amiable.

The Doctor's courtship with the Members of Parliament having now terminated, so far at any rate as further grants were concerned, and a *grant* of a much more tender nature being now within his reach, he began seriously to consider if he should not at once capitulate to Miss H., and exchange his beard and his Alcoran for a razor and the New Testament. After weighing matters deliberately, love prevailed, and he intimated by letter, in the proper vehemence of Asiatic passion, his determination to turn Christian, discard his beard, and, throwing himself at the feet of his beloved, vow eternal fidelity to her in the holy bands of matrimony. He concluded by requesting an interview in the presence of the young lady's confidant, a Miss Owen, who resided next door. His request was granted, and he repeated his proposal, which was duly accepted, Miss Hartigan stipulating that he should never see her again until the double promise in his letter was fully redeemed; upon which he might mention his own day for the ceremony. The Doctor having engaged to comply, took leave.

On the evening of the same day, a gentleman was announced to the bride-elect, with a message from Doctor Achmet Borumborad. Her confidential neighbour was immediately summoned; the gentleman waiting meantime in a coach at the door. At length Miss Hartigan and her friend being ready to receive him, in walked a Christian gallant, in a suit of full-dress black, and a very tall, fine-looking Christian he was! Miss H. was surprised; she did not recognize her lover, particularly as she thought it impossible he could have been made a Christian before the ensuing Sunday! He immediately, however, fell on his knees, seized and kissed her lily hand, and on her beginning to expostulate, cried out at once, 'Don't be angry, my dear creature! to tell the honest truth, I am as good a Christian as the Archbishop; I'm your own countryman, sure enough! Mr Patrick Joyce from Kilkenny county:—the devil a Turk any more than yourself, my sweet angel!' The ladies were astonished; but astonishment did not prevent Miss Hartigan from keeping her word, and Mr and Mrs Joyce became a very loving and happy couple.

The Doctor's great skill, however, was supposed to lie in his beard and faith;—consequently, on this *denouement*, the baths declined. But the honest fellow never had done any discreditable or improper act; none indeed was ever laid to his charge: he fully performed every engagement with the Parliament whilst he retained the power to do so.

His beauty and portly appearance were considerably diminished by his change of garb. The long beard and picturesque dress had been half the battle; and he was, after his transformation, but a plain, rather coarse, but still brave-looking fellow. An old memorandum-book reminded me of these circumstances, as it noted a payment made to him by me on behalf of my elder brother, who had been lodging in the bathhouse at the time of the *swimming match*.

RONALD KNOX

The Man Who Tried to Convert the Pope

Most of us are aware that, at intervals during the last three centuries, efforts have been made by well-meaning persons to realize the pathetic dream of a reunited Church, something not quite Protestant and not quite Catholic, based upon those principles of compromise which are so dear to the English heart. But none of them, I suppose, has ever been made with so little appreciation of the facts, so quaint a misunderstanding of values, as that described by its author in a book entitled *Journal of a Tour in Italy in 1850*, by George Townsend, D.D., Canon of Durham, published by Messrs Rivington in 1851.

I am suspected, I do not know why, of being infected with that April Fool's Day spirit which delights to palm off literary frauds on the public. Let me explain, then, that the volume really exists, and that my quotations are all genuine. Nor let it be supposed that I am the victim, any more than I am the author, of an imposture. Canon Townsend has his niche in the *Dictionary of National Biography*; he is no fiction of a Tractarian humorist, he is solid fact. A visit to Durham might even supply us with his portrait, but I have felt the pilgrimage to be unnecessary. I think I see the old gentleman well enough as it is; white-chokered, well-tailored, earnest, whiskered after the fashion of his time. He had got his canonry, I suppose, before 1840, and was not therefore affected by the findings of the Ecclesiastical Commission, which cut down its value to a beggarly thousand a year; he liked, clearly, to do himself well, and was not infected with the enthusiasm of the Evangelicals. But the Oxford Movement has equally passed him by; he was a Low Churchman of the old school, a complete fundamentalist in his attitude towards the Bible—as who was not, in his day?—and an Englishman *à outrance*. How did such a man condescend to take an interest in the corrupt politics of the Vatican, or the insanitary population of the Seven Hills?

I think it was due to an odd streak of logic in his composition, which drove him on from strength to strength, regardless of prudent counsels, and shaking of heads in high places. He realized, it seems, that the numerous prayers which an Anglican has to offer up in the course of his ministry for the welfare and guidance of the Universal Church cannot be said with any real meaning when your practical interest is centred entirely in the national church of one people, sparsely represented even in its dominions overseas. He wanted to do something about it; to establish an effective contact between the Christianity of his own country and Christianity on the other side of the Channel; and his sublime confidence in the rightness of his own position convinced him that there was only one course open—he must persuade the erring Christians of the Continent to change their minds. How he took the first steps in this direction had best be described in his own words:

> Ten years have elapsed since I commenced a laborious work on the Pentateuch, entitled 'Scriptual Communion with God'. The sixth and final part was completed at the end of last year (1849) immediately before I left England for Italy. As the reunion of Christians, or the establishment of the truth, unity and concord for which we pray, by unpoperizing the Church of Rome, was the frequent subject of my private prayers to God, the meditations on which those prayers were founded were embodied in various dedications, prefixed to the last four parts of that work. The third part was dedicated to Pope Gregory the XVIth. It related to the mode in which the work of the reunion of Christians might be commenced ... that as laws must be rescinded by the powers which enact them, and as the bulls of Popes have frequently been rescinded by their successors, the bull, therefore, which decreed that twelve doctrines be added to the Nicene Creed, as articles of faith, may be rescinded by the present Pope, or by any of his successors, without propounding any condemnation of the articles themselves. If this was done, the propositions which the Council of Trent commended to the approbation of the Roman Catholic Church might be reconsidered in another Council, summoned under the authority of Christian temporal princes, of whom the Bishop of Rome might be one; and in this mode the hope of a better state of Christianity might dawn upon the world.

The fourth part of the book was dedicated in the same sense to the sovereigns of Europe, the fifth to Queen Victoria, and the sixth to the Universal Episcopate. 'And the Dedication is concluded with the words of the despair with which I was conscious that I might as well have spoken to the dead themselves, for the present time at least'—he was addressing the Archbishop of Canterbury—'Can your Grace do nothing—nothing to remove the mutual hatred of Christians?'

It does not appear that either Gregory XVI or Queen Victoria, or Dr Sumner, made any reply to these overtures. The Pope must have been on his death-bed, I imagine, when his volume appeared. Queen Victoria was much occupied at the time with the cares of the nursery, and the remaining secular princes of Europe were mostly hurled from their thrones by the revolutions of 1848. Archbishop Sumner did not want to hear the word Rome mentioned at all; it was but a year or two since Newman had made his submission, and a storm was already brewing over the Gorham controversy which was to determine the ecclesiastical career of Archdeacon Manning. In fact, there could hardly have been a less opportune moment for Canon Townsend's activities; but the more distracted the state of Europe, the more confident he felt that the summoning of a new Council, to supersede and undo the Council of Trent, was the only remedy for every disorder.

At this point fate intervened. The labour of educing six volumes of spiritual consolation from the sometimes arid material of Leviticus and Deuteronomy could not but tell upon the constitution of the writer, though he were a man so tough of fibre as Canon Townsend. A change of scene and climate was the doctor's ultimatum—we are in the period when it was fashionable to recommend the Grand Tour. At first, the patient demurred; then a salutary thought struck him. Why not consent to travel, and make this the excuse for a personal interview with the head of the corrupt Roman Church?

'I would proceed to the Vatican,' he says—Canon Townsend is always sonorous in his phraseology—'and seek an audience of the Pope, whom I had so often addressed from a distance, as an almost imaginary personage; I would appeal to him ... to begin, and to commend by his great authority, the reconsideration of the past. In proportion to my magnificent independence, should be my extreme and deferential courtesy. In proportion to my zeal to serve the cause of peace, on the basis of Truth, should be my caution never to offend. The very attempt to gain admission to the Vatican would subject me, I well knew, to the charge of enthusiasm, fanaticism, and folly ... I well knew, that disinterestedness is always folly, in the opinion of the selfish, the formal, and the dull.'

A man who could thus imitate the style of Gibbon was not likely to be put off, it is clear, by any ordinary dissuasions.

But one curious difficulty he did experience. A stickler for the methods of primitive Christianity, as exemplified in St Paul's Epistles, he felt it would not be etiquette to demand an audience at the Vatican without a recommendation from some bishop nearer home. And this, he complains, was prohibited by the laws of his country. I find it difficult to believe that if Dr Sumner had furnished the Canon with letters of introduction, either of them would have been prosecuted under the act of King Henry VIII in restraint of appeals. I fancy the true difficulty lay rather in the Archbishop's attitude towards the journey; I cannot resist quoting Dr Townsend's account of it, because it is so beautiful a model of the attitude adopted by all Archbishops of Canterbury on all similar occasions.

> My venerable friend the Archbishop of Canterbury, though he declined to comply with my request that I might use his name, in the most general manner, as one desirous of the peace of the Church, when I should see the Bishop of Rome; and though he discouraged rather than encouraged my persevering, expressed to me, in his answer to my request, every kind and friendly wish.

That was all very well, but it was hardly a Pauline recommendation. Thereupon, Canon Townsend devised a scheme which does remarkable credit to his ingenuity. He would go over to Paris, call on the British Ambassador, get an introduction from him to the Cardinal Archbishop, and so extract from the Cardinal Archbishop the fortifying documents he needed. He realized, like others who have undertaken similar errands before and since his time, that an Englishman who goes round leaving cards, instead of sitting about in the lounge of his hotel, always goes down well on the Continent. Canon Townsend had little honour in his own country; Monsieur le Chanoine would carry all before him in the polite society of France.

There was a further difficulty which does not seem to have daunted him as it might have daunted the modern peacemaker. He had received, no doubt, an excellent public school education; but in those days there was no School Certificate; he could not speak a word of Italian, or a word of French. But he had a resource here of which neither the Archbishop of Paris nor the Pope of Rome could boast. Mrs Townsend must have been a remarkable woman; I am sorry that her husband's reticence makes it so difficult to form a distinct picture of her. But though there was no Somerville in those days, and no Girton, it is clear that she talked both French and Italian without difficulty. Had not Canon Townsend a right to carry about with him a sister, a wife, like the Apostles? Certainly he had, and I think it is quite possible that he would have found it difficult to organize the expedition without her. As she had got to go, she would come in very handy as an interpreter.

For the rest, her husband rightly argued that, if he talked his best school Latin to foreign ecclesiastics, they must at least show a polite affectation of understanding him. It is clear that he used this method a good deal. Between Valence and Avignon, for example, he travelled with a priest who, to his evident surprise, was 'neither vulgar nor slovenly in his appearance, nor sheepish in his looks or demeanour', and he opened up at once with the phrase 'Intelligisne Latinam, Domine?' The only trouble was the difference of pronunciation. Canon Townsend gives it as his opinion that 'the Continental pronunciation of the Greek is better, and of the Latin worse, than our own.' But, whether it was better or worse, it was inevitable that a man who read Latin 'as spelt' should tax the patience of his Continental interlocutors. However, he seems to have got on well enough. He did not, I think, make the mistake of adopting unnecessarily Ciceronian turns of phrase; his Latin was of a more pedestrian order. Thus, when his cabman pursued him into the cathedral at Naples, complaining that he had not received his full fare, the Canon ordered payment to be made, and explained to the priest who was awaiting him 'Ecclesia non locus est controversiae', a sentiment which was excellently received.

It was, then, in the guise of an ordinary English tourist, anxious to learn what these damn foreigners look like when they are at home, that Canon Townsend set out on his memorable journey. To the last, his friend Dr Gilly, the historian and advocate of the Vaudois, tried to dissuade him. He records, under January 22nd, the day of his sailing, the ineffectiveness of these protests.

If God could make Saul the persecutor Paul the Apostle, God can make the Bishop of Rome himself the opponent of the old Popery. Modern experience shall not destroy my faith that, in spite of all present appearances, men shall be one fold under the great Shepherd. I will never sacrifice Truth, but I will persevere to speak peace, as the will of Christ, and of God. Wednesday, the 23rd. Arrived at Meurice's Hotel in Paris, where we had previously ordered apartments.

It must be confessed that our hero did not emulate the unkempt appearance or the fanatical deportment of earlier agitators, like Peter the Hermit. He travelled in style, with at least two servants, I am not certain of the exact number, to wait upon himself and Mrs Townsend. And from the first he used, and found himself justified in using, the methods of a feudal class. Lord Brougham was staying at Meurice's, and Canon Townsend was well dug in with Lord Brougham. For Lord Brougham, it appears, had made some utterances in the celebrated case of King v. Williams which were unacceptable to the clergy; when he came to Durham, therefore, on circuit, the other canons did not ask him to dine; but, with a providential broadmindedness, Canon Townsend did.

> At eleven o'clock, the earliest hour permissible by the customs of society, I called upon Lord Brougham. The conversation was animated and interesting.

What Lord Brougham thought we do not know, but he promised to provide letters. And at eleven the next morning Canon Townsend was round again.

> At eleven I was with him, and, while he breakfasted, renewed the conversation of the preceding day. After a lively and interesting conversation on Wycliffe, and the ecclesiastical history of the Middle Ages ... his Lordship gave me some letters of introduction to his friends at Rome. 'I am not acquainted,' he added, 'with Pio Nono nor with the Archbishop of Paris, but here is a letter to the Marquis of Normanby' (then Ambassador in Paris) 'and most sincerely do I wish you success in your' (and he added some words of eulogy) 'mission.'

Next day the Canon is at Lord Normanby's. He 'observed that he read Lord Brougham's writing with some difficulty, as it was very peculiar, but that he saw something in the letter that referred to my going to Rome'. Poor Lord Normanby! He should have been more careful. As it was, he got a long allocution, in which the Canon explained his intentions in full detail. Under this treatment, like everybody else who met Canon Townsend, he succumbed; he would write a letter of introduction to the Archbishop of Paris. But he warned our hero to be careful.

> He informed me that at the present juncture there prevailed at Rome a great deal of jealousy on the subject of conversion; that any attempt in that direction would be looked upon with much suspicion.

Canon Townsend remained unperturbed.

I told his Lordship that my object, in one sense, was not conversion; that, in the commonly understood sense, I did not intend to put myself forward as the opponent of Popery ...

and so on, and so on, till Lord Normanby hastily agreed to see the Archbishop of Paris himself, and let Canon Townsend know the result.

The next day was Sunday. Lord Brougham called, with eye bandaged as the result of an accident, to say good-bye; it was due to this accident, he explained, that he was forced to travel on the Lord's Day. 'We wished him a pleasant journey, and a useful life.' Let it not be supposed from this that Canon Townsend was lax about Sunday observance. Here are his impressions of the Continental Sunday:

> If we had not been grieved and shocked, we should have been amused by the vivacity of the people in the streets, whom we passed on our way. They seem to imagine that religion being a very dull, uninteresting matter, they must chase away its dullness by external and most intense gaiety. They seem to be utterly ignorant of the delightful fact that a Christian's duty is a Christian's privilege, and that to keep the Lord's Day holily is only to keep the Lord's Day happily, to increase inward felicity, and to anticipate the pleasures of the immortality that is before us.

'If we had not been grieved and shocked, we should have been amused'; what more appropriate description of the Englishman in Paris? But I must not linger too much over Canon Townsend's impressions of Travel. It is enough to say that he faithfully admires every building, picture and view which his guide-book recommends to his admiration, but seldom without some melancholy reflections upon the local representatives of the human species, their ignorance of the Bible, and their superstitious veneration for the Virgin Mary.

The interview with Mgr. Sibour, then Archbishop of Paris, took place on the following Saturday. The interpreter was a gentleman not named, but described as 'the former Roman Catholic correspondent of *The Times*'. Canon Townsend appears to have been particularly careful on this occasion to observe his own principles of 'caution never to offend'. He wanted letters to the Pope, he said, that he might converse with him on the expediency of summoning, in conjunction with other sovereigns, another General Council. No word is spoken of the interdicted Bible or of the twelve articles added to the Creed by the corrupt Council of Trent. The Archbishop, however, seems to have scented an equivocation about the term 'Council', and asked on what principle Monsieur wished to see it assemble? The Canon talked vaguely about common Christianity and a common danger from the infidels; he referred to the negotiations in Queen Anne's time between Dupin and Archbishop Wake. Mgr. Sibour's next question was an unexpected one. 'And', said he, 'is Monsieur a Puseyite?' Canon Townsend has vividly depicted for us his annoyance.

'I was sorry,' he says, 'to be thought to have touched that pitch, and to be defiled with the touch; I was sorry to be regarded as one of those imbeciles, who imagine that either Christian peace or Christian holiness can be restored to the universal Church by bringing the Church of England into conformity with the Church of Rome,' etc., etc.

But he does not seem to have expressed his horror in very outspoken terms. All he said was, 'I am an Episcopalian Christian, and I can assume nor bear no other appellation.' It is doubtful whether the Archbishop was much enlightened; however, he promised the letters of recommendation to the Holy Father, and, sure enough, on the following Tuesday they arrived. In a fortnight Canon Townsend was off to Rome, with the key to the Vatican in his pocket.

By diligence all the way to Lyons, by steamer from Lyons to Avignon. At Valence he finds a golden inscription to Pio Nono; 'this marble monument,' he says to himself, 'with its inscription, shall be to me an omen of the reception I shall experience, and of the probability of the useful or useless results of my mission. I read the inscription. It was the memorial of the gratitude of the Canons of the cathedral of Valence to Pio Nono; for what, I exclaimed, for what reason is the gratitude? I could with difficulty believe the evidence of my senses, when I read that the gratitude of the Canons of Valence to Pio Nono was here commemorated, because he had permitted the bowels of his predecessor, who had died at Valence, to rest here, while the body was conveyed for its burial to Rome! ... What would be thought or said in England, if the Canons of Winchester had raised a memorial to Bishop Sumner, because he permitted them to retain the bowels of Bishop Tomline, while his body was buried at St Paul's? If this act would be deemed absurd in England, why not in Italy?'

Quite so, quite so; only somehow Bishop Tomline does make it funnier.

Undeterred by the sinister omens which the entrails provided for him, Canon Townsend pressed on for Rome. He went from Marseilles to Genoa by sea; for the rest, he was dependent on the diligence, and it was not till the twentieth, after four weeks of travel, that he set foot in the city. The time of his arrival was hardly propitious. For more than a year Pius IX had been absent from the city, owing to a popular insurrection, and it was not many months since French troops had entered the capital to restore order there. The Pope was still in Naples, and the date of his return uncertain. The English Consul recommended that Canon Townsend should proceed to Naples at once, without communicating his plan or his desire to anyone at Rome. This was too much to expect; nor did our hero's good fortune desert him. He made friends with Father Mesaheb, a Maronite Jesuit from Mount Lebanon—so at least he is described—was taken round by him, argued freely with him on theological points, and secured an introduction from him to the antiquarian, Cardinal Mai. The interview proceeded on the now familiar lines. Latin was spoken, with interpreters present in case Italian were needed.

> He bowed, and permitted me to proceed, as I had done with the Archbishop of Paris, I fear at some length, to submit to him the object of my visit to Rome ... [etc.]

The Cardinal seems to have insisted chiefly on the practical difficulties of summoning an international council to discuss the danger of infidelity and Socialism in the then state of affairs. But he took all the Canon's views in good part, and when, before leaving, his visitor pointed to some English books with the observation, 'it could not be expected that the nation which had produced such works could ever again be submissive to Rome', contented himself with replying *Paulatim.*

> He was evidently ... impressed with the conviction, which seemed indeed to be general among his brethren, that England was returning to the adoption of the Papal additions to the faith of Christ. I sighed at the mistake, and again expressed my conviction and my hope that this could never be; and he said again with emphasis, *Paulatim.*

There is something pathetically typical, in that troubled Rome of 1850, about the Canon's haste for action and the Cardinal's readiness to wait upon the future. They parted good friends, with a warm invitation to Cardinal Mai to come and stay at Durham any time when he was evicted from his country. They exchanged letters, which Canon Townsend comments, 'The only stumbling-block between us is this steady, invincible determination never to be

reformed.' He found, as others have found before and since, how
difficult it is to arrive at a complete agreement with a man who will
not adopt your own point of view.

It is actually on record that our Canon visited St Peter's on a Sunday
morning. 'Can I keep the Sabbath, or Lord's Day, holy, by going
there? Yes, I wish to see how the common Lord of the Sabbath is
honoured by those who assume to be more peculiarly His servants.'
The sermon was 'upon the whole, unobjectionable', but the line must
be drawn somewhere. 'I could not kneel at the elevation of the Host.'
It must not be supposed that his sturdy Protestantism was ever
stampeded by its alien surroundings. He was visited by one of the
English converts—I wonder which? He was not impressed: 'Discussion
in conversation, when there is but little or no previous reading, becomes tedious.' He is invited to attend the consecration of Cullen as
Primate of Ireland; 'I refused to sanction the insult to my Church
and country.' More profitably, he consents to perform a wedding
service in the Lutheran chapel.

> One of the princesses of Prussia had given a very beautiful covering
> for the altar, and had adorned it, in the most elaborate gold embroidery,
> with a grouping of the Cross, an anchor, and flowers. I congratulated
> the company present ... and reminded them that the flowers of life
> most abounded in beauty and fragrance when they were blended with
> a good hope of the future and entwined round the Cross ... Much
> enthusiasm was kindled by a few observations of this nature, and the
> Lord's Day was not desecrated, though all was cheerfulness, and joyous-
> ness, and smiles.

But he remained true to his purpose of working for reunion, and,
when taken to task by some gentlemen of the Scottish Free Church,
represented to them that, though some supporters of Popery might
justly be called serpents and a generation of vipers, 'this could not
be said of all'.

On Friday, the 12th of April, the Pope returned to the city, amid
the eager expectations of a large crowd, which knelt to receive his
blessing, and of Canon Townsend, who bowed. On the 13th an
audience was solicited; on the 25th, word was received that the Holy
Father would receive Signor Townsend the following day in private
audience, 'unitamente alla Consorte'. In just over three months the
indomitable peacemaker had triumphed over every obstacle, and
stood on the threshold of his great enterprise. There were minor
regrets; the Italian gentleman who was to have interpreted was unable

to be present, but Mrs Townsend readily volunteered to supply his place; and again

> I was sorry that I had not with me my academic dress. My wearing the robes of an English clergyman would have been but the more proper observance of the courtesy which was due to the Pope as a temporal Prince, and as the Bishop of the greatest of the Western Churches. I assumed the usual evening dress required by society in England.

At half-past five they were ushered into the presence. Why Pio Nono should have been dressed in 'the long white fine cloth Dominican robe' or wearing the 'Dominican cap on his head', I am unable to discover. He received them alone with the utmost graciousness, asked Mrs Townsend whether she had been to Italy before, whether she admired the country, what objects in Rome had interested her most, in what language her husband desired to converse? The the Canon was let loose; not, he hastens to assure us, in a speech, but in answer to the Pope's questions. He asked for a General Council of Christians, at which the Pope was to have precedence, though not jurisdiction. The usual practical difficulties were urged in reply. There was no discussion of details.

> It has been said, I know not why, that I alluded to the celibacy of the clergy, and the giving of the cup to the laity. I said nothing of the kind.

We learn from another passage that Mrs Townsend understood Latin; apart from that, it is quite clear that the Canon did not mean to suggest any programme of reform for the Roman Church until the Council should be already in session. He presented a document for the Pope to read, enshrining his appeal. 'I am a Protestant,' he explained, 'and I have always been an enemy to your Church, but there will not be found in this document any expression which will be personally offensive.'

Mrs Townsend hastened to reassure the Holy Father about this: 'No, no, mio marito è troppo buono' and so on. Many Christians in England, the Canon explained, would rejoice in the hope of the reunion of the Churches. I cannot find that he had much authority for this remark, for it appears that all his friends had discouraged the expedition. But it did service on this occasion as on others. 'Yes,' said Pio Nono, 'there are in England many persons of good will.' 'There are many good men there who would rejoice in peace,' replies the Canon, and explains in a footnote that the Pope was quoting from a false text of the New Testament when he talked about 'men of good will'. All modern scholarship, I fear, is against Canon Townsend and with the Pope on this point. Asked whether he knew Dr Wiseman, our hero cautiously explained that he lived in retirement, and was not personally known to him. Then, after a forty minutes' interview, the intrepid couple took their leave, bowing themselves out as if from the presence of the Queen. Some Cubans who were admitted after them 'both knelt down, as to God ... We had not done so. We had rendered every respect to the Pope as to an earthly sovereign; we could not venerate him as our God'.

The text of the memorandum left with the Pope is then given. It defines the object of the Council, 'restoring to the Catholic Church the ancient discipline and the primitive union', but says nothing about the Council of Trent, or the twelve popish additions to the Nicene Creed. In fact, it is a document which Dr Pusey might have written, and I suspect that Pio Nono took the Canon for a Tractarian. We learn, on the authority of an English gentleman who had an interview soon afterwards, that he thought the *Canone di Durham* an excellent and good man, but found his Latin difficult to follow; 'he did not think the proposal of summoning a Council would lead to the desired effect'. And here a misunderstanding seems to have arisen. The Canon had a visit next day from Monsignor de Mérode and Dr Grant, of the English college, who told him that 'His Holiness had read my memorial, and desired to converse with me further on the subject of its contents'.

It would appear, from what followed, that a mere polite expression of interest was somehow misconstrued into a summons for a fresh audience. It was with that hope that Canon Townsend left for Naples, promising to wait on the Holy Father on his way home.

I have no space to describe that splendid visit to Naples; how they were shewn round the Cathedral sacristy, and Mrs Townsend was not allowed to touch the chalices, though her husband was, on her assurance that he was a Canon too; how they attended the liquefaction of St Januarius's blood—the Canon, under the impression that Mr Neumann, a chemist of Berlin, had reproduced the alleged miracle in his own laboratory, saw the liquefaction perfectly, and bears witness to it. When they returned to Rome they found that the Pope was not expecting a fresh discussion with them, and did not like, on their side, to press for a second interview, since there was naturally a great press of business at the Vatican. Accordingly, on the 27th of May, they set out from Rome on their homeward journey.

Did Canon Townsend feel that he had failed? I think not, at the time. It is clear that there was one Catholic doctrine of which he had no appreciation—he did not realize that the decisions of a Council are irreformable. He thought of a Council—he uses the parallel himself—as if its decisions could always be changed later on, like the decisions of an English Parliament. And he believed, or at least tried to persuade himself, that a new General Council would find no more difficulty about repudiating Transubstantiation than a Labour Government might have about dropping the artificial silk duties.

But there are other passages, scattered throughout the book, which talk the language of despair. I do not like the methods of those critics who profess to find traces of different documentary strata in Canon Townsends' beloved Pentateuch. But I confess that I am inclined to apply the method to his own *Journal*, and suggest that these defeatist passages were put in later, when the book was preparing for the press, in the light of subsequent events. Both at Rome and at Naples he observes the volcanic character of the soil, and speculates whether Dr Cumming is not right in supposing that the whole of the south of Italy, from Rome to Naples, is shortly to be destroyed by fire.

> Oh, for that warning voice, which he who saw the Apocalypse heard cry in heaven, that I might be heard in my appeal to the Bishop of Rome when I say, Repent, Repent, rescind your additions to the religion of Jesus Christ!

But Dr Townsend *had* seen the Pope, and did not say anything of the kind. Again, as he looks back on Rome on leaving it, he breaks out into a tremendous denunciation of Rome, and of the traitorous spirits in England who encourage its pretensions.

> Go on, Church of Rome. The divisions of England strengthen thee! The traitors of England love thee, and give thee power. Fill up the measure of thy ancient iniquity. Send out the unrequired bishops to insult us, the unrequired priests to mock us. Go on! The government is indifferent, the people are torpid, the Church is silent.

And much more to the same effect. Now, why should a clergyman who has gone out to Rome to promote unity in Christendom, who has been received with the utmost kindness by an archbishop, two cardinals and the Pope himself, all of whom are content to point out that the time is not ripe just yet for the summoning of a General Council—why should such a man feel, as he leaves the city, so deep-rooted a grievance against its inhabitants?

The answer is that he did not feel it at the time; he put that part in afterwards. He went back to England with the consciousness that his memorandum lay on the table in the Vatican, wondering what reply it would provoke. On September 29th, little more than two months after his return, a bull was issued restoring the English hierarchy, and on October 7th Wiseman issued his pastoral from the Flaminian Gate. Poor Canon Townsend! Here was his journal, I take it, already advertised and undergoing its final process of polishing, with all the nice things he said about popes and cardinals, and all the nice things popes and cardinals said about him; and then suddenly, this official insult to Lambeth, this gratuitous affront to the feelings of Protestant England. He did the best he could; he put his journal into shape, let in a few passages to emphasize the hardheartedness and all-but irreformability of Rome; then he sent it to the press, tacking on at the beginning a preface in which he lets himself go.

It is a strange preface to such a work. He explains that the journal was written, with the exception of a few sentences, 'long before the promulgation of the late unscriptural, absurd and insolent bull of the Pope, whom I visited at the Vatican'. He expresses the hope that the Papists of the Continent will be brought to their senses by a fresh reformation. But how is this to be secured? By resisting papal aggression in England. The resistance, he assures us, must be of three kinds, Political, Christian and Ecclesiastical. First, by way of political resistance, we must repeal the Acts of Catholic Emancipation. Next, by way of Christian resistance, we must maintain our protest; our motto must be, No peace with Rome. I do not understand what he means by ecclesiastical opposition, and I am very doubtful if he did himself; the fact is, Canon Townsend was rattled.

> If I could have imagined the possibility of the folly and crime which the Pope has committed, I would never have entered Rome.

It would be possible to point or at least to suggest, all sorts of morals as a tail-piece to Canon Townsend's story. I prefer to leave it without comment, as the story of an honest Englishman who really did set out to do great things on his holiday, really did think that he could turn the Grand Tour into a grand slam, and failed so unexpectedly. He lived to 1857; he was not permitted, therefore, to see the summoning of the Council which he recommended, or to mourn the definition of Infallibility which was its principal result. And somewhere, I suppose, in the débris of the Vatican archives lies his memorandum to the Pope, all written fair in Italian, a document of our mortality, and a warning, should it ever be needed, to some new generation which has forgotten it.

LYTTON STRACHEY

Muggleton

Never did the human mind attain such a magnificent height of self-assertiveness as in England about the year 1650. Then it was that the disintegration of religious authority which had begun with Luther reached its culminating point. The Bible, containing the absolute truth as to the nature and the workings of the Universe, lay open to all; it was only necessary to interpret its assertions; and to do so all that was wanted was the decision of the individual conscience. In those days the individual conscience decided with extraordinary facility. Prophets and prophetesses ranged in crowds through the streets of London, proclaiming, with complete certainty, the explanation of everything. The explanations were extremely varied: so much the better—one could pick and choose. One could become a Behmenist, a Bidellian, a Coppinist, a Salmonist, a Dipper, a Traskite, a Tryonist, a Philadelphian, Christadelphian, or a Seventh Day Baptist, just as one pleased. Samuel Butler might fleer and flout at

> petulant, capricious sects,
> The maggots of corrupted texts;

but he, too, was deciding according to the light of his individual conscience. By what rule could men determine whether a text was corrupted, or what it meant? The rule of the Catholic Church was gone, and henceforward Eternal Truth might with perfect reason be expected to speak through the mouth of any fish-wife in Billingsgate.

Of these prophets the most famous was George Fox; the most remarkable was Lodowick Muggleton. He was born in 1609, and was brought up to earn his living as a tailor. Becoming religious, he threw over a charming girl, with whom he was in love and whom he was engaged to marry, on the ground that her mother kept a pawnbroker's shop and that usury was sinful. He was persuaded to this by his puritan friends, among whom was his cousin, John Reeve, a man of ardent temperament, fierce conviction, and unflinching holiness. Some years later, in 1650, two peculiar persons, John Tawny and John Robins, appeared in London. Tawny declared that he was the Lord's high priest, that it was his mission to lead the Jews back to Jerusalem, and that, incidentally, he was the King of France. Robins proclaimed that he was something greater; he was Adam, he was Melchizedek, he was the Lord himself. He had raised Jeremiah, Benjamin, and many others from the dead, and did they not stand there beside him, admitting that all he said was true? Serpents and dragons appeared at his command; he rode upon the wings of the wind; he was about to lead 144,000 men and women to the Mount of Olives through the Red Sea, on a diet of dry bread and raw vegetables. These two men, 'greater than prophets', made a profound impression upon Muggleton and his cousin Reeve. A strange melancholy fell upon them, and then a more strange exaltation. They heard mysterious voices; they were holy; why should not they too be inspired? Greater than prophets . . . ? Suddenly Reeve rushed into Muggleton's room and declared that they were the chosen witnesses of the Lord, whose appearance had been prophesied in the Book of Revelation, xi. 3. Muggleton agreed that it was so. As for Tawny and Robins, they were devilish impostors, who must be immediately denounced. Sentence of eternal damnation should be passed upon them. The cousins hurried off on their mission, and discovered Robins in gaol, where he had been lodged for blasphemy. The furious embodiment of Adam, Melchizedek, and the Lord glared out at them from a window, clutching the bars with both hands. But Reeve was unabashed. 'That body of thine,' he shouted, pointing at his victim, 'which was thy heaven, must be thy hell; and that proud spirit of thine, which said it was God, must be thy Devil. The one shall be as fire, and the other as brimstone, burning together to all eternity. This is the message of the Lord.' The effect was instantaneous: Robins, letting go the bars, fell back, shattered. 'It is finished.' he groaned; 'the Lord's will be done.' He wrote a letter to Cromwell, recanting; was released from prison, and retired into private life, in the depths of the country. Tawny's fate was equally impressive. Reeve wrote on a piece of paper, 'We pass sentence upon you of eternal damnation,' and left it in his room. The wretched man fled to Holland, in a small boat, *en route* for Jerusalem, and was never heard of again.

After this the success of the new religion was assured. But Reeve did not live long to enjoy his glory. In a few months his fiery spirit had worn itself away, and Muggleton was left alone to carry on the work. He was cast in a very different mould. Tall, thick-set, vigorous, with a great head, whose low brow, high cheekbones, and projecting jowl almost suggested some simian creature, he had never known a day's illness, and lived to be eighty-eight. Tough and solid, he continued, year after year, to earn his living as a tailor, while the words flowed from him which were the final revelation of God. For he preached and he wrote with an inexhaustible volubility. He never ceased, in sermons, in letters, in books, in pamphlets, to declare to the world the divine and absolute truth. His revelations might be incomprehensible, his objurgations frenzied, his argumentations incoherent—no matter; disciples gathered round him in ever-thickening crowds, learning, to their amazement and delight, that there is no Devil but the unclean Reason of men, that Angels are the only beings of Pure Reason, that God is of the stature of a man and made of flesh and bone, that Heaven is situated beyond the stars and six miles above the earth. Schismatics might arise, but they were crushed, cast forth, and sentenced to eternal damnation. Inquiring magistrates were browbeaten with multitudinous texts. George Fox, the miserable wretch, was overwhelmed—or would have been had he not obtained the assistance of the Devil—by thick volumes of intermingled abuse and Pure Reason. The truth was plain—it had been delivered to Muggleton by God; and henceforward, until the Day of Judgment, the Deity would hold no further communication with his creatures. Prayer, therefore, was not only futile, it was blasphemous; and no form of worship was admissible, save the singing of a few hymns of thanksgiving and praise. All that was required of the true believer was that he should ponder upon the Old and the New Testaments, and upon 'The Third and Last Testament of Our Lord Jesus Christ,' by Muggleton.

The English passion for compromise is well illustrated by the attitude of Charles II's Government towards religious heterodoxy. There are two logical alternatives for the treatment of heretics—to let them alone, or to torture them to death; but English public opinion recoiled—it still recoils—from either course. A compromise was the obvious, the comfortable solution; and so it was decided that heretics should be tortured—not to death, oh no!—but ... to some extent. Accordingly, poor Muggleton became a victim, for years, to the small persecutions of authority. He was badgered by angry justices, he was hunted from place to place, his books were burnt, he was worried by small fines and short imprisonments. At last, at the age of sixty-eight, he was arrested and tried for blasphemy. In the course of the proceedings, it appeared that the prosecution had made a serious blunder: since the publication of the book on which the charge was based an Act of Indemnity had been passed. Thereupon the Judge instructed the jury that, as there was no reason to suppose that the date on the book was not a false imprint, the Act of Indemnity did not apply; and Muggleton was condemned to the pillory. He was badly mauled, for it so happened that the crowd was hostile and pelted the old man with stones. After that, he was set free; his tribulations were at last over. The Prophet spent his closing years writing his autobiography, in the style of the Gospels; and he died in peace.

His doctrines did not die with him. Two hundred and fifty Muggletonians followed him to the grave, and their faith has been handed down, unimpaired through the generations, from that day to this. Still, in the very spot where their founder was born, the chosen few meet together to celebrate the two festivals of their religion—the Great Holiday, on the anniversary of the delivery of the Word to Reeve, and the Little Holiday, on the day of Muggleton's final release from prison.

> I do believe in God alone,
> Likewise in Reeve and Muggleton.

So they have sung for more than two hundred years.

> This is the Muggletonians' faith,
> This is the God which we believe;
> None salvation-knowledge hath,
> But those of Muggleton and Reeve.
> Christ is the Muggletonians' king,
> With whom eternally they'll sing.

It is an exclusive faith, certainly; and yet, somehow or other, it disarms criticism. Even though one may not be of the elect oneself, one cannot but wish it well; one would be sorry if the time ever came when there were no more Muggletonians. Besides, one is happy to learn that with the passage of years they have grown more gentle. Their terrible offensive weapon—which, in early days, they wielded so frequently—has fallen into desuetude: no longer do they pass sentence of eternal damnation. The dreaded doom was pronounced for the last time on a Swedenborgian, with great effect, in the middle of the nineteenth century.

JOHN FYVIE

The Author of 'Sandford and Merton'

The present generation of children are not so familiar with *The History of Sandford and Merton* as were their grandfathers and grandmothers. And even the latter, though they may have some hazy recollection of the judicious instruction which good Mr Barlow imparted to his two pupils, and of the very excellent stories with which he enlivened his moral discourses, have probably no idea whatever of the curious personality of the remarkable author of this once popular children's book. Unfortunately, the authorized biography of Thomas Day, which appeared in 1805, in spite of certain undeniable merits, was a rather dull performance; but its subject was so singular a specimen of ultra-individualistic humanity, that it may be worth while to tell his story anew. Mr James Keir, an old army captain turned scientist, who was deputed to write Day's *Life*, had his own notions of the duties of a biographer. He appears to have had some unaccountable objection to Dr Johnson's methods, as exhibited in that incomparable gallery of half-length portraits, the *Lives of the Most Eminent English Poets*; and even went so far as to declare that Johnson had been rightly punished for such a lamentable performance, by the way in which his own biographers had treated him. Keir's consequent determination not to display any of the 'follies and weaknesses (real or supposed)' of his hero, resulted in the suppression, among other things, of all details concerning Day's curious matrimonial experiments, which not only make a good story of themselves, but are absolutely essential to a right understanding of his life and character. Fortunately, however, all of Day's friends were not of the same way of thinking; and Keir's somewhat abstract, though eloquent, eulogium of the character of his friend in his public aspects, may be supplemented by many piquant details of his private and domestic history, which have been recorded in the *Memoirs* of his own life by Richard Lovell Edgeworth, and by Miss Annie Seward in her *Life* of Dr Erasmus Darwin. 'The Swan of

Lichfield', as Miss Seward was called, expressly tells us that she 'would deem it inexcusable to introduce anything fabulous; to embellish truth by the slightest colouring of fiction'; but it may be well to remember, that many inaccuracies in her *Life* of the elder Darwin have been pointed out by the author of the *Origin of Species*, and that, in spite of her disclaimer, she may be justly suspected of a constitutional tendency towards 'exaggerating singularities', and 'heightening what is extraordinary'. In most points, however, we are able to check her statements by a more trustworthy authority. Edgeworth's *Memoirs* were edited, and some details added to them, by his more famous daughter, Maria; and there is no reason to impeach their substantial accuracy.

Thomas Day was born in Wellclose Square, London, on June 22, 1748. Of his father nothing more is known than that he was a Collector of Customs, and that, when he died suddenly in July 1749, he left an estate at Bear Hill, near Wargrave in Berkshire, valued at £1200 a year, to his infant son, charging it with an annuity of £300 to the child's mother. Mrs Day, on account of the delicate health of her son, removed to the more salubrious neighbourhood of Stoke Newington; but, before the boy was more than seven years old, she became the wife of another officer of Customs, named Thomas Phillips. The step-father behaved more or less unkindly, as stepfathers not infrequently do. In after years, Day described him as 'one of those characters who seek to supply their inherent want of consequence by a busy, teasing interference in circumstances with which they have no concern'. Nevertheless, one of Day's first acts, on coming of age, was to raise his mother's jointure to £400 a year, and to settle this sum on his disagreeable stepfather for life. The mother seems to have been a woman of much strength of mind and character, who devoted great care to the education of her only son. He was first sent to school at the Charter-house, and then, in his sixteenth year, to Corpus Christi, Oxford. He resided at Oxford three years, and left without taking a degree. But 'plain living and high thinking' appears to have been his motto; and he certainly studied philosophy, after a fashion of his own, to such purpose that, in spite of passion, ambition, and the ridicule of others, he adhered throughout the whole of his life, with extraordinary consistency, to the Stoic principles imbibed during this period of his youth. Keir says that the character of Tommy Sandford is a transcript of the author's own mind in his younger days. On one occasion he saved the live of William Seward, a school-fellow, at the risk of his own; and on another, discovering that his antagonist in a schoolboy fight was no match for him, he at once stopped the fight, and offered to shake hands and be friends. Both Tommy Sandford and his prototype were undoubtedly inspired with a fine manly spirit; but there is also an unmistakable spice of the prig in both their constitutions. In his undergraduate time Day was a youth of great strength and activity, full of animal spirits, and not without humour. He was fond of taking walking tours through various parts of England and Wales; and on these occasions it was his habit to mix by preference with working people, because he believed human nature might be better studied amongst the unconventional 'lower orders', than amongst sophisticated fine ladies and gentlemen. Before leaving Oxford, he had made acquaintance with R. L. Edgeworth; and the latter, in his *Memoirs*, states that he counted this date as an era in his life. Day's exterior, says Edgeworth, was not at that time prepossessing, for 'he seldom combed his raven locks, though he was remarkably fond of washing in the stream'. The essential point of sympathy between them was a love of knowledge, and a freedom from 'that admiration of splendour which dazzles and enslaves mankind'. In other matters there was more of contrast than of resemblance. Day was melancholy, Edgeworth 'full of constitutional joy'. Day was not a man of strong passions; Edgeworth, by his own admission, was most emphatically so. Day was averse from, and even suspicious of, women; Edgeworth, on the other hand, was 'fond of all the happiness which they can bestow'. They became fast friends, however; and after Day's death Edgeworth declared that during twenty-three years of the most perfect intimacy, he had never known his friend to swerve from the strictest morality in word or action, adding: 'It is but justice, and not the partiality of friendship, that induces me to assert, that Mr Day was the most virtuous human being I have ever known.' When they first became acquainted, Edgeworth was already a married man, with an infant son, whom he was bringing up according to the principles of Rousseau's *Émile*. Day soon became an ardent convert to these principles, and, as we shall see later on, put them into practice in an even more thorough fashion than did his comrade. In the spring of 1768, these two young friends, accompanied by Edgeworth's infant prodigy, started on a tour to Edgworthstown, in Ireland. They travelled at their ease in a patent phaeton of Edgeworth's invention; and, by way of amusing themselves on their journey, he informs us:—

'We agreed that Mr Day should pass for a very *odd* gentleman, who was travelling about the world to overcome his sorrows for the loss of his wife; he was to be doatingly fond of his son, who was to be a most extraordinary child. We settled that I should pass for his servant and factotum; that, whilst I behaved with the utmost civility and attention towards my master, I should behind his back represent him as a humorist and a misanthropist; and that, while he appeared civil and easily pleased with common fare and ordinary attendance, I should give myself all possible airs.'

This simple and harmless hoax they determined to play on the good people of Eccleshall in Staffordshire. Their patent carriage was provided with a contrivance for letting off the horses instantaneously. Edgeworth drove rapidly up to the inn door, shouted vociferously for the ostler, disengaged his horses and conveyed them round the corner in a moment; and when the ostler appeared was seen, with his hat off, lifting out his little master, and then holding his arm with grave deliberation for his great master to descend from the mysterious chariot, which appeared to have arrived without horses. He then ordered cold meat for the master and a tart for the child, after which he peremptorily desired to inspect the larder, and ordered for himself every delicacy the house contained. This was followed up by the performance of a number of gymnastic feats by the child on the phaeton outside; and, as young Edgeworth's usual costume was a jacket and trousers of strange and novel pattern, with no stockings and bare arms, it is small wonder that the curious population of Eccleshall soon collected round the inn in a crowd. The volatile Irishman amused the crowd till near dinner-time with an extravagant account of his master's misanthropy and strange adventures by sea and land; and was on the point of inventing further mystifications for the benefit of the landlady inside, when the whole of his ludicrous plans were completely upset by the unexpected arrival of Dr Erasmus Darwin, and the consequent revelation of the true identity of the erratic travellers.

Edgeworth's father and sister were at first repelled by Day's unconventional manners; but, before three months were over, he had become Miss Edgeworth's avowed admirer, and she had acknowledged that, if he were of the same mind a year hence, she might be induced to give him her hand. Before the summer was over, he left Ireland to enter himself as a student of the Middle Temple, leaving Miss Edgeworth to study a course of works on metaphysics which he had recommended to her. But, before the winter of the same year, says the brother who had introduced them, they discovered that they were not suited to each other, 'a fact which all their friends had seen from the beginning of their acquaintance'. At a very early age Day appears to have conceived the notion of the possibility of raising the physical, intellectual, and moral status of posterity by the careful selection of proper partners in marriage—a doctrine which has recently been elaborated with more scientific precision by Mr Francis Galton. During one of his walking tours in the West of England, he wrote a poem embodying his own ideal of a wife. She was to be simply neat, with none of the 'deceitful glare' of a town nymph, but with a healthy bloom on her cheeks, and lustrous eyes, which spoke the genuine feelings of her soul. She was, moreover, to be heedless of the praise or blame of all mankind, save only her husband. He imagines that some such appropriate partner is possibly to be found in that beautiful part of England, wherefore he sings:

> 'Oh, gentle Lady of the West!
>   To find thee be my only task;
> When found, I'll clasp thee to my breast:
>   No haughty birth or dower I ask.
> Sequestered in some secret glade,
>   With thee unnoticed would I live;
> And if Content adorn the shade,
>   What more can Heaven or Nature give?'

He had so great a contempt for dress, external appearances, and the usages of polite society generally, that he definitely resolved upon a life of simplicitly and retirement, in which nothing was to be sacrificed to fashion and vanity, but much to benevolence. He was equally resolved on having a wife to share the simplicity and solitude with him; but ladies who love philosophy and despise dress and fashion were probably no more plentiful in Day's time than they are in our own. Whether any such lady was really discovered in the West does not appear; but we learn from Miss Seward, that, before the encounter with Miss Edgeworth, Day's mind had been wounded by the caprice of some unnamed young lady who 'claimed the triumph of a lettered heart', without knowing how to value and retain her prize; and in her *Life* of Erasmus Darwin the sentimental Swan prints 'a beautiful elegy', which Day composed on the occasion. He wanted a wife, she explains, 'with a taste for literature and science, for moral and patriotic philosophy'; and the lady was also required to be 'simple as a mountain girl, in her dress, her diet, and her manners; fearless and intrepid as the Spartan wives and Roman heroines'. His friend Edgeworth evidently thought it somewhat unreasonable that 'a person neither formed by nature nor cultivated by art to please' should yet expect to win a wife who would feel for him the most romantic and everlasting attachment, and even be content to—

> 'Go clad like our maidens in grey,
> And live in a cottage on love.'

And Day himself seems at last to have admitted that he would be somewhat unlikely to find the ideal creature ready made. But he thought he would at least be able to mould one for himself; and he formed a plan which Edgeworth mildly characterises as 'more romantic than we find in novels'. He determined to breed up two young girls, under his own eye, strictly according to the principles which he had imbibed from Rousseau, with the view of making the most suitable one his wife as soon as she arrived at a marriageable age.

In accordance with this extraordinary plan, he went off, in company with a friend, a young barrister named Bicknell, to the Orphan Asylum at Shrewsbury, and there chose a young girl of promising appearance, whom Miss Seward describes as 'an auburn brunette', and whom he named (after the river Severn and his favourite patriot) 'Sabrina Sidney'. A few days later, he paid a similar visit to the Foundling Hospital in London, and there chose another girl, with flaxen hair and light eyes, whom he named 'Lucretia'. For form's sake, these girls were bound apprentice to Edgeworth, who was a married man; and Bicknell became guarantee that Day would apprentice one of them, with a premium of £100, within a year, to some reputable tradeswoman, and that he would educate the other with a view to her becoming his wife. If, however, he did *not* marry her, he undertook to pay for her support in some creditable family until she married some one else, when he would pay down a dowry of £500. The two girls were eleven and twelve years of age respectively, and Day began their education at once. Instead of bringing them up in England, he decided to take them to Avignon, partly to avoid the curiosity and inquiries of his acquaintances, and partly because, as the girls spoke nothing but English, he would be better assured that no one but himself would have any influence over their minds. He taught his young pupils to read and write; and, says Edgeworth, 'by reasoning which appeared to me to be above their comprehension, backed up by ridicule, he endeavoured to imbue them with a deep hatred for dress, for luxury, for fine people, for fashion, and for titles, all which inspired his own mind with such an unconquerable horror'. Miss Seward says that the girls quarrelled and fought incessantly, and gave poor Day a thoroughly bad time of it, to say nothing of taking the small-pox, through which he had to nurse them, and falling from a boat during tempestuous weather into the Rhone, from which he had to rescue them at the risk of his own life. But in a letter which he wrote from Avignon in November 1769, there is a much more favourable account of them:

> You enquire after my pupils [he says]. I am not disappointed in one respect. I am more attached to, and more convinced of, the truth of my principles than ever.... I have made them, in respect of temper, two such girls as, I may perhaps say without vanity, you have never seen at the same age. They have never given me a moment's trouble throughout the voyage, are always contented, and think nothing so agreeable as waiting upon me (no moderate convenience for a lazy man).

And he transcribes the following letter from Miss Sabrina Sidney, which, he says, was dictated, word for word, by herself:

> Dear Mr Edgeworth—I am glad to hear you are well, and your little boy—I love Mr Day dearly, and Lucretia—I am learning to write—I do not like France so well as England—the people are very brown, they dress very oddly—the climate is good here. I hope I shall have more sense against I come to England—I know how to make a circle and an equilateral triangle—I know the cause of day and night, winter and summer. I love Mr Day best in the world, Mr Bicknell next, and you next.

All this, Day assures Edgeworth, he believes to be a faithful display of his little charge's heart and head. When, after eight months spent at Avignon, Day returned to England, Lucretia, who, according to Miss Seward, was 'invincibly stupid', was apprenticed to a milliner. It is satisfactory to know that she did well enough in that business, and ended by marrying a respectable linendraper. Sabrina, the favourite, was at this time a very pleasing girl of thirteen. Edgeworth says:

> Her countenance was engaging. She had fine auburn hair, that hung in natural ringlets on her neck: a beauty which was the more striking because other people then wore enormous quantities of powder and pomatum. Her long eye-lashes, and eyes expressive of sweetness, interested all who saw her; and the uncommon melody of her voice made a favourable impression upon every person to whom she spoke.

Day took a house in the little green valley of Stow, near Lichfield, and, as 'the Swan' expresses it, 'resumed his preparations for implanting in her young mind the characteristic virtues of Arria, Portia, and Cornelia'. When he came to Lichfield, in 1770, he was not more than twenty-two years of age; but 'the Swan' declares that he looked quite the philosopher. Powder and fine clothes were at that time the marks of a gentleman; but he wore neither. He was tall, full-bodied, though not corpulent, and deeply pitted by the small-pox. The curious mixture of awkwardness and dignity in his manners, his melancholy and meditative air, and his large hazel eyes, which, when he was excited to discussion, gleamed from beneath 'the shade of sable hair, which, Adam-like, curled about his brows', seem altogether to have made a strong impression, not only on the romantic Miss Seward, but also on the other members of that distinguished circle which revolved about Dr Erasmus Darwin. They found him to be 'less graceful, less amusing, and less brilliant' than his friend Edgeworth, who settled there for a while about the same time, but 'more highly imaginative, more classical, and a deeper reasoner'. The Swan describes, with an enthusiasm which nowadays strikes one as highly comical, a portrait of the young philosopher, painted about this time by Wright, of Derby:

> Drawn in the open air, the surrounding sky is tempestuous, lurid, and dark. He stands leaning his left arm against a column inscribed to Hampden. Mr Day looks upward, as enthusiastically meditating on the contents of a book, held in his dropped right hand. The open leaf is the oration of that virtuous patriot in the senate against the grant of ship-money demanded by King Charles the First. A flash of lightning plays in Mr Day's hair, and illuminates the contents of the volume.

Sabrina appears to have been a general favourite with the ladies of Lichfield; but Day's method of cultivating her mind and heart did not have quite the success which he so confidently expected. Miss Seward tells us that the young lady's spirit could not be armed against the dread of pain or the apprehension of danger. 'When he dropped melting sealing-wax upon her arms she did not endure it heroically; nor when he fired pistols at her petticoats, which she believed to be charged with balls, could she help starting aside, or suppress her screams.' Her fidelity in keeping secrets was also tried in Day's balance and found wanting; and she, moreover, showed little or no inclination for the study of books or the rudiments of science. The Swan puts her finger upon what was undoubtedly the cause of Day's failure, namely, that he was unable to supply his pupil with any adequate motive to exertion in these matters. He had endeavoured to keep from her any knowledge of the value of money, the reputation of beauty, and the love of dress, it being altogether against his principles to encourage the usual motives of pecuniary reward, luxury, ambition, or vanity. Nevertheless, he steadily persisted in his experiments for a year; but at the end of that time, finding he had made no progress, he sent Sabrina to a boarding-school at Sutton Coldfield, and turned his affections towards a charming and cultivated young lady of the Lichfield coterie, named Honora Sneyd. Day was aware that Edgeworth, whose married life was not at that time a very happy one, though he was living at home with his wife, had also been deeply smitten with Honora's charms. He therefore wrote him a letter, stating his intentions, and enlarging on the absurdity of a married man encouraging a hopeless passion, but at the same time declaring that he would go no further himself if his action were likely to divide him from his chosen friend. Edgeworth's reply to this Quixotic epistle was to post off to Lichfield to make personal protestation that he would view his friend's union with Honora, not only with pleasure, but with exultation. Being thus conveniently on the spot, he was employed to deliver Day's formal proposal of marriage, which appears to have been in the form of an essay on matrimony of sufficient length to make a bulky packet. Honora, after controverting at length the views of the rights of man set forth in this proposal, and giving in return her views of the rights of woman, admitted that she admired the young philosopher's talents and revered his virtues, but plainly said that she could not love him, and that she firmly declined to change her present mode of life, with which she was by no means dissatisfied, for the dark and untried system of seclusion from society and unbounded marital control which Mr Day had been good enough to propose to her. This disappointment, says Edgeworth, made Day ill for a short time; but Dr Darwin bled him, and he soon recovered. Just at this point Honora's less intellectually distinguished, but personally more attractive sister, Elizabeth, came upon the scene at Lichfield, and Day promptly commenced to pay his court to her. She received his addresses with rather more favour than her sister had done; but, telling him plainly that she attached little weight to his philosophical objections to those accomplishments of polite society which he had never endeavoured to attain, she gave him to understand that she would be much more likely to accept him for a husband if he were to acquire the manners of the world, and abandon his present austere singularities of air, habit, and address. A compromise was accordingly effected between the parties. Day promised to go to France and do all that could be done to acquire a pleasing deportment; while Elizabeth, on her part, promised not to go to London, or Bath, or any other public place of amusement until his return. In the meantime, she would also go through a prescribed course of reading. Edgeworth, whose passion for Honora had revived as soon as his friend's affections were transferred to her sister, and who judged that his only safety lay in flight, accompanied Day to Lyons. The latter gave up eight hours a day to learn the arts of dancing, fencing, and horsemanship; and, as his legs were not straight, was also condemned to sit pent up in durance vile for hours together, 'with his feet in the stocks, a book in his hands, and contempt in his heart'. Sad to relate, the crooked legs refused to be straightened out, in spite of these heroic efforts. Having learnt all that the French experts could manage to teach him, Day returned to England to claim the hand of Elizabether Sneyd. But that young lady was forced to confess that 'Thomas Day, *blackguard*' (as he used jestingly to call himself), was, after all, less unpleasing to hèr than 'Thomas Day, *gentleman*'; and she declined to marry him. Miss Seward evidently thought Elizabeth was not without excuse for her apparent capriciousness; for, says the Swan, Mr Day's efforts at society manners were more really ungraceful than his natural stoop and unfashionable air; and the showy dress in which he came back from France was most unbecoming to him. We are not here concerned with Edgeworth's many marriages; but it may be mentioned, in passing, that he ultimately wedded both these charming ladies who had refused his bosom friend. Four months after becoming for the first time a widower in 1773, he married Honora Sneyd; and, within eight months of Honora's death in 1780, he married her sister Elizabeth.

Day's fluctuating affections now returned for a time to Sabrina, who had developed into a very charming young lady. Edgeworth says that Day was certainly never more loved by any woman than he was by Sabrina, and that no woman was ever personally more agreeable to him. After his rejection by Elizabeth Sneyd, at any rate, he was just on the point of proposing to marry, after all, the favourite girl of his own rearing, when a trifling circumstance occurred to change his intention. He had left Sabrina at the house of a friend, under strict injunctions as to some peculiar fancies of his own respecting her dress. In what particular she gave offence does not appear. According to

Edgeworth, she neglected, or undervalued, or forgot something. She did, or she did not, wear certain long sleeves, or some handkerchief, which had been the subject of his dislike or of his liking. And he, considering this as a criterion of her attachment to him, as well as a proof of her want of strength of mind, quitted her for ever!

He then took up his residence in London, and commenced author with a poem, entitled *The Dying Negro*, in which he denounced the Americans for their maintenance of slavery. But as marriage was still the principal object of the young philosopher's consideration, his friend, Dr Small, of Birmingham, kept a continual look out for him, and never failed to report on the merits and qualifications of any suitable lady whom he might happen to see. At last, in Miss Milnes, of Wakefield, a young lady two or three and twenty years of age, of much culture, great benevolence, and the possessor of a considerable fortune, the match-making doctor believed himself to have found the ideal help-meet for his friend. Day's specified requirements seem to have been a combination of the spirit of a Roman matron, with the simplicity and physical health of a Highland mountaineer, and the culture of a London Bluestocking. But he wanted other things as well. When Dr Small discoursed of the incomparable lady from Yorkshire, Day at once inquired—'Has she white and large arms?'—'She has.'—'Does she wear long petticoats?'—'Uncommonly long.'—'Is she tall, and strong, and healthy?' This question could not be answered so satisfactorily; and after being forced to admit that the lady was small, and not particularly robust, Dr Small was constrained to argue: 'My dear friend, can you possibly expect that a woman of charming temper, benevolent mind, and cultivated understanding, with a distinguished character, with views of life congenial with your own, with an agreeable person, and a large fortune, should be also formed exactly according to a picture that exists in your imagination?' Day replied that his chief objection was her fortune, as he could hardly expect compliance with his ascetic plan of life from a person of such affluent circumstances. However, after some acquaintance with the lady, and a provisional courtship, during which he discussed with her every subject of opinion or speculation on which he held strong views, and on which it was possible for them to disagree, he was induced, in view of her evident tender devotion to his talents and his person, to propose marriage, on condition that they should retire together into the country, shun the infectious taint of polite society, abandon luxuries and all that the world calls pleasures, and, after supplying the ordinary comforts of life to themselves, devote the surplus of their fortunes to clothing the naked and feeding the hungry. Miss Milnes agreed to these strange terms of her eccentric lover, and in August 1778 they were married at Bath. Day insisted that his wife's fortune should be settled entirely beyond his control, in order that she might the more readily separate from him, if the experiment proved too much for her endurance. The reader will probably expect to learn that they parted before the year was out. But it is not the least extraordinary part of this extraordinary story, that Mrs Day remained a devoted wife to the day of her husband's death, and when he died was inconsolable for his loss.

It will perhaps be convenient at this point to state what became of Sabrina. When she left school, Day allowed her £50 a year, and continued to correspond with her paternally, but they do not appear to have often met. She was a general favourite in the various houses in which she lived, and was frequently the guest of Dr Darwin and other of Day's friends in Lichfield, especially of the Sewards at the Bishop's Palace. About two years after Day's marriage, and when Sabrina was twenty-three years of age, Mr Bicknell, now a barrister of some practice, happening to meet her after several years' absence, at once fell in love, and asked her to be his wife. She accepted him provisionally, but declared that she would not marry either him or anybody else without Mr Day's consent. Day wrote, rather ungraciously: 'I do not refuse my consent to your marrying Mr Bicknell; but remember you have not asked my *advice*.' One wonders whether his advice would have been that she should wait until his dear friend Edgeworth again became a widower, and wanted another wife! However that may be, he duly paid down the promised dowry of £500. Five or six years later Bicknell died, leaving her with two children, and little or no means for their support. Day then allowed her £30 a year, a not very munificent annuity, upon which the Swan of Lichfield comments—'To have been more bounteous *must* surely have been in his *heart*, but it was not in his *system*.' Sabrina was not named in Day's will, but Mrs Day continued the allowance of £30 a year, and bequeathed its continuance from her own fortune for Mrs Bicknell's life.

Mr and Mrs Day spent the winter of 1778–9 in lodgings at Hampstead, a place which, we must remember, was as much cut off from the life of the metropolis in those days, as the New Forest is now. Edgeworth and his second wife (the charming Honora) paid them a visit there, and the former declared—'I never saw any woman so entirely bent upon accommodating herself to the sentiments and wishes and will of a husband.' There was, nevertheless, he says, a continual flow of discussion between them, and Mrs Day was nothing loath to support on any occasion an opinion of her own. In 1779, Day bought a house and small estate called Stapleford-Abbot, near Abridge in Essex. The house was indifferent, and the land worse. The former had only one good room, and our self-sufficient philosopher proceeded, in characteristic fashion, to make some necessary additions to his little mansion. Edgeworth's account of this building experiment is as follows:

When Mr Day determined to dip his unsullied hands in mortar, he bought at a stall Ware's *Architecture*; this he read with persevering assiduity for three or four weeks before he began his operations. He had not, however, followed the occupation a week before he became tired of it, as it completely deranged his habits of discussion with Mrs Day in their daily walks in the fields, or prevented their close application to books when in the house. Masons, calling for supplies of various sorts, which had not been suggested in the great body of architecture which he had procured with so much care, annoyed the young builder exceedingly. Sills, lintels, door and window cases were wanting before they had been thought of; and the carpenter, to whose presence he looked forward, but at a distant period, was now summoned and hastily set to work to keep the masons going. Mr Day was deep in a treatise written by some French agriculturist, to prove that any soil may be rendered fertile by sufficient ploughing, when the masons desired to know where he would have the window of the new room on the first floor. I was present at the question, and offered to assist my friend. No—he sat immovable in his chair, and gravely demanded of the mason whether the wall might not be built first, and a place for the window cut out afterwards. The mason stared at Mr Day with an expression of the most unfeigned surprise. 'Why, sir, to be sure, it is very possible; but I believe, sir, it is more common to put in the window-cases while the house is building, and not afterwards.' Mr Day, however, with great coolness, ordered the wall to be built without any opening for windows, which was done accordingly.

The room in question, it appears, was intended for a dressing-room for Mrs Day, and the poor lady had always to perform her toilet by candle-light, for no window was ever put in up to the time of Day's disposal of the house. In 1781 they left Abridge, and settled at Anningsley, near Ottershaw, in Surrey. Of all the arts, agriculture, in Day's opinion, was the most beneficial to mankind; and the people employed in it he considered to be the stamina of the human species.

But, as he entered on his farming projects with little more preliminary information than sufficed him for his building operations, it is not surprising that the result was not a financial success. He was satisfied, however, to lose money, provided he improved his estate, and benefited the poor. Keir says, that if any in his neighbourhood wanted employment, Day provided it; if any were sick, Day supplied them with medicines, or with food and cordials from his kitchen; if any wanted advice, legal or other, Day was always ready to give it. He also sought every opportunity of converse with his poorer neighbours; and, being at some distance from any church, he always invited them to his house on Sundays to listen to his reading of family prayers. In 1789 he wrote from Anningsley to Edgeworth:

> Were I to give up farming I should have less care, but I should also become more sedentary ... and the very absence of that care would expose me infinitely more to hypochondriacism: which I am now totally free from. I have besides another very material reason, which is, that it enables me to employ the poor; and the result of all my speculations about humanity is, that the only way of benefiting mankind is to give them employment, and make them *earn* their money.

Considering the special vices of his age to be vanity, effeminacy, and the love of luxury, Day from the first had determined to make his rule of life a practical protest against these. His wife had no carriage nor maid, and gave up her harpsichord; while he denied himself all those gratifications from painting, sculpture, and architecture, to which his fortune might well have entitled him. He did, indeed, form a large library; but his choice of books was strictly regulated, not by the splendour or rarity of the editions, by considerations of fine paper, gilt leather, or old vellum, but solely by his estimate of the value of the ideas they contained. A collection of books was also, of course, a necessary part of his equipment as a publicist.

He took a keen interest in public affairs. During the eight years of his residence at Anningsley, he published, *Reflections on the Present State of England and the Independence of America*, in 1782; *The Letters of Marius; or, Reflections upon the Peace, the East India Bill, and the Present Crisis*, in 1784; *Fragments of Original Letters (written in 1776) on the Slavery of the Negroes*, in 1784; *Dialogue between a Justice of the Peace and a Farmer*, in 1785; and *A Letter to Arthur Young on the Exportation of Wool*, in 1788. He also joined a 'Society for Constitutional Information', and spoke with much effect at meetings in Essex, Surrey, and Berks. He advocated

Parliamentary Reform, because he believed, with Lord Chatham, that 'a portion of new health might be infused into the Constitution, to enable it to bear its infirmities'. But he could never be induced to stand for Parliament himself. In answer to certain representations on the subject, he wrote the following highly characteristic epistle to Dr Jebb:

> How is it possible that I should descend to the common meannesses of the bought and buying tribe, or stoop to solicit the suffrages of the multitude, more than I have hitherto done the patronage of the great. Whatever may be the common and flimsy pretensions of popular men, I believe that few entertain any doubt that their own interest or vanity is in reality the predominant principle of their exertions. It was not in the forum, amidst the tribe of begging, cringing, shuffling, intriguing candidates, but in their farms, and amidst their rural labours, that the Romans were obliged to seek for men, who were really animated with an holy zeal for their country's glory, and capable of preferring her interest to their own. I never pretend to the abilities of these illustrious men—whom we are more inclined to admire than imitate, but I pretend to all their indifference to public fame, and to all their disinterestedness. Be assured, then, that these principles, which have always been so wrought up into the groundwork of my character that they never can be separated without marring the little merit of the piece, will always be an invincible obstacle to my entering the list of public competition.

After a time, however, he came to despair of making any impression, either by reason or by ridicule, on the ingrained habits of grown men and women; and he consequently determined to throw all his energies into an attempt to form the minds of the rising generation, in accordance with what he held to be the principles of right reason and sound morality. With this object, he set about the composition of *The History of Sandford and Merton*, of which the first volume appeared in 1783, the second in 1787, and the third in 1789. In Day's view, the most prominent evil of his time was effeminacy of manners, and this he set himself to counteract; the greatest needs of the age were manliness, independence, and certain other sterling qualities of character, which he endeavoured to set forth with all the energy and eloquence at his command. It would be impossible in any available limits to give an intelligible idea of the work. Those who have never read it may be confidently recommended to make the attempt at once; and those who have read it, or who had it read to them in their childhood, will find it a pleasing experience to renew their acquaintance with an old favourite. In the words of the most eminent of recent literary critics, it is, 'in spite of its quaint didacticism, still among the best children's books in the language'; and it may perhaps be found both pleasant and profitable by children of a larger growth.

Soon after the appearance of the last volume of *Sandford and Merton*, its author came to a sudden and untimely end. A martyr to theory throughout his life, Day became a victim to theory in his death. On September the 28th, 1789, he started from Anningsley, riding an unbroken colt, with the intention of visiting his wife, who was staying with his mother at Bear Hill. He had always firmly held, that any animal could be controlled by kindness. Although not a good horseman, he disdained to employ a horse-breaker; and the animal he rode on this occasion was a favourite foal, which he had reared, fed, and, as he thought, tamed, with his own hand. During the journey, however, the colt shied, and Day was thrown on his head, receiving such injuries that he died within an hour. According to Miss Seward, Mrs Day never afterwards saw the sun. 'She lay in bed, into the curtains of which no light was admitted during the day; and only rose to stray alone through her garden when night gave her sorrows congenial gloom.' However that may be, it is certain that she survived her adored husband only two years, and then died, broken-hearted for his loss.

Day was certainly an original. Most people are as much alike as coins of the realm, and might almost have been struck out, like coins, with the same die. Day was more like a peculiar medal, of which the mould was broken after the first impression had been cast. It is small wonder that he was a puzzle to his contemporaries, or that widely divergent views were taken of his character. Keir says that some imputed his friend's unostentatious mode of life to avarice, although the greater part of his income was spent in generosity; others attributed his retirement to misanthropy, although his life was devoted to the service of mankind; and many were only able to explain his conduct to their own satisfaction as the result of an abnormal love of singularity and caprice, whereas it is abundantly evident that all his actions flowed from fixed principles, with a consistency seldom equalled. His biographer, who knew him intimately for twenty years, declares that he 'never showed the smallest inclination to appear more or less wise, good, or learned, or more or less anything, than he really was'. No service was too laborious to be undertaken for his friends; and he was uniformly kind and generous to the neighbouring poor, notwithstanding that his bounty was often rewarded by ingratitude. As Sir

Leslie Stephen says, 'his amusing eccentricities were indeed only the symptom of a real nobility of character, too deeply in earnest to submit to the ordinary compromises of society'. Edgeworth declares that he puts the singularities of his excellent friend on record, by way of a warning that we may have too much of even such a good thing as reason. He need have been under little apprehension on that score. The Νόμος is no less powerful in modern times than Grote represents it to have been amongst the ancient Greeks; exercising still plenary power, spiritual as well as temporal, over individual minds, and moulding emotion as well as intellect according to the local type. Men like Day, who evolve a code of morals for themselves, and consistently act upon it in defiance of the law and custom of their contemporaries, will never be very numerous. At the same time, their consistency in such a set of fixed principles is not necessarily wisdom. And it must be admitted that Day affords a striking example of the failure of one of the best-intentioned of men who ever lived, to compress human life within the rigid limits of a cast-iron system.

S. BARING-GOULD

The Snail-Telegraph

The writer well remembers, as a child, the sense of awe not unmixed with fear, with which he observed the mysterious movements of the telegraph erected on church towers in France along all the main roads.

Many a beautiful tower was spoiled by these abominable erections. There were huge arms like those of a windmill, painted black, and jointed, so as to describe a great number of cabalistic signs in the air. Indeed, the movements were like the writhings of some monstrous spider.

Glanvil, who wrote in the middle of the 17th century says, 'To those that come after us, it may be as ordinary to buy a pair of wings to fly into the remotest regions, as now a pair of boots to ride a journey. *And to confer, at the distance of the Indies, by sympathetic conveyances*, may be as usual to future times as to us is literary correspondence.' He further remarks, 'Antiquity would not have believed the almost incredible force of our cannons, and would as coldly have entertained the wonders of the telescope. In these we all condemn antique incredulity. And it is likely posterity will have as much cause to pity ours. But those who are acquainted with the diligent and ingenious endeavours of true philosophers will despair of nothing.'

In 1633 the Marquis of Worcester suggested a scheme of telegraphing by means of signs. Another, but similar scheme, was mooted in 1660 by the Frenchman Amonton. In 1763 Mr Edgeworth erected for his private use a telegraph between London and Newmarket. But it was in 1789 that the Optical Telegraph came into practical use in France— Claude Chappe was the inventor. When he was a boy, he contrived a means of communication by signals with his brothers at a distance of two or three miles. He laid down the first line between Lille and Paris at a cost of about two thousand pounds, and the first message sent along it was the announcement of the capture of Lille by Condé. This led to the construction of many similar lines communicating with each other by means of stations. Some idea of the celerity with which messages were sent may be gained from the fact that it took only two minutes to reproduce in Paris a sign given in Lille at a distance of 140 miles. On this line there were 22 stations. The objections to his system lay in its being useless at night and in rainy weather. The French system of telegraph consisted of one main beam—the regulator, at the end of which were two shorter wings, so that it formed a letter Z. The regulator and its flags could be turned about in various ways, making in all 196 signs. Sometimes the regulator stood horizontally, sometimes perpendicularly.

Lord Murray introduced one of a different construction in England in 1795 consisting of two rows of three octangular flags revolving on their axis. This gave 64 different signs, but was defective in the same point as that of Chappe. Poor Chappe was so troubled in mind because his claim to be the inventor of his telegraph was disputed, that he drowned himself in a well, 1805.

Besides the fact that the optical telegraph was paralysed by darkness and storm, it was very difficult to manage in mountainous and well-wooded country, and required there a great number of stations.

After that Sömmering had discovered at Munich in 1808 the means of signalling through the galvanic current obtained by decomposition of water, and Schilling at Canstadt and Ampère in Paris (1820) had made further advances in the science of electrology, and Oersted had established the deflexion of the magnetic needle, it was felt that the day of the cumbrous and disfiguring optical telegraph was over. A new power had been discovered, though the extent and the applicability of this power were not known. Gauss and Weber in 1833 made the first attempt to set up an electric telegraph; in 1837 Wheatstone and Morse utilized the needle and made the telegraph print its messages. In 1833 the telegraph of Gauss and Weber supplanted the optical contrivance on the line between Trèves and Berlin. The first line in America was laid from Washington to Baltimore in 1844. The first attempt at submarine telegraphy was made at Portsmouth in 1846, and in 1850 a cable was laid between England and France.

It was precisely in this year when men's minds were excited over the wonderful powers of the galvanic current, and a wide prospect was opened of its future advantage to men, when, indeed, the general public understood very little about the principle and were in a condition of mind to accept almost any scientific marvel, that there appeared in Paris an adventurer, who undertook to open communications between all parts of the world without the expense and difficulty of laying cables of communication. The line laid across the channel in 1850 was not very successful; it broke several times, and had to be taken up again, and relaid in 1851. If it did not answer in conveying messages across so narrow a strip of water, was it likely to be utilized for Transatlantic telegraphy? The *Presse*, a respectable Paris paper, conducted by a journalist of note, M. de Girardin, answered emphatically, No. The means of communication was not to be sought in a chain. The gutta percha casing would decompose under the sea, and when the brine touched the wires, the cable would be useless. The Chappe telegraph was superseded by the electric telegraph which answered well on dry land, but fatal objections stood in the way of its answering for communication between places divided by belts of sea or oceans. Moreover, it was an intricate system. Now the tendency of science in modern times was towards simplification; and it was always found that the key to unlock difficulties which had puzzled the inventors of the past, lay at their hands. The electric telegraph was certainly more elaborate, complicated and expensive than the optical telegraph. Was it such a decided advance on it? Yes—in one way. It could be worked at all hours of night and day. But had the last word in telegraphy been spoken, when it was invented? Most assuredly not.

Along with electricity and terrestrial magnetism, another power, vaguely perceived, the full utility of which was also unknown, had been recognized—animal magnetism. Why should not this force be used as a means for the conveyance of messages?

M. Jules Allix after a long preamble in *La Presse*, in an article signed by himself, announced that a French inventor, M. Jacques Toussaint Benoît (de l'Hérault), and fellow worker of Gallic origin, living in America, M. Biat-Chrétien, had hit on 'a new system of universal inter-communication of thought, which operates instantaneously'.

After a long introduction in true French rhodomontade, tracing the progress of humanity from the publication of the Gospel to the 19th century, M. Allix continued, 'The discovery of MM. Benoît and Biat depends on galvanism, terrestrial and animal magnetism, also on natural sympathy, that is to say, the base of communication is a sort of special sympathetic fluid which is composed of the union or blending of the galvanic, magnetic and sympathetic currents, by a process to be described shortly. And as the various fluids vary according to the organic or inorganic bodies whence they are derived, it is necessary further to state that the forces or fluids here married are: (*a*) The terrestrial-galvanic current, (*b*) the animal-sympathetic current, in this case derived from *snails*, (*c*) the adamic or human current, or animal-magnetic current in man. Consequently, to describe concisely the basis of the new system of intercommunication, we shall have to call the force, "*The galvano-terrestrial-magnetic-animal and adamic force!*"' Is not this something like a piece of Jules Verne's delicious scientific *hocus-pocus?* Will the reader believe that it was written in good faith? It was, there can be no question, written in perfect good faith. The character of *La Presse*, of the journalist, M. Jules Allix, would not allow of a hoax wilfully perpetrated on the public. We are quoting from the number for October 27th, 1850, of the paper.

'According to the experiments made by MM. Benoît and Biat, it seems that snails which have once been put in contact, are always in sympathetic communication. When separated, there disengages itself from them a species of fluid of which the earth is the conductor, which develops and unrolls, so to speak, like the almost invisible thread of the spider, or that of the silk worm, which can be uncoiled and prolonged almost indefinitely in space without its breaking, but with this vital difference that the thread of the escargotic fluid is invisible as completely and the pulsation along it is as rapid as the electric fluid.

'But, it may be objected with some plausibility, granted the existence in the snails of this sympathetic fluid, will it radiate from them in all directions, after the analogy of electric, galvanic and magnetic fluids, unless there be some conductor established between them? At first sight, this objection has some weight, but for all that it is more specious than serious.' The solution of this difficulty is exquisitely absurd. We must summarise.

At first the discoverers of the galvanic current thought it necessary to establish a return wire, to complete the circle, till it was found to be sufficient to carry the two ends of the wire in communication with the earth, when the earth itself completed the circle. There is no visible line between the ends underground, yet the current completes the circle through it. Moreover, it is impossible to think of two points without establishing, in idea, a line between them, indeed, according to Euclid's definition, a straight line is that which lies evenly between its extreme points, and a line is length without breadth or substance. So, if we conceive of two snails, we establish a line between them, an unsubstantial line, still a line along which the sympathetic current can travel. 'Now MM. Benoît and Biat, by means of balloons in the atmosphere,' had established beyond doubt that a visible tangible line of communication was only necessary when raised above the earth.

'Consequently, there remains nothing more to be considered than the means, the apparatus, whereby the transmission of thought is effected.

'This apparatus consists of a square box, in which is a Voltaic pile, of which the metallic plates, instead of being superposed, as in the pile of Volta, are disposed in order, attached in holes formed in a wheel or circular disc, that revolves about a steel axis. To these metallic plates used by Volta, MM. Benoît and Biat have substituted others in the shape of cups or circular basins, composed of zinc lined with cloth steeped in a solution of sulphate of copper maintained in place by a blade of copper riveted to the cup. At the bottom of each of these bowls, is fixed, by aid of a composition that shall be given presently, a living snail, whose sympathetic influence may unite and be woven with the galvanic current, when the wheel of the pile is set in motion and with it the snails that are adhering to it.

'Each galvanic basin rests on a delicate spring, so that it may respond to every escargotic commotion. Now; it is obvious that such an apparatus requires a corresponding apparatus, disposed as has been described, and containing in it snails in sympathy with those in the other apparatus, so that the escargotic vibration may pass from one precise point in one of the piles to a precise point in the other and complementary pile. When these dispositions have been grasped the rest follows as a matter of course. MM. Benoît and Biat have fixed letters to the wheels, corresponding the one with the other, and at each sympathetic touch on one, the other is touched; consequently it is easy by this means, naturally and instantaneously, to communicate ideas at vast distances, by the indication of the letters touched by the snails. The apparatus described is in shape like a mariner's compass, and to distinguish it from that, it is termed the *pasilalinic—sympathetic compass*, as descriptive at once of its effects and the means of operation.'

But, who were these inventors, Benoît and Biat-Chrétien? We will begin with the latter. As Pontoppidan in his History of Norway heads a chapter, 'Of Snakes', and says, 'Of these there are none,' so we may say of M. Biat-Chrétien; there was no such man; at least he never rose to the surface and was seen. Apparently his existence was as much a hallucination or creation of the fancy of M. Benoît, as was Mrs Harris a creature of the imagination of Mrs Sairey Gamp. Certainly no Biat-Chrétien was known in America as a discoverer.

Jacques Toussaint Benoît (de l'Hérault) was a man who had been devoted since his youth to the secret sciences. His studies in magic and astrology, in mesmerism, and electricity, had turned his head. Together with real eagerness to pursue his studies, and real belief in them, was added a certain spice of rascality.

One day Benoît, who had by some means made the acquaintance of M. Triat, founder and manager of a gymnasium in Paris for athletic exercises, came to Triat, and told him that he had made a discovery which would supersede electric telegraphy. The director was a man of common sense, but not of much education, certainly of no scientific acquirements. He was, therefore, quite unable to distinguish between true and false science. Benoît spoke with conviction, and carried away his hearer with his enthusiasm.

'What is needed for the construction of the machine?' asked M. Triat.

'Only two or three bits of wood,' replied Benoît.

M. Triat took him into his carpenter's shop. 'There, my friend,' he said, 'here you have wood, and a man to help you.'

M. Triat did more. The future inventor of the instantaneous communication of thought was houseless and hungry. The manager rented a lodging for him, and advanced him money for his entertainment. Benoît set to work. He used a great many bits of wood, and occupied the carpenter a good part of his time. Other things became necessary as well as wood, things that cost money, and the money was found by M. Triat. So passed a twelvemonth. At the end of that time, which had been spent at the cost of his protector, Benoît had arrived at no result. It was apparent that, in applying to M. Triat, he had sought, not so much to construct a machine already invented, as to devote himself to the pursuit of his favourite studies. The director became impatient. He declined to furnish further funds. Then Benoît declared that the machine was complete.

This machine, for the construction of which he had asked for two or three pieces of wood, was an enormous scaffold formed of beams ten feet long, supporting the Voltaic pile described by M. Allix, ensconced in the bowls of which were the wretched snails stuck to the bottom of the basins by some sort of glue, at intervals. This was the Pasilalinic-sympathetic compass. It occupied one end of the apartment. At the other end was a second, exactly similar. Each contained twenty-four alphabetic-sympathetic snails. These poor beasts, glued to the bottom of the zinc cups with little dribbles of sulphate of copper trickling down the sides of the bowls from the saturated cloth placed on them, were uncomfortable, and naturally tried to get away. They thrust themselves from their shells and poked forth their horns groping for some congenial spot on which to crawl, and came in contact with the wood on which was painted the letters. But if they came across a drop of solution of sulphate of copper, they went precipitately back into their shells.

Properly, the two machines should have been established in different rooms, but no second room was available on the flat where Benoît was lodged, so he was forced to erect both vis-à-vis. That, however, was a matter wholly immaterial, as he explained to those who visited the laboratory. Space was not considered by snails. Place one in Paris, the other at the antipodes, the transmission of thought along their sympathetic current was as complete, instantaneous and effective as in his room on the *troisième*. In proof of this, Benoît undertook to correspond with his friend and fellow-worker Biat-Chrétien in America, who had constructed a similar apparatus. He assured all who came to inspect his invention that he conversed daily by means of the snails with his absent friend. When the machine was complete, the inventor was in no hurry to show it in working order; however M. Triat urged performance on him. He said, and there was reason in what he said, that an exhibition of the pasilalinic telegraph before it was perfected, would be putting others on the track, who might, having more means at their command, forestall him, and so rob him of the fruit of his labours. At last he invited M. Triat and M. Allix, as representative of an influential journal, to witness the apparatus in working order, on October 2nd. He assured them that since September 30, he had been in constant correspondence with Biat-Chrétien, who, without crossing the sea, would assist at the experiments conducted at Paris on Wednesday, October 2nd, in the lodging of M. Benoît.

On the appointed day, M. Triat and M. Allix were at the appointed place. The former at once objected to the position of the two compasses, but was constrained to be satisfied with the reason given by the operator. If they could not be in different rooms, at least a division should be made in the apartment by means of a curtain, so that the operator at one compass could not see him at the other. But there was insuperable difficulty in doing this, so M. Triat had to waive this objection also. M. Jules Allix was asked to attend one of the compasses, whilst the inventor stood on the scaffold managing the other. M. Allix was to send the message, by touching the snails which represented the letters forming the words to be transmitted, whereupon the corresponding snail on M. Benoît's apparatus was supposed to thrust forth his horns. But, under one pretext or another, the inventor ran from one apparatus to the other, the whole time, so that it was not very difficult, with a little management, to reproduce on his animated compass the letters transmitted by M. Jules Allix.

The transmission, moreover, was not as exact as it ought to have been. M. Jules Allix had touched the snails in such order as to form the word *gymnase*; Benoît on his compass read the word *gymoate*. Then M. Triat, taking the place of the inventor, sent the words *lumiere divine* to M. Jules Allix, who read on his compass *lumhere divine*. Evidently the snails were bad in their orthography. The whole thing, moreover, was a farce, and the correspondence, such as it was, was due to the incessant voyages of the inventor from one compass to the other, under the pretext of supervising the mechanism of the two apparatuses.

Benoît was then desired to place himself in communication with his American friend, planted before his compass on the other side of the Atlantic. He transmitted to him the signal to be on the alert. Then he touched with a live snail he held in his hand the four snails that corresponded to the letters of the name BIAT; then they awaited the reply from America. After a few moments, the poor glued snails began to poke out their horns in a desultory, irregular manner, and by putting the letters together, with some accommodation CESTBIEN was made out, which when divided, and the apostrophe added, made *C'est bien*.

M. Triat was much disconcerted. He considered himself as hoaxed. Not so M. Allix. He was so completely satisfied, that on the 27th October appeared the article from his pen which we have quoted. M. Triat then went to the inventor and told him point blank, that he withdrew his protection from him. Benoît entreated him not to throw up the matter, before the telegraph was perfected.

'Look here!' said M. Triat; 'nothing is easier than for you to make me change my intention. Let one of your compasses be set up in my gymnasium, and the other in the side apartment. If that seems too much, then let a simple screen be drawn between the two, and do you refrain from passing between them whilst the experiment is being carried on. If under these conditions you succeed in transmitting a single word from one apparatus to the other, I will give you a thousand francs a day whilst your experiments are successful.'

M. Triat then visited M. de Girardin who was interested in the matter, half believed in it, and had accordingly opened the columns of *La Presse* to the article of M. Allix. M. de Girardin wished to be present at the crucial experiment, and M. Triat gladly invited him to attend. He offered another thousand francs so long as the compasses worked. 'My plan is this,' said M. de Girardin: 'If Benoît's invention is a success, we will hire the *Jardin d'hiver* and make Benoît perform his experiments in public. That will bring us in a great deal more than two thousand francs a day.'

Benoît accepted all the conditions with apparent alacrity; but, before the day arrived for the experiment, after the removal of the two great scaffolds to the gymnasiums—he had disappeared. He was, however, seen afterwards several times in Paris, very thin, with eager restless eyes, apparently partly deranged. He died in 1852!

Alas for Benoît. He died a few years too soon. A little later, and he might have become a personage of importance in the great invasion of the table-turning craze which shortly after inundated Europe, and turned many heads as well as tables.

CORNELIA OTIS SKINNER

Robert de Montesquiou– The Magnificent Dandy

In a charming book of memoirs Elisabeth de Gramont, the Duchess de Clermont-Tonnerre, tells of leaning on the railing of her upper balcony one bright spring morning, gazing down onto the Avenue 'when,' she writes, 'I was suddenly struck by the appearance of a tall, elegant personage in mouse-gray, waving a well-gloved hand in my direction as he emerged swiftly from the green shadow of the chestnut trees into the yellow sunlight of the sidewalk.' This early caller must have been in an unusually conservative frame of mind that day to have appeared in mouse-gray. He might, likely as not, have turned up in sky-blue, or in his famous almond-green outfit with a white velvet waistcoat or in yet more startling examples of his extraordinarily colored and perfectly tailored wardrobe. He selected his costume to tone in with his moods and his moods were as varied as the iridescent silk which lined some of his jackets. Sir William Rothenstein once met him at an all–von Weber concert wearing a mauve suit with a shirt to match and a bunch of pale violets at his throat in place of a necktie 'because,' he explained, 'one should always listen to von Weber in mauve.' His scarfpins, when he wore a scarf, were exotic examples of the jeweler's art, ranging in motif from an emerald butterfly to an onyx death's-head. On a smooth tapering forefinger he wore a large seal ring set with a crystal that had been hollowed out to contain one human tear—whose, he never revealed.

This sartorial eccentric was the Comte Robert de Montesquiou-Fezensac, royalist, social snob, literary dilettante and Symbolist poet ... of sorts. There is little doubt that he served as a partial model for Proust's Baron Charlus although in many ways J. K. Huysmans' fantastic Des Esseintes, the hero of *A Rebours*, comes closer to being a direct portrait and Rostand is said to have created the character of the Peacock in *Chantecler* with him in mind. With ease and contemptuous elegance, he assumed an exalted position in both fashionable and literary circles. Graham Robertson, the English artist who painted appalling portraits but wrote delightful memoirs, said that Montesquiou was 'a typical member of that curious little world of amateurs which hangs midway between the worlds of art and society'. The categorizing would have outraged the count, who considered his own literary output anything but that of an amateur. And yet he would never have lowered himself socially to the level of being considered a professional writer. Even his association with certain genuine men of letters was done with somewhat the condescending attitude of the drawing-room liberal who mixes with the working classes.

Slim and graceful as a Siamese cat, he was absurdly handsome, with dark, wavy hair and a silky mustache beneath a proud Roman nose which Jules Renard in his gleefully acid journal likens to the beak of a bird of prey nurtured on vanity. There was something definitely artificial about his skin and Léon Daudet, Alphonse Daudet's clever and snobbish son, describes him as being 'ageless, as though varnished for eternity, every line of his brow cleverly ironed out'.

The count and his family were direct descendants of the dukes of Gascony and it pleased this exquisite to trace his haughty ancestry back through some early crusaders to the barbaric majesty of the Merovingian kings. Touchily proud, and at the same time sublimely self-assured, he held lyrical sway like a perfectly groomed Apollo over a worshipful band of muses, titled ladies with literary aspirations, poetry-conscious society women and a number of effete young Symbolists. He was invited everywhere, to the houses of the high-born and wealthy, into many of the leading salons, he even had entrée into circles of serious literature. He was often asked by the generous and lovable Alphonse Daudets to their apartment on the rue de Bellechasse for one of their Thursday dinners to which the literary world flocked. Edmond de Goncourt, the exquisite and aristocratic old *maréchal de lettres*, was his good friend. The only genuine symbolist of the whole vaguely irresponsible movement, Stephane Mallarmé, welcomed him in his humble flat up four flights of stairs on the smoky rue de Rome where all the intellectual youth of Paris crowded into a small bourgeois salon that could accommodate fifteen with difficulty for those shimmering and golden Tuesday evenings of the best of philosophical and aesthetic talk and rich discussion. Such evenings might amuse the count but not for long. His native milieu was the world of smart aristocracy to which he felt himself to be of prime importance. When he invited any distinguished men of letters to special ceremonies of his own devising, his engraved invitations, topped with the family crest, invariably wound up with the reassuring information 'Ladies of society will be present'. These special ceremonies included his flowery funeral oration over the casket of Leconte de Lisle, his speech at the unveiling of a statue he had arranged to be erected to the memory of the neglected poetess Marceline Desbordes-Valmore and he sent out announcements that he would be present at the funeral of Paul Verlaine, that tragic and sumptuous farce when the persons who had spurned Verlaine in life paid him expensive homage in death. The count also sent out engraved invitations to much of smart Tout Paris asking them to be present at the ceremony of the christening of his cat.

Robert de Montesquiou had a constantly shifting set of mannerisms. At the beginning of any conversation, he'd remove one glove and start a series of gesticulations, now raising his hands towards the sky, now lowering them to touch the tip of one perfectly shod toe, now waving them as though conducting an orchestra. His conversation was hardly conversation at all but long monologues filled with exotic anecdotes, mysterious allusions and obscure classical quotations all told with a rich vocabulary 'at the end of which', according to Léon Daudet, 'the count would burst into the shrill laughter of an hysterical woman, then suddenly, as though seized with remorse, he'd clap his hand over his mouth and rear back until his inexplicable glee was controlled ... as though he were coming out of laughing gas.' Probably the reason for his clapping his hand over his mouth was that for all his arrogant handsomeness, the count's teeth were small and quite black. Many of his hangers-on and admirers ... for absurd as this man was, he had a definite magnetism and could exude great charm when he wanted to ... aped his mannerisms of speech and gesture. Proust, who was to be his devoted slave, even went so far as copy his laugh and his gesture of hiding his teeth, although in contrast to the count's, Proust's teeth were even and white. Regarding his conversation, Jules Renard found it 'very refined, very precise, very insignificant'. Gustave Kahn in an article for the *Revue Blanche* called him 'the world's most laborious sayer of nothing' and Sir William Rothenstein said that Montesquiou had the affectation of Oscar Wilde without Wilde's touch of genius and without his geniality and sense of fun. And certainly without that Irishman's capacity for friendship, for the count himself is quoted as saying, 'However amusing it may be to speak ill of one's enemies, it is even more delectable to speak ill of one's friends.' His talk was mostly on the subject of himself, a subject he treated with respect and elaboration. He once told Mme. de Clermont-Tonnerre (Elisabeth de Gramont) that he was like a Greek temple with exquisite sculptured friezes that were hidden by climbing vines and that now he was about to unveil himself to the world. Mme. de Gramont found his conversation at times sparkling, at other times funny. Full of strange imagery—a combination of erudition and frivolity. It could be startling too as when he asked her if she hadn't been sprinkling aphrodisiac on her furniture as 'the armchairs seem to want to embrace the small chairs, the library is opening out rapturously to receive the piano.'

In later years, Robert de Montesquiou was to reside in the rue Franklin in a house which he chose to name 'The Pavilion of the Muses'. During the '90's, he lived on the top floor of his father's Quai d'Orsay mansion in a remote suite of rooms that were reached by climbing a dark, twisting staircase and passing through a carpeted tunnel lined with tapestry. The quarters into which a visitor emerged were partly Japanese, partly *Arabian Nights* and partly God knows what. Each room, he would explain, was decorated so as to fit a mood and thus he could move from one to the other. The first was painted and hung in tones of red which went from deep crimson to shell pink. The adjoining chamber was a symphony in gray with gray hangings, gray upholstery on gray furniture and four immense gray urns for which he ransacked Paris every week in a desperate search for gray flowers. The search was seldom successful. In a further sitting room, on a spotless polar-bear rug stood a large Russian sleigh while overhead from the beams of a vaulted roof there hung a collection of ancient musical instruments, lutes, rebecs and some objects handed down from an early Montesquiou troubadour which their owner said were mandores and theorbos. Maybe they were. High lancet windows with panes of seventeenth century glass shed a dim and not too religious light by day and at night there were curious electrical effects which went by the title of 'Sunlight through tropical water' or 'Moonlight on northern snow'. At one special soirée, the host, by way of entertainment, plunged the room into almost complete darkness and served his guests a series of liqueurs which supposedly blended with gusts of perfume which by some mysterious means were wafted into the room, while the only illumination came from the jewel-encrusted shell of a live turtle who crawled disconsolately about the Persian-carpeted floor, gleaming with genuine diamonds, sapphires and amethysts. The guests survived the ordeal. The less fortunate turtle turned over onto its Fabergé'd back and expired.

Montesquiou's library was housed in a glass conservatory where the works of his favorite authors, Baudelaire, Swinburne and his friend Goncourt, were displayed on low shelves as a background for a small forest of Japanese dwarfed trees, a rare collection of miniature oaks, century-old pines, and tiny delicate maples ... all no bigger than cabbages. Goncourt, who had been one of the 'discoverers' of things Japanese, said that seeing them, one was tempted to stroke them as if caressing the back of a dog or a cat. The count's bedroom was an Arabian nightmare of heavy curtains, low sofas, satin cushions and hanging brass lamps with colored glass. The bed was fashioned out of a mammoth ebony dragon on which the pillow nestled into a coil of the tail while, serving as a footboard, reared the monster's head with savage ivory teeth and glaring mother-of-pearl eyes.

Edmond de Goncourt was one of the few elect to be allowed a view of this exquisite's bathroom. All gauze curtains of muted blues, green walls painted with vague, dreamlike fish, it must have resembled a Gordon Craig setting for an allegorical play by Maeterlinck. Behind a diaphanous hanging with gold and silver flecks was the tub, an immense Moorish bowl whose water was heated by a brass boiler of oriental repoussée. The dressing room was a pretty folly known as the Hortensia Room, partly in tribute to Louis Napoleon's mother Queen Hortense from whom Montesquiou claimed descent, partly because stylized hortensias along with water lilies were the current rage in 'art moderne'. Here, painted, molded, carved, cast in green bronze, hortensias bloomed, climbed, writhed and swooned in fashionable convulsions. The door to the count's clothes cupboard was of clear plate glass behind which a floodlight could be turned on for the dramatic exhibition of one hundred neckties 'aux nuances les plus tendres', their owner's fond description. The ties were hung like banners on either side of a blown-up photograph of a certain La Rochefoucauld ... not the seventeenth century duke famous for his maxims, but an acrobat of the Cirque Molier, famous for his muscles and the erotic uses to which he could put them. The photograph, which was hand tinted, showed him in bright pink tights exhibiting what Goncourt called 'his elegant ephebic form'.

In every room were elaborate gewgaws ... Dresden china, Venetian glass, mounted butterflies, perfumed fans to wave as one sipped Russian tea and bouquets of peacock feathers ... 'the influence of my dear friend Whistler,' he would say. What Whistler said about him is to be conjectured. Montesquiou's very absurdity may have appealed to that acid genius. Among the treasures he had after he moved into his Pavilion of the Muses were a number of strange keepsakes ... the bullet that killed Pushkin, a cigarette partially smoked by George Sand, a tear (dried) once shed by Lamartine and the slippers of the last love of Lord Byron, the Countess Guiccioli. He kept Mme. de Montespan's pink marble tub in his garden, filled with rambler roses, and he would show admiring visitors a birdcage that had once housed Michelet's pet canary, along with a jewel box containing a single hair from the beard of the same historian. On special occasions he might, with great reverence, exhibit a bedpan used by Napoleon after Waterloo. He had also acquired a plaster cast of the knees of Mme. de Castiglione, the *femme fatale* of the Second Empire Court who, in her rosy time, had had herself photographed one hundred and ninety times. Montesquiou, not to be outdone, had himself photographed one hundred and ninety-nine times.

Here in the home of this exquisite who termed himself a Symbolist poet, one looked vainly for a desk. The inquisitive visitor rash enough to ask him where he did his writing would be given the languorous answer, 'My servants bring me the necessary things.' (One is reminded of the remark of Villiers de l'Isle Adam's hero Axël: 'Live? Our lackeys will do that for us.') The 'necessary things' were a small eighteenth century writing table, a pen made of a peacock feather and ink ... mauve or green according to the poet's mood ... kept in a jade phial that was half buried in a goblet of rose petals.

This was the period when the Symbolist Movement was at its height with Mallarmé its leader and prophet, Verlaine its incomparable song-bird, Maeterlinck its dramatist, while across the Irish sea was Yeats, its English interpreter. Certainly de Montesquiou's verse abided by Mallarmé's tenet that 'Symbolism is a mystery to which the reader must find the key.' It is doubtful if there were a key to be found to this man's poems which appeared in select privately printed editions under the titles of 'Bats', 'Peacocks', 'Bending Reeds', 'The Blue Hortensias' and 'The Chief of Subtle Odors' (*Le Chef des Odeurs Suaves*). They were brought out in costly print and with startling bindings. *Le Chef des Odeurs* had a cover of midnight blue satin, embroidered with golden griffon wings, while *Chauves-Souris* was bound in gray moiré decorated with a flight of bats made of jet beads. Their author managed to persuade certain amazingly well-known artists to do the illustrations. *Chauves-Souris* had illustrations by Forain, Gandara and Whistler and *Les Hortensias Bleus* was fancifully enlivened with sketches by the popular painter Helleu.

These exotic publications enjoyed a brief success of curiosity in the literary world and of snobbery in social circles. Ladies of fashion flocked to hear the poet read selections from his works, sighed 'How exquisite!' over the darkly turgid passages they could not remotely have understood and fairly swooned over the names of classical personages culled from their author's own private mythology . . . Anabaxare and Anacyndaraxe, Parameizes and Planiandrion.

He took adulation as his due, for his vanity was as prodigious as his exaggerated sense of importance. He had a habit of saying, on his way to the table at a dinner party, 'The place of honour is where I find myself.' He once made a trip to England telling all his Paris circle for weeks in advance that he would be traveling 'incognito,' a curious precaution since he could hardly have been of serious interest to the British public, few of whom had so much as heard of him. When he got to London, he adopted fantastic aliases, wore strange disguises and stalked like a stage assassin in the shadows of buildings, occasionally darting furtively down side alleys. His friend Graham Robertson said of his visit that 'Montesquiou was so wrapped about in thick mystery, no intelligent acquaintance within the three-mile radius could possibly have failed to notice him.'

The same preposterous vanity prompted him to commission innumerable portraits of himself. Jean Lorrain in his 'Pall Mall' column said that every season the Salon of the Champs de Mars exhibited, for the delight of an admiring public, a Montesquiou immortalized by the current artist in vogue. And he added that the princely subject always invited some five hundred 'intimate friends' from Tout Paris to the unveiling. Jacques Blanche painted him on a narrow panel in tones of gray, to hang later in his Gray Room amid those elusive gray flowers. He posed for La Gandara in a Chinese robe, clasping his knee with tapering jeweled fingers and Mandarin nails. Whistler obligingly made two studies of him. In one he wore black and carried a fur stole over his arm. For the other study the count selected a pearl-colored coat with an edging which was, he said, 'of a shade, a shade which cannot be expressed but which my own eyes epitomize.'

There was one portrait which led to a *cause célèbre* of the drawing rooms that became known as 'The Affair of the Cane.' The artist was the popularly facile Boldini 'who painted the way gypsy violinists play czardas'. In this canvas, the count was seated in a dashingly insolent pose, holding out before him a turquoise-handled walking stick. This gave the boulevard wags a perfect opening for double-meaning comment. They titled it 'l'Homme á la Canne' and Jean Lorrain went further (and in print), saying it should be called 'Indecision', or 'Where Shall I Put It?' then went on to say, 'Monsieur de Montesquiou takes communion before his cane ... swooning before it as Narcissus might swoon before a mirror,' and added the lines:

> Nous avions l'Homme au Gant,
> Nous avions l'Homme à la Canne,
> A quand, Messieurs, l'Homme à l'Encensoir?[1]

To all such venomous prattle, Montesquiou was superbly indifferent. He brushed it off, saying, 'It is better to be hated than unknown.' But then came the incident during the tragic aftermath of the Charity Bazaar Fire, a ghastly holocaust which occurred in 1897 on the afternoon of May 4. The Charity Bazaar was a big annual event sponsored by society and the Church which attracted not only Tout Paris but throngs of ordinary people eager to rub elbows with the high-ranking females whose names appeared daily in the social columns. For this worthy cause, fashionable hostesses and Faubourg Saint-Germain duchesses came down from their pedestals to serve as saleswomen and waitresses at the various booths and counters. That year the bazaar was held near the Place des Vosges in the rue Jean Goujon and set up in a temporary structure of canvas and plywood with floors of Norwegian pine. The overall décor represented a section of medieval Paris with little twisting lanes lined by house façades of painted scenery. On either side of the narrow passageways were some twenty-two booths and counters gay with banners, bright-coloured buntings and paper festoons. The most popular attraction was a primitive motion-picture exhibit. It was a great novelty at the time and every session was jammed. The projection machine was a crude affair which, for some obscure reason, required occasional doses of ether, an open bottle of which was beside the mechanic. A spark from the sputtering mechanism fell into the ether bottle, which exploded and shot a geyser of flame through the flimsy wall. It caught the ribbons and draped laces of an adjoining booth, ran like lightning up the paper streamers to the roof and in seconds the entire place was a roaring inferno. Blazing pieces of wood and smoldering tatters of canvas fell onto the crowd of some two thousand below, igniting women's tulle ruffs and feather boas, setting

[1] We had the Man with the Glove,
  We had the Man with the Cane,
  When, Gentlemen, shall we have the Man with the Incense Burner?

fire to straw hats and taffeta capes. Smoke and roaring flames made it impossible to see and indescribable panic ensued. People crowded toward the single exit in desperate attempts to escape, most of them ending up in an ever increasing pile of humanity. The screams were frightful and most horrible of all, according to one witness, 'every now and then the sound of a loud report . . . a skull cracking from the hideous heat.' Amid the frenzy there were scenes of heroism and heartbreaking pathos. The Duchesse d'Alençon, sister of the Empress of Austria, refused the help of a worker who wanted to carry her out on his shoulders. 'Because of my title I had to be the first to enter here. I shall be the last to go out,' she said and sat quietly behind her booth awaiting an unspeakable death. And there was the Sister of Charity in charge of a group of blind orphans who held to her smoldering skirts their pitiful whimpering heads while she intoned the prayers for the dying.

The real heroes of this dreadful day were, as always, men of the French laboring class. Some workmen on a nearby scaffolding and the cooks, waiters and porters from the Hôtel du Palais rushed time and again into the raging furnace, their own clothes and hair on fire and dragged out whomever they could reach, saving over a hundred and fifty. Many of the coachmen and *valets-de-pied* from the private carriages of the bazaar patrons waiting outside in the street made their way through the holocaust to save their employers. A cabdriver named Eugène Geordès grabbed General Munier as he ran down the street his clothes ablaze and flung him into the watering trough of the Rothschild stables at 26 rue Jean Goujon. Levelheaded rescue work was done by an intrepid butcher the back of whose shop was adjacent to one of the burning walls. With his cleaver he bashed out the bars of a window, formed his men into a lifeline and saved two hundred people. Other heroes included a plumber named Piquet, a street sweeper named Gustave Dhuy and a roof tiler named Léon Déjardins. The disaster was over in half an hour during which time it literally carbonized one hundred and twenty-seven human beings. Only five of these were men. Amid the heroism of the rescuers and the fortitude of some of the victims, the cowardly behavior of the dandies and young clubmen who had come to patronize the fair was a shocking disgrace. When the fire broke out, they ran like rats to save their well-tailored hides, beat their hysterical way to the exit, using their canes as cudgels, stepping on the bodies of the wretched woman and children they had knocked down. This became an immediate public scandal and roused violent resentment among the *peuple* who said, 'If it had happened in Montmartre, we would have saved our women.'

The rumor got about that Robert de Montesquiou was among the cowards who had fought their way to freedom. This was not true, for at the time of the conflagration he was nowhere near the rue Jean Goujon. The next day, however, he did turn up at the Palais de l'Industrie where the bodies had been laid out for identification. It was a gruesome spectacle, for most were charred beyond recognition. A desperate husband identified his young wife by bits of her new red corset, a dowager was recognized by the pearl dog collar about her blackened neck and pretty Mme. de Luppé's gold wedding ring was found thrust into her heart as though at the last moment she had held her hand over it and the intense heat had annealed the gesture.

Montesquiou, under the pretext of looking for possible friends but doubtless attracted by the macabre, minced along with the line of frantic relatives and agonized mourners. Before each laid-out corpse, he paused and lifted the covering sheet with the tip of his elegant cane. A gendarme on guard duty watched him as long as he could stand it, then cried out in anguish, 'One does not touch the dead with the end of a cane, Mr Clubman! If it disgusts you, I can do the unveiling!'

Jean Lorrain got wind of the incident and lost no time in publishing an account of it in his column 'Pall Mall' and the Montesquiou cane became again the subject of the gibes of the drawing rooms and boulevard cafés. This gave rise to the count's one affair of honor, not with Lorrain, but with the courteous and aristocratic writer Henri de Régnier, a charming and tactful person 'and such a gentleman,' it was said, 'one would never take him for a poet.' Régnier on one occasion had set tact aside long enough to announce at a soirée of the Baronne Alphonse de Rothschild that instead of a cane, Montesquiou would do better to carry a muff. The remark was repeated to the count, who lost no time in challenging the poet to a settlement with swords. This was a dauntless step to prove his courage after the Charity Bazaar libel and also because he had the assurance that his adversary was as inexperienced a duellist as he.

They met at an early hour in a deserted park at Neuilly. The park didn't remain deserted for very long, however, for the count had sent out invitations to all his friends and acquaintances and they arrived on the premises in varying states of sincere concern or of wild amusement. One palpitating titled lady had brought along her family chaplain to administer a possible last sacrament. Some hundred or more, they flocked to the scene as though to an outdoor pageant. The pageant must have been well worth the ten-kilometer trip. Neither contestant had the remotest idea of how to handle a sword. After the signal to start, Montesquiou leaped to and fro posturing like an amateur d'Artagnan, Régnier stood stiff and pallid, his monocle shaking visibly. Eventually Régnier managed to snip Montesquiou in the thumb, an indulgent surgeon pronounced the slight incision to be a wound, the onlookers applauded and the count retired to a hero's couch (that carved dragon affair) from which he received a steady steam of worshipful visitors. He himself announced that it was the best party he had ever given. The next day, cool, collected and perfectly groomed in faun color, he gave a conference on d'Annunzio.

Most people found Robert de Montesquiou fantastically absurd. Yet many toadied to him for he had entrée everywhere ... through the doors of the most exclusive clubs and restaurants, into the drawing rooms of the Plaine Monceau, past the crumbling posterns of the old aristocratic houses of the Faubourg Saint-Germain. He was a welcome guest in the salon of that beautiful and unchallenged sovereign of sophisticated Paris, the Comtesse de Greffulhe as well as in that leading intellectual cénâcle on the Avenue Hoche which Mme. de Caillavet maintained for the pleasure of Anatole France. He went occasionally to Mallarmé's Tuesday evenings but couldn't have enjoyed them much because Mallarmé and not he was the respected deity of these occasions. Edmond de Goncourt was as close a friend as ever Montesquiou could have had and was often his champion, yet he seldom patronized that author's literary Sundays in his famous *grenier*, finding them 'trop vulgaire.'

That he should make such a comment about the Goncourt gatherings was a typical Montesquiou affectation. Edmond de Goncourt was a polished 'aristo' from the tips of his fine fingers to the points of his white mustache and his *grenier* was anything but *vulgaire*. It wasn't an attic at all, but a perfectly appointed salon of his elegant flat in Auteuil. This 'grenier' was in the best of what then was considered intellectual good taste. It was filled with original drawings and crayons by Chardin, Boucher and Gavarni, Japanese bronzes, delicate porcelains and, above all, carefully preserved records and testimonials of whatever pertained to his dead brother Jules. This sentiment for the person with whom he wrote the first nineteen years of the famous Journal and with whose sensitive collaboration such excellent novels were produced, was probably the only great love of Edmond de Goncourt's life. Twenty-odd years after the death of Jules, Edmond seemed constantly to be turning to his younger brother for the joint observations and opinions they had shared for so long. They had always given the impression of being one single entity even to the point when if one of them started referring to himself in the first person singular, he'd instinctively and almost immediately go into the first person plural ... 'I saw such-and-such and we thought,' etc. Whereas in their stupendous Journal, the two merge into one in a continuous first person singular ... 'I saw' ... 'he wrote me,' etc. It was a strange relationship, almost like Siamese twins of the mind and spirit. At one period, they even shared the same mistress and felt no compunction in admitting it. Emile Bergerat once wrote:

> Did you ever watch Edmond de Goncourt going down a street? He isn't going straight ahead, he's following someone. It's a habit he acquired years ago with Jules during their *observation promenades*. The younger man alive, petulant, nervously darting on everything the fire of his black eyes, always ten paces ahead. The elder brother, more absorbed, less tender, more docile toward the overall and more apt to coordinate, kept his distance. They never exchanged a word during this ambulatory work. Only when something extraordinary struck Jules, he'd half turn to consult Edmond with a mere look; the latter had caught whatever it was at the identical second and had it classified. It was 'in the basket'! Jules took the clippers and Edmond the basket ... one was the poet, the other the philosopher. Today, the elder man had kept the habit of this four-legged march. The genius of Jules still drifts ten paces ahead, and even sometimes turns back; the accord takes place, the annotations made and entered in the workroom at the double desk. Edmond writes with both hands and does double work.

Goncourt's *grenier* meetings lacked the warmth of the good and simple gatherings at the hospitable hearth of his close friend Alphonse Daudet. They also lacked the intellectual stimulus of Stephane Mallarmé's Tuesday evenings in his bourgeois little apartment on the rue de Rome where the schoolteacher poet conducted a brilliant cénacle of advanced young intellectuals who sat in worship at his feet. The leader of the Symbolists and author of *l'Après-Midi d'un Faune* held forth with the appealing simplicity of an Athenian philosopher. William Rothenstein, who never missed a Mallarmé Tuesday, said of this profound aesthete that 'while his poetry was obscure and rather difficult, his conversation was crystal-clear.' The atmosphere of Goncourt's *grenier* was more conventional, more formal. His assemblage included, in addition to Alphonse Daudet, Joris-Karl Huysmans, François Coppée, Clemenceau, occasionally Ernest Renan and sometimes Mallarmé himself, in addition to any amount of young writers who shook with terror when the master of the house entrusted their awkward hands with a fragile and precious bibelot to admire. With a white scarf wound about his aristocratic neck, Edmond de Goncourt received them all with a manner both cold and courteous. During the 1890's he was a beautiful old man with silver hair, an aristocrat in bearing and intellect ... anything but a liberal, a passionate collector of art especially of the smaller art objects. Whatever his shortcomings, he has bequeathed to his country the Prix Goncourt which, even if he did bequeath it in a certain spirit of spite against the Academy to which he was never admitted, stands for one of the country's most coveted rewards for literary merit. And to the world in general he—and Jules too for the time he was alive to collaborate—have left the fine novels and the incomparable Journal. The Journal begun by the two brothers in 1851 was originally intended not to be published until after their death. After Alphonse Daudet persuaded Edmond into letting some of it appear in the *Figaro Illustré* in '85, Renan protested that such publicizing was indiscreet (and anyone who has dabbled in the Journal can vouch that in many entries it is not only indiscreet but downright salacious). To this Goncourt replied, 'Ever since the world has existed, any interesting memoirs have been written by the Indiscreet. My only crime is that I am still alive.'

In the estimation of certain people, mainly himself, Robert de Montesquiou passed for a wit. He undoubtedly had wit of a rather satanic sort. Certainly he had the talent for making amusing and rather lacerating remarks, and was, to quote his own words, 'Addicted to the aristocratic pleasure of offending.' A frivolous little society woman of questionable morals was the mother of five small children and he called her house 'La rue des Cinq Pères.' He couldn't abide bores and when one fatuous old dowager blocked his way into an art exhibit with an exuberant 'Ah, mon cher comte, comment allez-voux?' the 'cher comte' answered, 'Très vite, madame!' and beat a hasty retreat. He had an obsessive loathing for all social climbers. When one parvenue hostess tried to wheedle him into procuring her an entrée into a particular salon because, she said, it was so exclusive, de Montesquiou snorted, 'Impossible, madame! For the moment you appear there, it will cease to be exclusive!'

Living in Paris was a Mrs Kate Moore, an American millionairess, kindly, generous, socially ambitious and not a little absurd. Like other American international hostesses even down to our present day, she was an easy target for the fashionable wags. She entertained lavishly and those same fashionable wags accepted her invitations with alacrity. For the series of the Italian operas held yearly at the Châtelet, she bought a subscription that included thirty grand tier boxes all of which she filled nightly with the people who formed the trellis for her constant climbing. At one of her dinners, Mrs Moore suddenly burst into floods of tears saying that she had swallowed a tooth, an announcement which convulsed her guests whose muffled laughter deeply offended her. The maître d'hôtel got control of the situation by announcing in calm and all too clear tones: 'Rest assured, madame. Madame has not swallowed her tooth, she only forgot it and left it on the dressing table. La voilà!' and he handed her the porcelain incisor on a gold platter. Mrs Moore was determinedly out for titles. The more dukes, duchesses and princes she could snare for her parties, the happier she was. The great triumph of her life was when she finally managed, after machiavellian maneuvering, to get Edward VII for dinner in her Biarritz palace which she called her 'Folly.' The King was amused by her good-natured vulgarity and her blatant social ambition. 'You should have lived in the days of Louis XIV, madame,' he said. 'In those days there were kings everywhere.' Kate Moore was not above making munificent gifts of money or negotiable art objects to certain people who could get her into soirées in the upper circles, and those certain people were not in the least bit above accepting the gifts. When she died, the kind silly woman in a number of legacies remembered generously those who had managed to hoist her up a rung or two of the society ladder. Montesquiou's comment was: 'Mrs Moore has departed from life as she would from the Ritz, handing out tips.'

When another American, the Princesse de Polignac, formerly a Miss Winarella Singer and heiress to the Singer Sewing Machine fortune, sent the count an invitation to a buffet supper which was then called 'supper at little tables' he accepted, saying 'It will, I know, be charming, your supper at little sewing machines.' Needless to say, Robert de Montesquiou was anti-Semitic along with most of the social snobs, and during the Dreyfus commotion he proudly flaunted his prejudice. He did stoop low enough in his own estimation to ask a Jewish banker he knew—a man generally admitted in social circles—to lend him some jewels to wear for a costume ball in which he wanted to appear as a

Persian prince. The banker politely excused himself on the grounds that the pieces Montesquiou wanted were family jewels, to which the count coldly commented, 'I knew you had jewels. I didn't know you had a family.'

It gave him infinite delight to entertain with huge receptions and outdoor fêtes. Not the least of the delights was the making up of two lists of people: one, the 'inviteds,' the other the 'excluded,' the latter affording him endless glee. Though never a person of great means, he spared no expense for these fabulous galas. Debts meant nothing to him and he was quoted as saying 'It is bad enough to have no money. It would be worse if one had to deny one's self anything.' During one season he rented a seventeenth century house at Versailles where at an elaborate housewarming, with the grand manner of Louis XIV distributing favors, he received an array of titled *gratin*, men of letters, actresses and sycophants. In his torchlit garden was a small marble amphitheatre where Sarah Bernhardt and Julia Bartet recited poems. The poems were written by the host, of course, and one can imagine the tongue-in-cheek languor of the divine Sarah as she intoned:

> *J'aime le jade*
> *Couleur des yeux d'Hérodiade,*
> *Et l'améthyste,*
> *Couleur du sang de Jean-Baptiste.*[1]

Montesquiou adored Bernhardt and she was curiously fond of him. He was even reported to have had a twenty-four-hour love affair with this incandescent and unpredictable woman, followed, alas, by a week of vomiting. But despite this unfortunate interlude, if indeed it was true, theirs was a warm friendship until some years later when Sarah opened in *L'Aiglon*. The actress's appearance as a young man in white skin-tight trousers offended the count's aesthetic sensibilities and he felt that, regretfully, he must never speak to her again.

It was around 1898 that Robert de Montesquiou found Marcel Proust . . . or rather that Proust found him. They met in the salon of Madeleine Lemaître, a popular woman artist who had, according to the young writer, 'created more roses than anybody after God.' She painted pretty pictures which sold well, illustrated a number of books with

---

[1] I love jade,
  Color of the eyes of Herodias,
    And amethyst,
  Color of the blood of John the Baptist.

equally pretty sketches and watercolors and she ran a pseudo-intellectual salon where one met the better-born of the literary set and ate delicious little cakes. Madeleine Lemaître was said to be less famous for her paintings than for her *petits fours*.

Montesquiou proved to be one of the most rewarding finds for that insatiably observant chronicler of times past. The count, with magnificent condescension, allowed himself to be a patron of the pale, delicate author with his oriental features, his hacking asthma and his religious passion for the upper crust. It was a passion not so much that of the social climber as of the watchful student constantly gathering material and endless minutiae of customs, dress and décor for his meticulously detailed writings. The fashionable world was Prousts's field of study. Léon Daudet said perceptively that 'the *monde* mattered to him as flowers matter to a botanist, not as they count to the man who buys the bouquet.' Montesquiou was the passkey to that hitherto off-limits zone of the genuine remaining aristocracy living in their elegant *hôtels privés* of the fashionable Right Bank or desiccating with austere formality behind the peeling walls of the Faubourg Saint-Germain ... fabulous personages to the dream-struck novelist, behind whose ancient titles he beheld all the pageantry of the great families of France. They were the prototypes for his Guermantes, his Villeparisis, his Swann. And yet, Proust's characters are none of them direct portraits ... he took the type of one person, gave it the character of a second, added the mannerisms of a third and gradually made up the entire person. Swann was probably partly the Prince de Polignac and a greater part Charles Haas, that popular man-about-town whose charm alone gave him entrée everywhere for he had neither fortune nor family; moreover he was a Jew, the only one in the Jockey Club or the Cercle Royale except the Rothschilds. He was a close friend of the Prince of Wales and the Comte de Paris, a steady member of the Comtesse de Greffulhe's coterie as well as the salon of the Princesse Mathilde and when he journeyed to England he always went out to Twickenham to pay his respects to the Empress Eugénie.

Prouste's Duchesse de Guermantes was also a composite, the main components being the two most enchanting hostesses in Paris—the Comtesse de Chevigné and the Comtesse de Greffulhe—and added to them the occasional flashes of wit of Mme Straus. Laure de Sade, the Comtese de Chevigné, was a noblewoman whose family dated back to twelfth century Avignon and her ancestress that other Laura, the inspiration of Petrarch. She was spirited and satirical, courageous and gracious. She dressed with simplicity and style and continued to dress in the same style which, even when it was no longer in vogue suited her royally as Queen Mary's manner of dressing suited her. Mme de Chevigné, lithe, energetic, took a brisk two-hour walk every day of her life, wearing a smart tailored suit from Creed's and a tiny hat with a veil. Young Proust waiting in the shadow of a building to see her daily emergence into the rue d'Anjou, as later the narrator of *Guermantes' Way* would wait for the sight of his unattainable duchess, said that she made of her morning walk 'an entire poem of elegance'. When she was well over seventy some housepainters on a scaffolding watched her slim, graceful back and her free stride of a girl of eighteen, and one of them called out in admiration, 'Ah, la belle gonzesse!' to which the countess cheerfully called back in her husky voice, 'Attends un peu, mon petit. Tu n'as pas vu le devant!'[1] She had a way of addressing people, even those she didn't know, in the intimate second person singular. For all her noble bearing, there was a lot of the *gamine* in her and something completely beguiling about her cracked voice of the heavy smoker that she was. When Proust met her, she was no longer young. Before their introduction, he had written her a note saying, 'Madame, you live a few houses from me but far more, whether you will or no, you live in me in the light of an eternal summer.' And when at last they did meet and he saw at close hand the clarity of her wise blue eyes and the shimmer of her softly piled hair, golden red like that of Petrarch's Laura, he felt that this ageless lady had drunk less at the Fountain of Eternal Youth than at the Fountain of Eternal Loveliness and paid her the graceful compliment: 'You were as lovely years ago as you are today.'

Laure de Chevigné was homeloving and liked to receive her friends informally in her own drawing room. Her husband Adheaume de Chevigné, an elderly Royalist who was in the active service of the Comte de Chambord and a tireless worker for the King-in-exile, returned every day for lunch, departed immediately afterward for his club, and at two on the dot, the countess's faithful coterie would arrive ... elderly adorers who came daily to perch on uncomfortable little chairs in a small, dark drawing room for two hours, partly through blind devotion to their lively and lovely friend, partly through blind jealousy of each other. They were for the most part some of the more intellectual 'aristos' and politicians. They were so used to this daily ritual that they hardly greeted each other or even their hostess. The talk would be relaxed and

[1] 'Ah, the beautiful babe!' and the countess replied. 'Wait, little one, you haven't seen the front view!'

witty. No refreshments were ever served. Laure de Chevingé would chain-smoke Caporal cigarettes in an amber holder and occasionally one of her elderly beaux would help himself to a Vichy pastille from a candy box kept open for the use of the dyspeptic. Sometimes distinguished visiting Europeans would drop in, the Grand Duchess Wladimir, a British viscount or a titled Italian. Mme de Chevigné had friends all over Europe. She started the Cercle Interallié and was its president until it began to have too many members. Sometimes young Jean Cocteau would put in an appearance and Proust came as often as she'd allow him to. Her interests were varied and never precious. She liked to hear about new trends in the arts, but didn't go overboard about them. There was something distinctly earthy about this exquisite noblewoman who would undoubtedly have far preferred the Bouffes Parisiennes to the Russian Ballet.

The sponsor of the Russian Ballet who was first responsible for bringing Diaghilev to Paris was the other ingredient of Proust's duchess. She was the beautiful Comtesse de Greffulhe, leader of the smart intelligentsia and unchallenged queen of the upper *monde*. Besides the ballet, she had brought Chaliapin out of Russia, she had been the backer of Moussorgsky and Stravinsky, an early devotee of Richard Strauss and the discoverer of Caruso. Earlier she encouraged Debussy by heading the subscription committee which made possible the first performance of *Pelléas et Mélisande*. Her interests were countless. She organized exhibits for impecunious but always worthy artists, including an 'Apotheosis Showing' of the works of Alfred Stevens at the Georges Petit gallery where she herself pushed the old painter around in a wheelchair. She made greyhound racing popular and she arranged, through President Poincaré, for the physicist Edouard Branly to receive the Osiris prize at the Pasteur Institute for his invention of the radio-conducting tube, a first step toward the wireless.

Mme Greffulhe carried out most of these activities at a distance, for she seldom went beyond the elegant confines of her mansion and gardens on the rue d'Astorg. She and the guests who flocked regularly to her salon were known as the 'd'Astorg Set'. They were very pro-British and very smart. Elisabeth de Gramont in describing Mme Greffulhe's life, which was anything but a constant social whirl, says: 'One cannot be frivolously pleasure-seeking and be the most beautiful woman in France.' She was that indeed, she couldn't help but know it and she went only to functions where she would be the chief attraction. Her entrance into her box at opera or theatre was like that of royalty and when she passed through a drawing room, it was with the swiftness and grace of a doe. Her litheness was almost legendary. A Diana by Houdon which stood by her mantelpiece was her double. Her daughter, who later married the Duc de Guiches, wrote poems at the age of six to her lovely mother. One of them goes:

> Maman walks like a flower.
> I would like to plant her in my garden.
> But I would never pluck her
> For to break the stem would break my heart.
> Her feet and hands are leaves.
> How beautiful, beautiful she is!

The count, her husband, was a fine sportsman and an art connoisseur who every morning would make the rounds of the galleries and antique dealers to keep his eye trained ... as he'd explain: 'One must correct one's aim and keep firing tirelessly.' The count was also a gay blade and another of his daily rounds was a series of calls on those charmers his wife called 'the little women who enjoy performing on mattresses'. His calls were done with such regularity that his horses would stop of their own accord before the door of each of his houris.

Mme de Greffulhe was a cousin of Robert de Montesquiou, who took Proust to one of her outdoor fêtes. The writer was immediately struck by that incomparable loveliness which made Boldini, László and all the portraitists of Europe want to paint her. 'All the mystery of her beauty,' he wrote, 'is in the enigmatic light of her eyes. I have never seen a woman as beautiful.' He loved her bell-like laugh, which he likened to the carillon of Bruges. The countess didn't especially take to young Proust, and didn't ask him to her house, but in one quick encounter he was able to make a mental sketch to help construct his final portrait of Oriane de Guermantes.

Robert de Montesquiou initiated Proust into what he termed the 'poetry of snobbery'. He himself, in all unconsciousness, posed for much of the unforgettable portrait of Baron Charlus. The 'sittings' cost the artist much patience and incessant blows to his self-respect for Montesquiou treated him with insolence and sometimes with cruel mockery. But the indefatigable disciple put up with it for the sake of study of his model and the further models this patron made available. Moreover, according to André Maurois, Proust 'understood the thirst for admiration with which Montesquiou burned and quenched it generously.' Polite, self-effacing, ingratiating, he trotted meekly in the

wake of the ambivalent eccentric, lavishing those extravagant compliments which made people who received them call him 'the hysterical
flatterer'. His letters to Montesquiou are embarrassingly fervent. 'Your
mind is a garden filled with rare blooms,' he says in one, signing it 'Your
humble, ardent and wholly fascinated Marcel Proust.' In another,
referring to the count's rented villa at Versailles, Proust effuses: 'When
will you return to that Versailles of which you are the pensive Marie
Antoinette and the conscious Louis XVI? I salute your Grace and
Majesty.' The pensive Marie Antoinette and conscious Louis XVI took
such flowery adulation in his mincing stride and Proust kept following
his guide 'through the inferno or paradise of aristcratic society' and
storing up reams of notes. As Elisabeth de Gramont points out, 'Proust
flattered him like the fox in the fable. Montesquiou opened his large
beak and out fell the prize.'

Marcel even went so far as to write a short eulogy entitled 'The
Simplicity of the Count de Montesquiou.' Be it a testimonial to the
integrity of the Paris press that no newspaper would ever publish it.

STANLEY HYLAND

The Private Enterprise
of Anne Hicks

I

Lord Seymour, the Honourable Member for Totnes in the County of
Devonshire, the son and heir of the eleventh Duke of Somerset and her
Majesty's First Commissioner of Woods and Forests, had a field-day on
Tuesday, the 29th of July, 1851. With a very light heart, a conscience
lighter still, and a jaunty and unassailable brief, which was guaranteed
to get the laughs it deserved, he went down to the House of Commons
and his place on the Treasury Bench.

Behind him, in responsibility though not in presence, towered the
comforting and all but legendary figure of His Grace the Duke of
Wellington, 'the Hero in a Hundred Fights', as they called him, the
grand old gentleman who could do no wrong if he tried, and he never
tried.[1] If the Duke was not enough, alone, to save him from censure,
there was also an Act of Parliament, the tenth of George the fourth,
chapter fifty.[2]

Seymour had no need to fall back on these constitutional buttresses
(though, in fact, he did fall back on them) because the House guffawed
and roared itself into uncritical endorsement of his uncharity. One
Member only refused to laugh and when he hit back at Seymour a week
later, the House roared with laughter again. The House always laughed
at Colonel Charles de Laet Waldo Shibthorp, 'our friend Sibby'.

Behind Sibthorp, in petition if not in presence, cowered the unhappy
woman at whom all this blast of Parliamentary amusement was
directed, Mrs Anne Hicks. Mrs Hicks herself was not laughing; for just
short of a fortnight she had had nothing at all to laugh about.

On the 16th of July, Anne Hicks, a woman between forty and fifty

---

[1] See, however, 'The Duke of Wellington's Miss J.'—Ed.
[2] 'An Act to consolidate and amend the Laws relating to the Management and Improvement of His Majesty's Woods, Forests, Parks and Chases, etc.'

years old, had been charged before Mr Hardwick, the Magistrate at Marlborough Street. The *Times* which in those days reported court cases, even small cases in small courts, with a special and curious relish, described her as looking 'Woe-begone and very shabby in appearance ... with a basket of three-a-penny cakes upon her arm.' She had been 'charged with the offence of attempting to sell her humble wares near the Crystal Palace' in Hyde Park.

Her story was unlikely but, because of that, sensational. She had gone back to Hyde Park, she said, because she had worked and lived there all her life by royal grant and grace. About a hundred years before, her grandfather had 'had the good fortune to assist in extricating His Majesty King George the Second from the Serpentine', and, in return for this smart act of loyalty, he had been granted a permanent trading concession on the banks of the Serpentine river. After spending sixty-nine profitable years selling apples and nuts and soft drinks to children playing in the park, her grandfather had died, passing his stall and his privilege down to his son, Anne's father. His son had stayed and worked and prospered there for another forty-nine years before departing the Serpentine and this life and handing over to his daughter, Anne. She had lived there all her life, and had worked on the stall since she was five years old.

Her last seven years there had been particularly comfortable years for her, because the Chief Ranger of the Park, Lord Lincoln, had allowed her to build herself a nice comfortable house into which she had sunk all her savings—a lot of money, about a hundred and thirty pounds in all.

Business had been good and her life happy. And then, suddenly, business looked like getting very good indeed, and her life happier still. She had been quick to see the advantage of having a shop on the trade route to and from the Crystal Palace. 'She thought her lodge's proximity to the Exhibition,' said the *Times* reporter, 'might be turned to account in affording accommodation to ladies.' So she wrote to the Board of Woods and Forests in excited anticipation, and had the wit to enclose in her letter a formal petition signed by forty genteel mothers of some of her regular customers.

On the 1st of November, 1850, she got a reply from Lord Seymour, the First Commissioner. It was cold and formal and a cruel blow to her. 'Lord Seymour has received Mrs Hicks' application dated the 20th ult. As Mrs Hicks is aware, she has been served with a notice to quit and deliver up possession of the place she occupies. Lord Seymour conceives the serving of that notice to be an answer to her application. The Board of Woods and Forests has immediate occasion for her removal and they can do nothing, therefore, to assist her in extending the accommodation of her present dwelling. Lord Seymour is prepared to recommend the Board to make an allowance to Mrs Hicks for house rent for a short period after her removal in the event of her complying with the notice served upon her. Of course, if the Board are driven to expense in taking legal steps in dispossessing her, she must abide by the consequences.'

That was the first of a number of letters and notices and written orders to quit sent to her not only by Seymour but also by the thunderous and formidable Duke of Wellington who became involved on the side of law and order because he was by that time the Chief Ranger of the Park. In ten days, the letters moved through distaste to intimidation.

'The utmost Lord Seymour can do will be to promise means for the removal of her furniture and to allow her at the rate of five shillings a week, which he is advised is amply sufficient for lodings, for a twelve-month after she shall have quitted. He can do nothing more, and if Mrs Hicks shall not have appointed with Mr Mann, the Surveyor of the Park, before four o'clock tomorrow, the 11th of November, 1850, a time for the removal of her things and for delivering up her place, the Law must take its course and he will not consent to make her any allowance whatsoever.'

Anne Hicks was out of her house by four o'clock on the eleventh; the house was demolished immediately and Mrs Hicks received her *ex gratia* compensation of five shillings a week for the next twelve months. By some mysterious principle of contemporary accountancy she actually received £12 19s. 6d., which was sixpence short by anybody's arithmetic.

That was all she got, though she sent sixteen letters to Lord Seymour in a rising wave of frustration and anger, asking for compensation in cash for the bricks and stone which had cost her £130 seven or eight years before. She got no reply to any of her sixteen letters, and no compensation. She then wrote to the Queen for help and got an answer signed, with due rigid formality, by the private secretary to the Private Secretary to Her Majesty:

Madame,—I am directed by Colonel Phipps to express the Queen's regret that the very numerous pressing claims on Her Majesty's private bounty prevent a compliance with the request contained in your letter of the 2nd inst. Your obedient servant, Doyne C. Bell.

All that had happened nearly eight months ago. And now, said the reporter from the *Times*, in July, 1851, her money all spent and 'starvation staring her in the face, she took a basket to the Park to find her old customers'. Instead of finding her old customers, she had come up against a park-keeper who had led her straight to Marlborough Street and Mr Hardwick.

The Magistrate was reasonably kindly but very firm; and he tried several times to make her promise not to hawk her cakes in the park again. How would she support herself and her child, then? she asked him, and he had no answer. 'She supposed her fate would be the same as had attended the other poor creatures who had been turned out of their bread by the Commissioners,' wrote the *Times* man, 'One who had kept a stand for 20 years at the Victoria Gate had gone out of her mind in consequence of this eviction, a second was in the Kensington Workhouse, a third was in St George's Workhouse, and she met a fourth that morning nearly broken-hearted trying to sell medals in the park.'

Mr Hardwick waited until she had finished and then asked her again to promise not to take her cakes to the Crystal Palace. 'All right,' she said, 'if I can't sell cakes, I shall beg.' But if she went begging, said Mr Hardwick, patiently, she would be brought back again to his court. And in the end she promised not to do that either. She left the court 'woebegone and very shabby in appearance ... with her basket of three-a-penny cakes upon her arm,' and weeping as she went.

II

Two days later, a gentleman who described himself as 'A Stroller in the Park', wrote a letter to the *Times* about it. It was engagingly libellous.

Anne Hicks is part of Hyde Park. Most strollers there know her; most of us have heard her story. She has her faults, is poor and obstinate; but, without question, since the time of George II, her grandfather, father and herself have exercised certain privileges in Hyde Park, originally granted by personal leave of the Crown for personal service rendered. She has no deed of grant, no charter or sign manual, but possession, use and enjoyment since the days of George II. She is not, however, popular with the modern park-keepers and looks on them all as interlopers and herself as part of the park. In a moment Lord This or That, some Commissioner, comes, looks round, is displeased with her cottage built by herself in lieu of that her father and she had occupied; it is ordered to be pulled down and Anne Hicks is turned out to ruin and starvation as a usurper on Crown property.

A Scotch laird, an ancestor of the Earl of Haddington, as we read in the 6th and 7th Victoria, c. 64,[1] received a charter from Charles II as Hereditary Keeper of the Royal Park at Holyrood, with the power to appoint underkeepers and to enjoy all the privileges of his office. This Head keeper and his heirs, as deer and game disappeared from Auld Reekie, appropriated the grazing of the park to themselves, let in sheep etc. on their own behalf and, in short, gradually these Keepers kept the whole park to their own use. A more monstrous and flagrant usurpation on the Crown was never committed, but the representative of these encroachers was a peer and a Minister of State, not a poor old woman letting out tumblers and selling apples and cakes for her living. My Lords Commissioners of Woods etc. take a different view of the case. Instead of turning Lord Haddington's sheep out of the Queen's Park and, as Lord Seymour says, 'letting the law take its course', they refer the whole matter to arbitration, and £40,000(!)[2] is awarded and paid as compensation for abolishing the office of hereditary Keeper of the Park at Holyrood—an office which honestly could never have been worth £50 per annum with all its just and honest perquisites!

These two cases are examples of the working of Commissioners in general and the Woods and Forests in particular—at once oppressive to those without influence, and jobbing and compliant to those *with* influence. And Lord Haddington's is also an example of how very easy it is to carry through a scandalous job with all the forms of arbitration, inquiry and Parliamentary sanction, but with none of the reality of honest regard for the public rights and interests.

'Stroller in the Park' trailed his coat to much less effect than he presumably hoped. The ninth Earl of Haddington refused to follow him into the *Times*, but the letter must have encouraged Anne Hicks, because she jumped in where Haddington had disdained to tread.

On the 21st of July, five days after her appearance at Marlborough Street, she wrote this to the editor:

Honoured Sir,
Having by sad experience found that I have many foes, and though I have ever told the truth as far as I knew facts, I must humbly hope you will not let any mistake in my tale of want and sorrow be the cause of my being suspected of saying that which is not true. I beg to say that I told

---

[1] 'An Act for carrying into effect an Agreement between the Commissioners of Her Majesty's Woods and the Earl of Haddington for the Purchase and Surrender of the Office of Hereditary Keeper of the Royal Park of Holyrood House.'
[2] The Stroller's exclamation mark, not mine.

the Gentlemen at the police office on last Wednesday that Lord Dudley Stuart had kindly endeavoured to get me some money for my bricks and tiles belonging to my cottage and that Lord Seymour could or would not grant Lord Dudley Stuart's request.

I am still indebted to Mr Harrison of Millbank-row £8 10s. for the last work done to my cottage, and had but £3 10s. in the savings bank when I commenced to build my cottage.

But Mr Botten, 10 Exeter-Street, Sloane-Street, can tell what I suffered to get my cottage built. I lived then in his house and have been a lodger in his house five different times. I was residing at No. 7 Gray-St., Manchester-square, when Lord Dudley Stuart took up my cause and I have been a lodger in that house six different times within 20 years. I likewise said that I heard such sad facts about the poor people that were turned out of the park on the 11th of last November, but that I knew that the poor old man who had sold cakes etc. near the Duke of Wellington's statue was in Kensington Workhouse. I heard last night that the poor people who sold at the tent at Grosvenor-gate had had their furniture taken for rent, as well as myself.

I have not one bit of bread to give my child this day, or a penny to get it. Yet if I sell in Hyde-park I am to be sent to a prison. I have enclosed a copy of my petition sent by me to the Duke of Wellington on the 25th December. I have since been driven to send one to those kind friends who know the cause of my want and my sorrow, of which I send a copy enclosed.

I could not have been understood by the gentleman at the police office as I could not keep from crying all the time I spoke; and no wonder, for I had a sick, hungry little girl to go home to, and I have never earned but one shilling out of Hyde-park for more than 20 years; that I earned at my needle at the Crystal Palace on the 25th of April, and when I got home my all was taken for five weeks' rent, after my poor son having starved himself almost to death to pay eight shillings all the winter thinking I could get a living there in the summer following.

I can be seen at 10 Exeter-street, Sloane-st., Chelsea, any day if any persons wish to see me, and I shall be ever grateful to you, Sir, for your kindness to me in letting my case be known.

I remain, as in duty,
Anne Hicks.

Mrs Hicks was, of course, doing in style and the *Times* what she had promised Mr Hardwick she would not do in the streets, and her begging letter was immediately successful. The very day it was printed, a gentleman sent his man round to Printing House Square with a cheque for three guineas and a letter, signed 'P', promising to send some more when those three were spent. Within forty-eight hours, £18 7s. 6d. had been subscribed, most of it anonymously, though one man, Mr Alderman Salomons, presented his compliments, contributed two pounds and saw his name printed alongside his regret that Mrs Hicks had been turned out of her house and home. Mr Salomons was just then having great difficulty himself in persuading the Commons to let him take his place in their House and Home.[1]

Then, as the Anne Hicks Fund grew,—and it grew very quickly indeed until, within a fortnight, it had topped £70—a churlish correspondent moved in to attack Mrs Hicks and her benefactors and to defend the Duke of Wellington. He called himself *Incredulus*. 'A good deal of fine writing,' he wrote, 'and a score or two of sovereigns have been expended upon the case of Anne Hicks. The Duke of Wellington (for it is by his authority as Ranger of Hyde Park and not by that of Lord Seymour that this interesting martyr to free trade has been expelled from its precincts) has been held up to the public as a merciless tyrant who, for no imaginable reason, has, with more than celtic ruthlessness evicted the interesting "nymph of the Serpentine".'

The whole tone of the correspondence was changed in a flash of malice. Disiniterested benevolence collapsed before *Incredulus*'s observant arithmetic. Mrs Hicks had made a mistake, he pointed out. In the police court she said she had spent £130 on her house; in her letter to the *Times* £130 had shrunk to £3 10s. 'Now,' said *Incredulus*, '£13 given to her by the Board of Woods and Forests would be very good compensation for £3 10s., though very bad compensation for £130.' What exercised him, he added, was why people like 'P' got themselves taken in in this way.

'P' was saved the embarrassment of explaining the discrepancy between £130 and £3 10s. by his convenient discovery that Mrs Hick's case had found its way on to the Order Paper of the House of Commons, so in proud self-denial he confined himself to answering *Incredulus* in broad principle.[2] 'We Quixotics,' he claimed, 'have many a time snatched deserving persons from despair and have proved (not a useless matter) that there is a ready sympathy between those at their ease and

[1] David Salomons was returned as a Liberal for Greenwich in June, 1851. He was a Jew and unable, therefore, to take the oath 'on the true faith of a Christian'. Without taking the oath, he voted in three divisions in the House and he was fined £500 for doing it. He entered the House in 1859 after the form of oath had been altered, and he stayed there, representing Greenwich, until he died in 1873.
[2] P's refusal to discuss the matter before the House of Commons had debated it is a very early example of a freely accepted 14 days' rule.

those in destitution. This intercourse is not without some *political* benefit, to say nothing of duty, for it helps to fill the chasm so long said to yawn between the rich and the poor.' He then turned from broad principle to narrow pattern, telling the happy story of an old soldier whose 'age, hardship and labour had stooped his shoulders and shortened his stature' so much that he had shrunk to less than the statutory height and did not qualify for an official pension. Private benefactors— the Quixotics—had set him up for life with a proper competence.

The Hicks affair in the *Times* was now little more than an excuse for a sleepy contest in stylish disputation, *Incredulus* and 'P' exchanging tasteful and elegant references to 'our late Egeria' in two duty-watches, day and day about, decorating their crystal prose with Latin maxims of the best period. The sting had gone out of it all.

Anne Hicks and her story were all but forgotten in this devitalized and expiring correspondence. And then, one day, on the 29th of July, Mr Bernal Osborne, an Honourable Member for Middlesex, rescued Anne Hicks from the pages of the *Times* and put her down, so to speak, but only so to speak, on the floor of the House of Commons.

It was then that Her Majesty's Chief Commissioner of Woods and Forests, Lord Seymour, putting his jaunty and unassailable brief upon the despatch-box on the Treasury side, stood up and prepared to enjoy his field-day. He did enjoy it, and the House of Commons had its funniest half-hour for many a year. Anne Hicks was crushed (in her absence) by science and artfulness and a jolly Minister of the Crown who knew when he was on to a very good thing.

Seymour began, quietly, by denying that Mrs Hicks had ever had a house by gift of His Majesty King George the Second, or by gift of any other Royal Personage for that matter. What is more, he argued, Mrs Hicks had herself forgotten this interesting and memorable deed of gift until she had been away from Hyde Park for several months. It came to her, he said, as a very late afterthought. Nobody, incidentally, pointed out to him that he was mis-representing the lady. She had never said the house was hers by Royal Gift, just the trading site on which the house had been built a century or so later. The actual house (and she had made this quite clear) was built on a building licence she got from Lord Lincoln, the Chief Ranger.

This permission to build was, as Seymour admitted, the main issue. It was given piecemeal and by gradual extension over a number of years; and every time an inch of concession was made, Mrs Hicks had taken several yards. His Lordship explained how she did it.

In 1843, Anne Hicks, like a number of other persons, had a little stall where she sold apples and gingerbeer in the park. Before that she had occupied one of the old conduits there. She wrote to the commissioners of Woods and Forests asking permission to build a place she could leave her gingerbeer bottles in, and in the end, after a good deal of correspondence, she was given permission to build a stall of wood. Some time later, she thanked the Commissioners for her very useful stand but could she possibly replace it with one built of bricks? Wooden huts, she protested, are insecure. There was some more correspondence, and in the end she got her bricks.

All this time (it took several months of creeping negotiation) and in all these letters, Mrs Hicks never referred to George II's short moment of gratitude and generosity: she had, on the other hand, made occasional references to her fifteen children.

The next thing she did was to write to the Commissioners and point out that her brick-built stand was a great and constant joy to her but it was a bit small if anything. Could she please make it bigger? She had so many gingerbeer bottles, she added, that she did not know what to do. Again, the Commissioners gave way but would Mrs Hicks kindly take care not to get the stand built more than five feet high?

Both sides then took a breather which lasted a few months before Mrs Hicks moved into action again. She was very much obliged for the splendid little hut she had had built, it was a great accommodation to her and she had no intentions of making it into a residence but she took the liberty of saying that it would be a real act of kindness if the Commissioners let her have a little fireplace put in it. She was one, it seemed, for her cup of tea.

This time, however, the Commissioners stood firm on an immediate no. Even if it meant no cups of tea, still no fireplaces. That hut was built for gingerbeer bottles and for nothing else.

Anne Hicks saw the storm cones and did not press for her fireplace. Very soon afterwards, however, she was writing again. Her shed's roof had started leaking, could she get it put right? Yes, they said, please do, but no alterations.

A week or two later the hut had a new roof, a chimney and a fireplace; and there was Mrs Hicks and her indeterminate number of children, snug and warm and dry, drinking tea in front of a fire. When Lord Seymour came into office as First Commissioner in 1850, the hut had not only a roof and a chimney but also a garden round it. Anne Hicks said she had put the railings round because it was very disagreeable having people peering in at her window when she was having her cup of tea.

After a time, the park-keepers noticed that the garden was a bit bigger every time they went past it. They went and argued with her now and again but, as Seymour put it, 'she made so much noise and abuse about it that none of the park authorities cared to meddle with her.'

It was then that Lord Seymour decided that something would have to be done, officially and legally, about Mrs Hicks. There was no doubt at all that she was trespassing. The Act of Parliament which controlled the Royal Parks (this was where he brought up his first big gun, 10 Geo. IV, cap. 50) was specific and unambiguous about this. No one, Seymour and the statute said, had the right to build dwelling houses on the Royal land—not even, he added, with the permission of a Royal personage unless Parliament went to the trouble first of amending 10 Geo. IV, cap. 50. Prince Albert, it is true, he went on, has special persmission to have a model cottage built for a model artisan as a sort of appendix to the Great Exhibition, but that would not be going up without the signed affidavit that it would be shifted (with or without the model artisan) as soon as the Exhibition was over.[1]

Then Seymour brought up his other big gun, the Duke himself who, as Chief Ranger, had been consulted before Anne was evicted. Wellington 'with that consideration which he gave to the minutest details' came up to town, took a look at Anne Hicks and her illicit establishment and said yes, put her out.

That is what they did, giving her five shillings a week for a year, so that she could find something less illegal to live in. That, Seymour went on, was not all. The Commissioners discovered that when they evicted Mrs Hicks she had not paid for her chimney and they had to give her £6 extra to pay the debt. Here was the final perfidy. 'Instead of paying the debt with the money I gave her, she spent it in getting some placards printed and placing them about the Park, charging the Commissioners of Woods and Forests with hardship and oppression towards her.' Unfair to Anne Hicks.

The bubble, a big bubble, of public sympathy for Anne Hicks was burst by His Lordship the First Commissioner's funny story in the House of Commons. At the end of it there was only one friend left to

[1] It was removed soon afterwards to Kennington Park. It is still there. It looks different now because the wide alcove in the front of the house, His Royal Highness's special architectural conceit, has been faced over to make more rooms.

her in the House, Colonel Sibthorp, and there is plenty to suggest that
he loved her so much only because he hated the Crystal Palace so much
more still. One of the very first contributions to Anne's fund was
announced in the *Times* as: 'M.P., a consistent opponent of the Crystal
Palace, £5.' That must have been Sibby.

To give him the fullest credit, he did raise her case again in the House,
but everything was against him. Even his oratory—a strange, energetic
apostrophe as it always was, 'Oh, the liberality of the Liberals!' he
mourned—could not prevent the matter from falling off the Table of
the House (or being pushed off it) into the long deep silence of a
Parliamentary recess which started the next day and lasted almost six
months. The whole bunch of relevant papers which Lord Seymour
agreed to lay on the Table, so that they could be printed and published
to the world outside Westminster, somehow failed to find their way to
the printing office. Anne Hicks had become nothing more important
than a big joke specially kept for the day when the House would be
breaking up for the summer holidays.

Anne Hicks, had, however, one good, true and uninhibited friend
outside the House. He was a Mr Henry Dywell Griffiths, the self-elected
secretary of the North and West London Anti-Enclosure and Social and
Sanitary Improvement Association. He wrote to the Duke of Wellington telling him in almost as many words that he ought to be ashamed
of himself. The Duke was stung into one of his ponderous and famous
letters: 'Field-Marshal the Duke of Wellington presents his compliments to Mr Griffiths; he has received his letter and the enclosed printed
paper. The Duke declines to have any epistolary correspondence with
the secretary of any private society as to the subject of his performance
of his duties to the public.'

Mr Griffiths wrote back asking the Duke how he came by Apsley
House.

That drew blood, a good deal of it, hot and steaming. 'Field-Marshal
the Duke of Wellington present his compliments to Mr Griffiths; he has
received his letter of the 20th instant. Although the Duke again declines
to enter ino any discussion with the secretary of a self-appointed and
self-authorized association upon the details of his duty as Ranger of the
Park ... the Duke does not exactly understand what connexion is
supposed to exist between his House in Piccadilly and Mrs Hick's
cottage. The Duke purchased his property in Piccadilly from the
Crown; Mrs Hicks is neither more nor less of a squatter on the banks
of the Serpentine River. The Duke has frequently considered it his duty

to inquire, and he could never find that Mrs Hicks had any authority whatever to establish herself there.'

The Duke's touchiness vastly amused *Mr Punch*, who from the beginning had been on Anne Hicks's side (he printed two long and sentimental and very turgid ballads on her story[1]) but he reserved his sourest comment for the Lord S-ym--r.

Lord S-m--r,
Mrs Hicks sees by the papers that Lord S-ym--r has put his keepers in the Park in livery: green frocks—gilt buttons—and red stripes. Mrs Hicks has no doubt that they look very fine; but for her own part, she wonders how Lord S-ym--r can look upon those buttons without thinking of the widow's tears (who was *no* squatter) and to conclude, how he can behold those scarlet stripes without taking to his bed, and dreaming of an unprotected bleeding heart.

[1] There is also some evidence that he helped her to emigrate to Australia.

CHARLES KINGSTON

The Converted Murderer

The Gallery of Hypocrites is so overcrowded that the figure of James Cook, the Leicester murderer, is almost unnoticed. At first sight he seems out of place in it, and yet I am not sure that the oily little tradesman, with clasped hands and with the whites of his eyes showing towards the stars, is not greater than the kings and emperors, statesmen and prelates, *littérateurs* and philanthropists who out-glisten him. And if the test be supremacy in the not too easy art of hypocrisy in the condemned cell he is king of them all, a repelling, nauseating king, but all the same a veritable monarch.

No historian has ventured yet to enclose in a boundary of dates that elusive and illusive period to which dealers in clichés are fond of referring to as 'the good old times'. Only recently has it been proclaimed that by permitting the 'writing-up' of 'popular murderers' by the press we are violating the good taste of that visionary epoch when perfection was attained so easily as to leave nothing for criticism. But whatever that period was it was not the early part of the nineteenth century when James Cook, of Leicester, committed a diabolical crime which might have been completely forgotten by now had it not been for the orgy of canting and ranting hypocrisy with which his alleged conversion was surrounded. Murderers of to-day may weary us because of the garrulity of their daily biographers, but it is no longer possible to bestow on an occupant of the condemned cell the halo of a saint and the crown of a martyr. Public opinion would not tolerate it for a moment even if we had a repetition of the phenomenon of a girl of good family brushing aside the prison chaplain and in an ecstasy of fanaticism hero-worshipping a loathsome murderer. Charles Dickens created two supreme hypocrites, Silas Pecksniff and Uriah Heep, and when he wanted material for the latter he embodied something of James Cook in his character.

However, before I develop this feature of a once famous case I will

THE CONVERTED MURDERER 163

give a brief account of the crime. In the early part of the summer of 1832 Cook was a bookbinder with a workshop in Wellington Street, Leicester, a small, detached building which was overlooked on every side. He was twenty-two, and he had the reputation of being rather a good young man; in fact, he had been such an industrious apprentice that his master had left him his business. That he was quiet and inoffensive we can believe, and had he been as dependable as a master as he had been when an employé he might have attained a certain degree of prosperity. But Cook had grown tired of discipline before he became a man in the eyes of the law, and therefore he did not discipline himself, working only when the mood seized him, which was infrequently and usually at night. Business grew scarce and debts inevitably accumulated, and the end—bankruptcy—was in sight the morning he received a letter from Mr John Paas, of High Holborn, London, informing him that the writer would call in person in the course of the week for settlement of his account. Mr Paas was a brass ornament manufacturer who had supplied Cook with tools to the value of eight pounds, and the debtor knew that failure to settle would destroy his credit at one stroke. The young book binder, however, quickly reconciled himself to the thought of losing his business. It did not require much intelligence to arrive at a conclusion that he had no chance of rehabilitating himself. Quite apart from a disinclination for work of any kind he had lost the greater part of his connection, and whatever else happened it was certain that he would have to begin all over again and at a place remote from his native town.

He began to contemplate the possibility of emigrating to America where fortunes were to be made so easily, for your failure is fully persuaded that he has not failed because of his lack of merit but solely because of misfortune. But Cook was practically penniless and in debt, and emigration required capital. Once, however, the heavy, slow brain of the stoutish young man of medium height began to deal with the financial problem it gave birth to evil schemes, and when the letter from Mr Paas arrived immediately found fresh inspiration in it. Cook rapidly conjured up a picture of Mr Paas and his doings in Leicester. The London tradesman would have at least a dozen accounts to collect, and if it so happened that he was induced to call last at the workshop in Wellington Street, he would have a goodly sum in his pockets—perhaps a hundred pounds in coin and notes—for everybody in Leicester with whom the London manufacturer did business paid him in cash. What easier task than to kill Mr Paas, destroy his body in a furnace, and before the mystery of his disappearance was solved—if ever it was solved—emigrate to America, make a fortune, and at the same time rebuild his reputation for respectability.

No sooner was the desperate and dangerous plot conceived than its author accepted it as certain of success. He was not gifted with any great intelligence—the weakness of his expression was a severe handicap to features otherwise pleasing—and he conceded society less. He knew it would be necessary to prepare for his crime by hoodwinking his neighbours in Wellington Street, but all he did was, on the evening before he was due to receive Mr Paas, to light an unusually large fire in his workshop and leave it blazing away after he had locked up the premises. To his joy the bait took, the occupant of the house close by remonstrating with him for risking a conflagration which might have destroyed the street.

'The furnace is perfectly safe,' Cook answered glibly. 'I banked it up myself. I am very busy just now and I may have to work late to-morrow night.'

Having thus prepared the way he was quietly confident when on the evening of May 30th, 1832, the boy he employed ushered Mr Paas into the workshop. His visitor was a tall, well-built man of fifty, red-faced and amiable-looking, and he towered over the young bookbinder, who welcomed him with the intimation that he had the money ready to settle his debt. The boy was present during this preliminary conversation, but he heard no more, for Cook sent him away on an unnecessary and futile errand and told him to report the next day.

Within five minutes of the boy's departure Mr Paas was a corpse, Cook creeping behind him and striking him on the back of the head as the older man was bending over the table affixing his initials to a receipt. The furnace was waiting, and the murderer, having removed all the money from the unfortunate man's pockets—it amounted to nearly sixty pounds—and taken his gold watch, rings and other articles of jewellery, proceeded to do his clumsy best to destroy every vestige of his crime. Of course he was not successful, and where an anatomical expert like Dr Webster failed it was hardly necessary to record that in his efforts to destroy evidence Cook merely created proofs of his guilt. But he worked as he had never worked before, and only when he was completely exhausted did he take a rest. Then, fearful that his continued absence might bring one of his relations to the workshop—his father actually did call and knock, but receiving no answer went away—he went home at nine o'clock, but at one o'clock in the morning after four restless hours he declared that he must return to the workshop because he had an important commission to finish. That was Thursday, and he kept the furnace in full blast all day. Pedestrians saw the reflection of the flames through the covered window, and those who knew Cook marvelled that he should be so industrious. His more nervous neighbours talked of remonstrating with him again, but they did not interfere until late that evening. Meanwhile, Cook, in need of food and rest, went across to the 'Flying Horse', and having obtained both, flourished a handful of gold and silver in front of the landlord as he paid him. Then he sought recreation and diversion in a game of skittles. At eleven o'clock he was in bed at home when he was startled by a sudden ingress of excited men who told him that the landlord of the 'Flying Horse' had broken open the door of the workshop, having been alarmed by the fire, and that he was wanted there because something suspicious had been found.

The murderer was fuddled by drink, but he regained his wits during the short walk, and although it must have been a terrible moment for him he displayed no terror when conducted into the room where he had murdered Mr Paas and was confronted by a police constable.

The Leicester Dogberry of those days was known by the name of Measures, and from all accounts he must have been a very juicy specimen of the stage policeman. It was the settled opinion of Mr Measures that crime could not be detected without the aid of beer, and he was further convinced that the peace of Leicester would be destroyed if he failed to inspect his favourite public houses at least three times a day. He was in the half-way stage of one very lengthy inspection when he was dragged to the workshop in Wellington Street, and now he had just sufficient sobriety to be able to stand on his own legs as he was being shown the smouldering flesh before he was presented to the suspect. Mr Dogberry Measures shook his head gravely and murmured that there was reason for suspicion, and when Cook protested that the cause of all the pother and bother was merely horseflesh the semi-inebriated sleuth shook his head again and decided that the only thing to do was to postpone the investigation until he was sober and the flesh could be examined by a doctor.

'I must have security for your presence at the investigation to-morrow,' he said thickly. Cook promptly produced his father, who said he would go bail for him. That satisfied Dogberry, and Cook, having entered his father's cottage by the front door, gathered together a few necessary articles and went out by the back, unwilling to distress Measures by the pathos of a long farewell.

By the time a surgeon had seen the remains in the workshop and identified them as human, Cook was in a coach on the way to Liverpool, and with railways very much in their infancy the start he had was a great advantage which with a little luck he might have turned into complete victory over his pursuers. But when he arrived in Liverpool and went to the docks there was no boat leaving immediately for America and he was compelled to hide for a couple of days. By then the police were at his heels, and although, with the aid of the money he had obtained by his crime, he induced a boatman to take him out to one of the western-bound ships, he was intercepted by a boat containing his pursuers and forced to return to land. There he was made a prisoner as he was in the act of pressing a bottle containing laudanum to his lips.

There was never, of course, any doubt as to his guilt, although he had destroyed the greater part of his victim's body; indeed, there were so many proofs of his guilt that no one cared very much whether he confessed or not. But all Leicester was in a ferment at his capture, and the inquest was deemed important enough to be attended by the mayor and corporation, while the Home Secretary was kept informed daily of the progress of the investigation. Murderers are never original, and Cook, of course, denied that he had murdered Mr Paas in cold blood. Allowing his imagination to proceed on the usual conventional lines he told of a quarrel which had been terminated by a struggle and in which Mr Paas had received—accidentally, of course—mortal injuries. That had compelled the unfortunate young man to commit the body to the flames because he feared that no one would believe his version of the tragedy. Many murderers have since 1832 unconsciously repeated this absurd story, adapting it to their own ends and never succeeding in finding a believer except an occasional crank out for notoriety.

For the time being, however, James Cook, the Leicester bookbinder, was the chief topic of conversation throughout England, dimming for a time the interest taken in the great Reform Bill. From the moment he was lodged in Leicester Jail he became a sort of national figure, and with that tolerance which is unknown in our more enlightened age he was permitted to receive visitors—chiefly sightseers—every day and enjoyed a freedom which was scarcely hampered by the chains he was compelled to wear. Strangers who had come considerable distances to gaze upon him were amazed at the mildness of his expression and the humility of his manner, for, like Uriah Heep, Cook was always ' 'umble', and if he was now and then driven into fits of ill-temper he soon recovered his suavity, having duly discovered that humility was the nearest way to the good graces of his indulgent jailers. But he was going to be luckier than he ever anticipated, for amongst those who read of his crime and arrest was a Miss Payne, of Sulby Manor, Northampton, a member of a well-known family. Highly-strung and under the influence of a religious emotionalism which was too much for her weak frame, she suddenly came to the conclusion that it was her mission in life to save the soul of James Cook, and once she got the idea firmly planted in her mind she spared neither herself nor her purse until she began her divinely appointed—as she believed—work of salvation.

Who was Mrs Lachlan? A hundred year ago the *Morning Post* said of her that her numerous writings 'eminently entitled her to the sincere gratitude of parents and guardians', and she may claim the minor distinction of being the first author to dedicate a book to the princess who afterwards became Queen of England. The latter was only thirteen when Mrs Lachlan gave forth to the world a novel bearing the name of *The Twins of Chamouni*, 'dedicated by special permission of the Duchess of Kent to H.R.H. the Princess Victoria.' She wrote several other volumes, but the most curious of all is that which relates in pious detail the story of the conversion of James Cook. It is an extraordinary compilation, and although the good lady says very little about herself one can deduce from it sufficient to provide material for a pen picture of her. To begin with, she lived in Euston Square, which was, in the year of grace 1832, dull, acrid, dreary, but eminently respectable. I picture her as a stout, full-faced dame in the fifties, addicted to bombasine and bonnets challengingly unfashionable. She probably employed three servants, who were overworked on weekdays and overpreached at on Sundays, on which day they would not be allowed to do any work not considered necessary by their employer. No doubt, a nice hot dinner for Mrs Lachlan was a necessity, and was therefore not vetoed, but nothing so sinful as hot vegetables was allowed in the kitchen. No. 22 Euston Square may have been involved in a fog of religious depression every Sunday, but its mistress would have enjoyed it in her own calm way. Intensely loyal, she is sure to have had pictures of the royal family on the walls; and, as she was deeply religious, they would contest for her artistic appreciation with quarter-acre engravings depicting scenes from the Old Testament; while, solidly respectable as she was, her furniture would be weighty, gigantic and with horsehair in profusion. Mrs Lachlan prided herself on being a champion of poor girls—a female prototype of the gentleman in *The Chimes* who was the champion of poverty irrespective of sex. But she had a lively appreciation of class distinctions, and the only time she was moved to wrath during her championship of Miss Payne was owing to a newspaper referring to Mrs Paas—'the widow of a tradesman'—as a 'lady', and to Miss Payne as 'a Leicester woman'. But Mrs Lachlan's greatest passion was for the Church of England. It would be a mistake to describe her as a fanatic, for she lacked the youthfulness of spirit and the elasticity of mind necessary to militancy. Besides, she was too respectable, and although her book shows that she was well in advance of her time and a champion of the rights of her sex she was for the most part stately, staid and superior. The horsehair sofa, the quarter-acre engravings and all the rest of the paraphernalia of a sheltered life passed in dullness and extreme respectability made Mrs Lachlan what she was—a woman of very high principles, good-natured in a frozen way, a hater of lies who was outraged by shams, and deeply religious without any taint of hypocrisy. Completely devoid of a sense of humour, she judged the world by her rigid moral standard, and with the Bible in her hand looked forward with confidence to the next world, believing that all those who agreed with her would go to heaven and those who did not would find themselves in hell. That was Mrs Lachlan, the friend of Miss Payne, of Sulby Manor, Northampton, and the author of one of the queerest books in the English language, a volume which would revolt one's sense of decency were it not obvious that every line was written with perfect sincerity and inspired by the best of motives.

The book is entitled:

Narrative

of the

Conversion

(By the instrumentality of Two Ladies)

of

James Cook

The Murderer of Mr Paas:

in

Letters Addressed to a Clergyman of the

Established Church,

and is dedicated to James Thomas Holloway, described as 'the conscientious preceptor of a select number of young gentlemen.' Dr

Holloway was also Mrs Lachlan's parochial clergyman, and she informed the world that she dedicated her book to him because he was her ideal of a Christian clergyman—the qualification is her own, and is characteristic.

In reality, however, the book is Miss Payne's, for that portion occupied by Mrs Lachlan in expounding her evangelical theories is not of absorbing interest. But the adventures of Miss Payne and her companion while converting Cook is a revelation of fanaticism on one side and hypocrisy on the other without a parallel in history or literature.

According to her own statement Miss Payne was not in the habit of reading newspapers and it was quite by chance that she alighted upon an account of the murder at Leicester. At this time she was recovering from an illness and her mind was just in that condition to be influenced by the supernatural. Possessing none of Mrs Lachlan's masculinity, her natural piety worked itself up into a religious exaltation which she could not control, and when she decided that heaven had selected her to achieve the salvation of James Cook she threw herself into the task with a fierce energy, which plainly foreshadowed a complete breakdown when the inevitable reaction ensued.

Her first act was to send a long letter to the prisoner exhorting him to repentance and assuring him that if he did so he would go straight from the scaffold to heaven. Cook, who was by no means lacking in shrewdness, seized the opportunity presented and responded with a request that Miss Payne and her friend should visit him. The powerful and wealthy family of Payne of Sulby Manor could not have been unknown to him, and he had every reason for enlisting the sympathy and help of an influential person. Had Miss Payne been troubled by doubts as to the propriety of her mission they would have been removed by the receipt of Cook's invitation. It threw her into a state of ecstasy, for she saw in it a divine confirmation of her mission, and a few days later she and her companion arrived in Leicester, armed with Bibles, a basket of fruit, a dozen cambric handkerchiefs and other articles which she hoped would lessen the severity of his unfortunate situation. Cook, who had had plenty of time for rehearsing his part, received her with a humility which he tempered with a pretence of indifference to religion. The young scoundrel did not intend to make his conversion too cheap, and when on closer acquaintance he realized that his conversion had become the strange young lady's passion he played up to her with a cleverness which would have done credit to a professional actor, and at the right moment dropped his 'hardness of heart' pose and declared himself converted. He had nothing to lose by doing so and he stood to gain a great deal, and when he was asked to prove his conversion by confessing his crime he did so with an alacrity which would have opened the eyes of anyone except a girl who wished to be deceived. The murderer knew very well that the prosecution regarded a confession as quite unnecessary. There was sufficient evidence to convict him a dozen times over, but the confession he wrote at the instigation of his fair chaplain sent her into a paroxysm of joy, and she hastened to inform Mrs Lachlan of her triumph. The brutal murderer of Mr Paas became in a twinkling a Christian hero, and the callous, ignorant youth was henceforth an object of almost indolatrous adoration. Nothing could be more eloquent of her state of mind than her own account of his conversion.

'When I entered the prison,' she wrote to Mrs Lachlan, 'I fell on a text which gave me a powerful assurance that Cook would be saved; and though I saw in him much to discourage us, yet I never doubted. The assurance followed me that he would be saved, and I knew there was nothing too hard for the Lord. O what an instance of the stony heart becoming a heart of flesh! He is ripening so fast for heaven, that such a sight I never could have imagined I should behold on earth. Could you but see him! He takes the Bible and astonishes us with his beautiful child-like remarks. He does indeed answer the description of receiving the kingdom of God as a little child. In fact, words can never give you an idea of the amazing wonderful change in this being. Christ shines in every look and every word. He seems to feel that God sent us to him, and says he longed to make a full confession to us the first day we saw him, but that the devil prevented him, and that what we had said had such an effect on him, that he never rested till he had confessed. His ripening for Heaven is the most rapid and wonderful thing I ever beheld. He is the brightest child of God I ever saw. He looks on death with a smile. His exceeding holiness in word, look, and manner, exceeds anything I ever beheld in man. It excites me too much to tell you a hundredth part of what we hear and see. We are the instruments intended to strengthen him for death. What an undertaking! But so it is; and I think he will glorify God to such a degree, that such a death has hardly, if ever, been on record. He has particularly desired to have all the particulars printed, and we intend to have this done. Pray that I may be supported under the trial, for my health is still delicate. I think Christ's coming is close at hand; pray that we may be found among the wise virgins watching for our Lord, loving His appearance. Blissful exchange of earth for Heaven! The nearness of the comet, too, which is expected next October, calls for our serious attention. This world is to be burnt up, and I think it will be at that time. What bliss, to be changed in the twinkling of an eye, and be for ever with the Lord!'

'The brightest child of God' turned to instant advantage the fanaticism and credulity of his patroness, and when the prison chaplain, Dr Fancourt, tried to discourage her visits, Cook prayed for his conversion also, thereby earning from Miss Payne further paeans of praise for what she termed his 'Christian charity and forgiveness'. On another occasion when a tactless sightseer referred, within hearing, to Cook as a murderer and the prisoner immediately lifted up his voice and prayed for the tactless one's conversion, Miss Payne could not express in words her wonderment and delight.

'I will forgive my enemies ten times seventy times seven,' he said, rubbing his hands together and elevating his eyebrows. 'I am not sorry for myself—only for the millions who are not converted, for I am going to heaven and they are going to hell.'

In a very short time, thanks to Miss Payne's influence and her daily consignment of luxuries to the prisoner, Cook became the king of the castle, and the jailers his subjects. Every luxury that money could procure found its way into his cell, and the jailer whose turn it was to watch him was very grateful when permitted to make a meal off the remnants of roast chicken and other dainties provided for the murderer by his patroness. But Cook never committed the blunder of abandoning his pose of humilty, and he applied himself to the richly-bound Bible— a special gift from Miss Payne—with such diligence that he was soon an expert in the art of quotations from the Scriptures, able at a moment's notice to find a text for any and every occasion.

In any other environment he would have been a perfect prototype of Chadband, but as he was within shadow of death all the time he was something more remarkable.

'What sort of a life do you think you would now lead if that were to be spared?' Miss Payne asked him.

'A life of holiness,' he answered. 'Yes, it would be a useful life. I should be an ornament to society.'

That was a feeler, of course, for behind the hypocrite's mask there was always the hope that the influence of his dupe might obtain a reprieve for him.

Later as she rose to go he implored her to sing another hymn with him, and when it was ended murmured that he intended to spend the next two hours on his knees praying for Mrs Paas and her family. We may be sure that that brought more presents the next day and more adulation for the loathsome hypocrite.

The next morning, when asked how he had passed the previous evening he replied, 'Oh, I had such a beautiful night; we read and prayed and sang prayers to God, and then we departed in peace, and met again with love this morning.'

His word was now law in the prison, and with an imperiousness which was concealed artfully by an affectation of humility he occasionally demanded the presence of the jailer and his family so that they might sing hymns together! These performances were always timed to coincide with the arrival of Miss Payne and her companion, and when, as sometimes happened, the hymns were succeeded by prayers for Mrs Paas, the snivelling hypocrite was surrounded by admirers who whispered to one another hoarsely their amazement at his goodness and charity.

When the keeper of the jail transferred him to another apartment because the ordinary cell seemed scarcely worthy of his distinguished daily visitor, Cook implored Miss Payne to use her influence to have the arrangement cancelled.

'But it's much nicer than the cell,' she expostulated, thinking that her convert was unnecessarily anxious to embrace discomfort. Of course the roast chicken, the jellies, the wine and the weekly gifts of fine linen she did not consider as luxuries.

'That cell is the dearest spot on earth to me,' he murmured, with a saccharine hypocrisy which was revolting, 'because it was the scene of my conversion by you.' Bursting into tears he added, 'I shall break my heart if I stay here.'

All his conversations with Miss Payne were religious, and all the time he was 'showing off', to use a schoolboy expression. For he knew that the only way to keep the infatuated woman up to the mark and guarantee the continuance of her gifts was to quote Scripture lavishly and base every topic on his conversion.

'With this blessed book in my hand,' he exclaimed one day, holding the Testament towards her, 'I can declare that if my chains were taken off and all the prison doors were opened I would not attempt to escape. I bless God for bringing me into this prison. I am sorry for everybody outside. There are thousands who would be all the better if they were here.'

One can hear the voice of Uriah Heep in this, and I will quote from *David Copperfield* to show that Charles Dickens must have had James

Cook in mind when he depicted Uriah Heep in prison. The scene is from the sixty-first chapter.

'Now, Twenty-Seven,' said Mr Creakle, entering on a clear stage with his man, 'is there anything that any one can do for you? If so, mention it.'

'I would 'umbly ask, sir,' returned Uriah, with a jerk of his malevolent head, 'for leave to write again to mother.'

'It shall certainly be granted,' said Mr Creakle.

'Thank you, sir! I am anxious about mother. I am afraid she ain't safe.'

Somebody incautiously asked, what from? But there was a scandalized whisper of 'Hush!'

'Immortally safe, sir,' returned Uriah, writhing in the direction of the voice, 'I should wish mother to be got into my state. I never should have been got into my present state if I hadn't come here. I wish mother had come here. It would be better for everybody, if they got took up, and was brought here.'

This sentiment gave unbounded satisfaction—greater satisfaction, I think, than anything that had passed yet.

'Before I come here,' said Uriah, stealing a look at us, as if he would have blighted the outer world to which we belonged, if he could, 'I was given to follies; but now I am sensible of my follies. There's a deal of sin outside. There's a deal of sin in mother. There's nothing but sin every-where—except here.'

'You are quite changed?' said Mr Creakle.

'Oh, dear, yes, sir!' cried this hopeful penitent.

'You wouldn't relapse, if you were going out?' asked somebody else.

'Oh de—ar no, sir!'

'Well!' said Mr Creakle, 'this is very gratifying. You have addressed Mr Copperfield, Twenty-Seven. Do you wish to say anything further to him?'

'You knew me a long time before I came here and was changed, Mr Copperfield,' said Uriah, looking at me; and a more villainous look I never saw, even on his visage. 'You knew me when, in spite of my follies, I was 'umble among them that was proud, and meek among them that was violent—you was violent to me yourself, Mr Copperfield. Once, you struck me a blow in the face, you know.'

General commiseration. Several indignant glances directed at me.

'But I forgive you, Mr Copperfield,' said Uriah, making his forgiving nature the subject of a most impious and awful parallel, which I shall not record. 'I forgive everybody. It would ill become me to bear malice. I freely forgive you, and I hope you'll curb your passions in future. I hope Mr W. will repent, and Miss W., and all of that sinful lot. You've been visited with affliction, and I hope it may do you good; but you'd better have come here. Mr W. had better have come here, and Miss W. too. The best wish I could give you, Mr Copperfield, and give all of you gentlemen, is, that you could be took up and brought here. When I think of my past follies, and my present state, I am sure it would be best for you. I pity all who ain't brought here!'

He sneaked back into his cell, amidst a little chorus of approbation; and both Traddles and I experienced a great relief when he was locked in.

But after all Heep was merely a shadow of a greater hypocrite. 'Thank God I was detected,' cried Cook to a little audience of admiring men and women; 'I shall be in heaven this day week.'

The 'bright ornament of society' had by now been informed that the country had been so roused against him that after his condemnation the question of a reprieve would not even be discussed, and so he made the most of his last few weeks on earth, the fear of death overcome by an anxiety lest there should be a sudden stoppage of the luxuries supplied by Miss Payne.

'Don't grieve for me,' he said to her, and she certainly seems to have grieved for his fate unnecessarily. 'I am simply going to heaven first, and who knows when you die I may be your guardian angel.'

Shortly before his trial the jailers came to take a respectful farewell, and the head jailer and his wife he made supremely happy by informing them that he regarded them as his parents.

'I hope I shall meet you in heaven,' he said, for although certain about his own migration there he could not be so positive about such earthy beings as prison warders. 'I shall shine as a star in the firmament of heaven, and I hope that you may all inherit a crown of glory.'

We may be sure that the jailers shared in the good things provided by Miss Payne, and we can only marvel that in an age when penal methods were for the most part savage and merciless that one of the most callous and cowardly murderers should have been permitted so much liberty and licence in the weeks preceding his trial and execution. It is all the more remarkable in Cook's case because, save for the little group of admirers in the precincts of the jail, there was not a man or woman in the country who was not eager to see him punished. Now and then there was a reference in the papers to the activities of Miss Payne and she was the object of considerable sarcasm and criticism, but it was all wasted on her. The girl who had persuaded herself that the coming comet was heaven's preliminary to the destruction of the world and the end of all things could not be turned aside from her purpose by the ravings of persons she looked upon as lost souls. To her Cook was no longer a murderer—he was a saint. He no longer bore the image of a mere man—he was the counterpart of Christ. He was, in fact, in his new guise an innocent man, and was not to be held responsible for the misdeeds of his previous existence. And if ever her faith in him showed signs of weakening Cook played his part manfully and off went another letter to Mrs Lachlan extolling his perfection.

'You will be present at my trial, won't you?' he implored, as he stood in a humble attitude before her. 'You are my only comfort and I can't do without you.'

A less expert hypocrite might have diluted his religion with a little worldly lovemaking, but Cook was crafty enough to remember always the great difference in their respective social positions, and he was therefore ever very ''umble'. He must have known that this daughter of a well-known family was completely under his influence and would have faced execration and death for his sake, but he agreed with Uriah Heep that 'ambition was sinful' and not suitable to an ''umble person like myself, Mr Copperfield', and behaved accordingly.

The day before his appearance in court he presided in his cell at three religious services, and Miss Payne's parting gift was a book of devotions and a cambric handkerchief which he was to flourish as soon as he recognized her in court.

When she parted from him for the last time Miss Payne found consolation in writing out in full all his favourite hymns. There she despatched to Mrs Lachlan, before preparing herself for an ordeal which she would have been wise to spare herself. But fortified by her admiration for her convert she was present when Mr Justice Park took his seat in court and Cook having been formally called upon to plead answered in a firm voice that he was guilty. Just previous to this he had taken out his handkerchief and shaken it and thereby made glad the heart of the young lady who stared at him with shining eyes and then kissed her hand to him.

Mr Justice Park was fond of describing himself as a 'Christian judge', but his Christianity was of a more robust and practical kind than Miss Payne's, and before he sentenced Cook to death he delivered an address to the convict which was a mixture of sermon and reproof. In language which must have hurt the susceptibilities of the Christian hero and his admirer he described the brutality of the crime, and ignoring the rumours which must have reached him of the extraordinary religious orgies in Cook's cell, implored him to turn from his wickedness and seek forgiveness from Above. This might have been resented by the alleged convert had it not been that throughout the whole of the address he studied the little book of devotions which was Miss Payne's last gift, but the book was not the only thing that was studied that morning, and those who caught a glimpse of the pallid face of the prisoner as he descended from the dock detected genuine terror in it.

On reaching the condemned cell he collapsed, and, aware that Miss Payne would not be permitted to see him again, gave vent to his real feelings. But he had practised hypocrisy too long to be able to discard it at once, and when one of his former jailers visited him he was almost himself again.

'How do you feel now?' he was asked by his visitor.

'Happier than ever,' he answered, in the old humble attitude. 'Why should I not be happy when I am about to exchange these chains for a crown of glory? There is only one thing that distresses me,' he added, after a pause.

'And what is that?'

'I hope that poor Mr Paas has forgiven me,' he murmured , 'otherwise it will be so awkward for both of us when we meet in heaven.'

The remark proved that he was once more in his old form, and right up to the moment he stood before the crowd, outwardly as fearless as the most heroic of Christian martyrs, he mouthed Scriptural texts which, coming from such a brute, must have sounded the worst of blasphemies in the ears of any decent person. A short time before Cook's execution the government had decided in their wisdom that it was necessary to revive the barbarous custom of hanging in chains. The abolition of this revolting post-mortem punishment had been followed by an increased number of murders, and the Home Office experts of the day decided that Bill Sikes and Co. had lapsed into murderers because their remains could not be exhibited in public after execution. It was a fantastic and ridiculous excuse for a return to methods of barbarism, and even the universal detestation of Cook could not justify the horrible spectacle. There was some sympathy for the convict who seemed to dread hanging in chains even more than death, but by the time he arrived on the scaffold he had regained all his courage, and, fortified by a determination to 'die game'—that is, so far as he could do so consistently with his affectation of ''umbleness'—assumed an attitude of patronage towards the sheriff and his retinue, tempered with Heep-like subserviency. It is said that he actually thanked the hangman for being the means by which his mortality was to be changed into immortality and that his last words were an expression of confidence in ultimate glory phrased in such a way as to contain a broad hint to the officials that unless they changed drastically the course of their lives they would never have the pleasure of meeting him in heaven. Then with a glance of pity at the crowd he took his place under the beam and met death without flinching.

His remains were gibbeted in Saffron Lane, and twenty thousand persons, fully representative of the scum of the nation, assembled round the gibbet and held festival until one of the severest rainstorms the country has ever known sent them scuttling back to their slums. Booths were erected and every form of intoxicant and innumerable and incredible edibles dispensed to the multitude which had gathered together to celebrate the death of a murderer.

A goodly proportion of that crowd was quite equal to emulating Cook, but the vicious are never more virtuous than when denouncing crime, and every scoundrel for twenty miles around doubtless felt incumbent upon him to show by attendance at Saffron Lane that he was on the side of law and order. But when towards the night the wind rose and the moving corpse seemed to be shrieking in unison with it there were many cries of terror from the women, and an immediate trek was begun homewards. Everybody fled from the swinging corpse, and through the long hours until dawn, as the elements played their Satanic and ironic game with it, there were no spectators of the contest between infuriated nature and brutalized man.

The disgraceful scenes in Saffron Lane were reported to the government, with the immediate result that an order was issued for the taking down of the body and its interment, and, as a paper remarked at the time, this meant that never again would a criminal be gibbeted in England, for a custom abolished in the case of the greatest of murderers could not be enforced to punish an inferior criminal. The abolition of the gibbet has been ascribed since to humanitarianism, but those who by virtue of their position abolished it did so not because they disbelieved in its efficacy but solely because they feared the scandal which must arise out of a sudden aggregation of thousands of ruffians and their kind within a comparatively small area.

With the execution of Cook his patroness, Miss Payne, returned to that genteel obscurity which distinguished the well-bred young lady of a hundred years ago. Physically she was weaker than ever, but a quiet confidence in the divinity of her mission and its success brought her a sense of peace which enabled her to wait with patience for the coming of the comet which she was sure was to presage the end of the world. Almost daily she wrote lengthy letters to her beloved friend, Mrs Lachlan, who rushed to give them to the world in the book to which I have referred already. Miss Payne found a sombre pleasure in reading the queer letters which were showered on her daily from the time a Leicester paper revealed the reason for her visits to Leicester Jail. The majority were abusive, and in these she took delight, regarding them as the thorns in the crown of glory which had been awarded to her on earth. Newspaper references to herself she treasured, and as these were invariably offensive it required a thickening of her religious skin to read them with equanimity. In those days English journalism had a robustness about it which, even accompanied as it was with coarseness, gave it a flavour not altogether unattractive. If journalists did not exactly call a spade a spade they found a synonym for it as startling as it was eloquent and descriptive, and Mrs Lachlan, anxious to illustrate the attitude of her friend's critics—'children of Satan' she called them—preserved for us an extract from the 'Age', a paper which was known to dabble in blackmail.

'The following remarks,' wrote Mrs Lachlan, 'and a great deal more, appeared in the *Age* of Sunday:

MURDER AND PIETY.—Cook, the murderer of Mr Paas, of Holborn, pleaded guilty, was sentenced to be hanged, and hanged accordingly. A more hard-hearted and depraved ruffian never dropped from a gallows—and the penny-a-line men report him, of course, as dying firm, undaunted, heroic, etc., etc. The greater the scoundrel, the greater the favourite with them. Thurtell was their especial hero. However, they, poor devils, are only labouring in their trade; and we shall not quarrel with them through endeavouring to obtain the price of an extra pint of beer by a few extra lines; but there is something to us infinitely disgusting in the interference of some Leicester woman, particularly a Miss Payne, in the case. What have women to do with a beastly murderer, who was not a degree above the New Zealanders? Some snuffling saint will answer—she was impelled by piety! Stuff. Had not he spiritual advice enough without her volunteer assistance? She might have left the business to the chaplain. This vagabond, on his trial, never took his eyes off a book he was reading but once, and that was to ogle Miss Payne who sat on the bench—and on his leaving the dock he kissed hands to her. We suppose she had a lock of his hair as a memento. It was on the whole a most disgusting exhibition of cant and hypocrisy.'

But when the *Age* imputed hypocrisy and the desire for notoriety to

Miss Payne it was wrong. The self-appointed missionary to James Cook was wholly sincere and animated by the best of motives. She was misguided and illogical, but that she believed herself to be inspired admits of no doubt. Every religion appears absurd to the unbeliever, and if Miss Payne's special cult was a rigid Calvinism she acted with the best intentions. In common with her friend, Mrs Lachlan, she believed in a literal interpretation of every sentence in the Bible, and for one so gentle and refined it is remarkable that she could see no way of escape from the literal fires of hell for all those who did not share her beliefs. She must have derived immense satisfaction and consolation from Mrs Lachlan's story of her Leicester crusade, for that good lady completely demolished all opposition—in her own opinion—and by means of a dialogue with a gentleman of her acquaintance (who took the opposite side) demonstrated to her own satisfaction that no one except an avowed adherent of the devil could discover the least fault in the converter of the murderer of Mr Paas.

I have not delved into Miss Payne's history subsequent to the execution of Cook. Whether or not she was disappointed by the survival of the world after the appearance of the comet I cannot say, but I can imagine her waiting serenely for a catastrophe which she believed would enable her to renew her acquaintance with Cook and see for herself the fulfilment of all her promises of heavenly happiness which she had made to him in the dismal prison cell. It is now nearly a hundred years since Miss Payne penned her prophecy of the end of all things, but the world goes on in much the same old way, and I have no doubt that every generation has produced its Miss Payne, with her fanaticism and bad taste inspired by the best of motives. She is, however, no longer able to practise upon a condemned murderer owing to the rigid seclusion in which the condemned are shrouded in the interval between sentence and execution. Some of them tried to make a hero of Dr Lamson, the loathsome poisoner, and their protests were as indignant as they were tearful when they were informed that the flowers they had sent to decorate his cell with had never been seen by the criminal. That was just half a century after the 'canonization' of Cook, and it proved that in one respect at least we had improved on an age which will soon be distant enough to be referred to as 'the good old times'.

THOMAS DE QUINCEY

The Female Infidel

At the time of my father's death, I was nearly seven years old. In the next four years, during which we continued to live at Greenhay, nothing memorable occurred, except, indeed, that troubled parenthesis in my life which connected me with my brother William—this certainly was memorable to myself—and, secondly, the visit of a most eccentric young woman, who, about nine years later, drew the eyes of all England upon herself, by her unprincipled conduct in an affair affecting the life of two Oxonian undergraduates. She was the daughter of Lord le Despencer (known previously as Sir Francis Dashwood); and at this time (meaning the time of her visit to Greenhay) she was about twenty-two years old; with a face and a figure classically beautiful, and with the reputation of extraordinary accomplishments; these accomplishments being not only eminent in their degree, but rare and interesting in their kind. In particular, she astonished every person by her *impromptu* performances on the organ, and by her powers of disputation. These last she applied entirely to attacks upon Christianity; for she openly professed infidelity in the most audacious form; and at my mother's table she certainly proved more than a match for all the clergymen of the neighbouring towns, some of whom (as the most intellectual persons of that neighbourhood) were daily invited to meet her. It was a mere accident which had introduced her to my mother's house. Happening to hear from my sister Mary's governess that she and her pupil were going on a visit to an old Catholic family in the county of Durham (the family of Mr Swinburne, who was known advantageously to the public by his 'Travels in Spain and Sicily', &c.), Mrs Lee, whose education in a French convent, aided by her father's influence, had introduced her extensively to the knowledge of Catholic families in England, and who had herself an invitation to the same house at the same time, wrote to offer the use of her carriage to convey all three—*i.e.*, herself, my sister, and her governess—to Mr Swin-

burne's. This naturally drew forth from my mother an invitation to
Greenhay; and to Greenhay she came. On the imperial of her carriage,
and elsewhere, she described herself as the *Hon*. Antonina Dashwood
Lee. But, in fact, being only the illegitimate daughter of Lord le
Despencer, she was not entitled to that designation. She had, however,
received a bequest even more enviable from her father—viz., not less
than forty-five thousand pounds. At a very early age, she had married
a young Oxonian, distinguished for nothing but a very splendid person,
which had procured him the distinguishing title of *Handsome Lee*; and
from him she had speedily separated, on the agreement of dividing the
fortune.

My mother little guessed what sort of person it was whom she had
asked into her family. So much, however, she had understood from Miss
Wesley—that Mrs Lee was a bold thinker; and that, for a woman, she
had an astonishing command of theological learning. This it was that
suggested the clerical invitations, as in such a case likely to furnish the
most appropriate society. But this led to a painful result. It might easily
have happened that a very learned clergyman should not specially have
qualified himself for the service of a theological tournament: and my
mother's range of acquaintance was not very extensive amongst the
clerical body. But of these the two leaders, as regarded public consideration, were Mr H——, my guardian, and Mr Clowes, who for more
than fifty years officiated as rector of St John's Church in Manchester.
No men could have been found who were less fitted to act as champions
in a duel on behalf of Christianity. Mr H—— was dreadfully common-
place; dull, dreadfully dull; and, by the necessity of his nature, incapable
of being in deadly interest, which his splendid antagonist at all times
was. His encounter, therefore, with Mrs Lee presented the distressing
spectacle of an old, toothless, mumbling mastiff, fighting for the household to which he owed allegiance, against a young leopardess fresh
from the forests. Every touch from *her*, every velvety paw, drew blood.
And something comic mingled with what my mother felt to be paramount tragedy. Far different was Mr Clowes: holy, visionary, apostolic,
he could not be treated disrespectfully. No man could deny him a
qualified homage. But for any polemic service he wanted the taste,
the training, and the particular sort of erudition required. Neither
would such advantages, if he had happened to possess them, have at
all availed him in a case like this. Horror, blank horror, seized him
upon seeing a woman, a young woman, a woman of captivating
beauty, whom God had adorned so eminently with gifts of person

and of mind, breathing sentiments that to him seemed fresh from the mintage of hell. He could have apostrophized her (as long afterwards he himself told me) in the words of Shakespere's Juliet—

> Beautiful tyrant! fiend angelical!

for he was one of those who never think of Christianity as the subject of defence. Could sunshine, could light, could the glories of the dawn, call for defence? Not as a thing to be defended, but as a thing to be interpreted, as a thing to be illuminated, did Christianity exist for *him*. He, therefore, was even more unserviceable as a champion against the deliberate impeacher of Christian evidences than my reverend guardian.

To him, being such a man by nature and by habit, it was in effect the lofty Lady Geraldine from Coleridge's 'Christabelle' that stood before him in this infidel lady. A magnificent witch she was, like the Lady Geraldine; having the same superb beauty; the same power of throwing spells over the ordinary gazer; and yet at intervals unmasking to some solitary, unfascinated spectator the same dull blink of a shaky eye; and revealing, through the most fugitive of gleams, a traitress couchant beneath what else to all others seemed the form of a lady, armed with incomparable pretensions—one that was

> Beautiful exceedingly,
> Like a lady from a far countrie.

The scene, as I heard it sketched long years afterwards by more than one of those who had witnessed it, was painful in excess. And the shock given to my mother was memorable. For the first and the last time in her long and healthy life, she suffered an alarming nervous attack. Partly this arose from the conflict between herself in the character of hostess, and herself as a loyal daughter of Christian faith; she shuddered, in a degree almost uncontrollable and beyond her power to dissemble, at the unfeminine intrepidity with which 'the leopardess' conducted her assaults upon the sheepfolds of orthodoxy; and, partly also, this internal conflict arose from concern on behalf of her own servants, who waited at dinner, and were inevitably liable to impressions from what they heard. What chiefly she feared, on behalf of her servants, was either, first, the danger from the simple *fact*, now suddenly made known to them, that it was possible for a person unusually gifted to deny Christianity: such a denial and haughty abjuration could not but carry itself more profoundly into the reflective mind, even of servants, when the arrow came winged and made buoyant by the gay feathering of so many splendid accomplishments. This general fact was appreciable by those who would forget, and never could have understood, the particular arguments of the infidel. Yet, even as regarded these particular arguments, secondly, my mother feared that some one —brief, telling, and rememberable—might be singled out from the rest, might transplant itself to the servants' hall, and take root for life in some mind sufficiently thoughtful to invest it with interest, and yet far removed from any opportunities, through books or society, for disarming the argument of its sting. Such a danger was quickened by the character and pretensions of Mrs Lee's footman, who was a daily witness, whilst standing behind his mistress's chair at dinner, to the confusion which she carried into the hostile camp, and might be supposed to renew such discussions in the servants' hall with singular advantages for a favourable attention. For he was a showy and most audacious Londoner, and what is *technically* known, in the language of servants' hiring-offices, as 'a man of figure'. He might, therefore, be considered as one dangerously armed for shaking religious principles, especially amongst the female servants. This conscientious apprehension on account of the servants applied to contingencies that were remote. But the pity on account of the poor lady herself applied to a danger that seemed imminent and deadly. This beautiful and splendid young creature, as my mother knew, was floating, without anchor, or knowledge of any anchoring grounds, upon the unfathomable ocean of a London world, which, for *her*, was wrapped in darkness as regarded its dangers, and thus for *her* the chances of shipwreck were seven times multiplied. It was notorious that Mrs Lee had no protector or guide, natural or legal. Her marriage had, in fact, instead of imposing new restraints, released her from old ones. For the legal separation of Doctors' Commons, technically called a divorce, but a divorce simply *à mensâ et thoro* (from bed and board), and not *à vinculo matrimonii* (from the very tie and obligation of marriage), had removed her by law from the control of her husband; whilst, at the same time, the matrimonial condition, of course, enlarged that liberty of action which else is unavoidably narrowed by the reserve and delicacy natural to a young woman whilst yet unmarried. Here arose one peril more; and, secondly, arose this most unusual aggravation of that peril—that Mrs Lee was deplorably ignorant of English life; indeed, of life universally. Strictly speaking, she was even yet a raw untutored novice turned suddenly loose from the twilight of a monastic seclusion. Under any circumstances, such a situation lay open to an amount of danger that was afflicting to contemplate. But one dreadful exasperation of these fatal auguries lay in the peculiar *temper* of Mrs Lee, as connected with her infidel thinking. Her nature was too frank and bold to tolerate any disguise: and my mother's own experience had now taught her that Mrs Lee would not be content to leave to the random call of accident the avowal of her principles. No passive or latent spirit of free-thinking was hers—headlong it was, uncompromising, almost fierce, and regarding no restraints of place or season. Like Shelley, some few years later, whose day she would have gloried to welcome, she looked upon her principles, not only as conferring rights, but also as imposing duties of active proselytism. From this feature in her character it was that my mother foresaw an *instant* evil, which she urged Miss Wesley to press earnestly on her attention—viz., the inevitable alienation of all her female friends. In many parts of the Continent, my mother was aware that the most flagrant proclamation of infidelity would not stand in the way of a woman's favourable reception into society. But in England at that time this was far otherwise. A display such as Mrs Lee habitually forced upon people's attention would at once have the effect of banishing from her house all women of respectability. She would be thrown upon the society of *men*—bold and reckless, such as either agreed with herself, or, being careless on the whole subject of religion, pretended to do so. Her income, though diminished now by the partition with Mr Lee, was still above a thousand per annum; which, though trivial for any purpose of display in a place so costly as London, was still important enough to gather round her unprincipled adventurers, some of whom might be noble enough to obey no attraction but that which lay in her marble beauty, in her Athenian grace and eloquence, and the wild impassioned nature of her accomplishments; by her acting, her dancing, her conversation, her musical improvizations, she was qualified to attract the most intellectual men; but baser attractions would exist for baser men; and my mother urged Miss Wesley, as one whom Mrs Lee admitted to her confidence, above all things to act upon her pride by forewarning her that such men, in the midst of lip homage to her charms, would be sure to betray its hollowness by declining to let their wives and daughters visit her. Plead what excuses they would, Mrs Lee might rely upon it, that the true ground for this insulting absence of female visitors would be found to lie in her profession of infidelity. This alienation of female society would, it was clear, be precipitated enormously by Mrs Lee's frankness. A result that might, by a dissembling policy, have been delayed indefinitely would now be hurried forward to an immediate crisis. And in this result went to wreck the very best part of Mrs Lee's securities against ruin.

It is scarcely necessary to say that all the evil followed which had been predicted, and through the channels which had been predicted. Some time was required on so vast a stage as London to publish the fact of Mrs Lee's free-thinking; that is, to publish it as a matter of systematic purpose. Many persons had at first made a liberal allowance for her, as tempted by some momentary impulse into opinions that she had not sufficiently considered, and might forget as hastily as she had adopted them. But no sooner was it made known as a settled fact that she had deliberately dedicated her energies to the interests of an antichristian system, and that she hated Christianity, than the whole body of her friends within the pale of social respectability fell away from her, and forsook her house. To *them* succeeded a clique of male visitors, some of whom were doubtfully respectable, and others (like Mr Frend, memorable for his expulsion from Cambridge on account of his public hostility to Trinitarianism) were distinguished by a tone of intemperate defiance to the spirit of English society. Thrown upon such a circle, and emancipated from all that temper of reserve which would have been impressed upon her by habitual anxiety for the good opinion of virtuous and high-principled women, the poor lady was tempted into an elopement with two dissolute brothers; for what ultimate purpose on either side was never made clear to the public. Why a lady should elope from her own house, and the protection of her own servants, under whatever impulse, seemed generally unintelligible. But apparently it was precisely this protection from her own servants which presented itself to the brothers in the light of an obstacle to their objects. What these objects might ultimately be, I do not *entirely* know; and I do not feel myself authorized, by anything which of my own knowledge I know, to load either of them with mercenary imputations. One of them (the younger) was, or fancied himself, in love with Mrs Lee. It was impossible for him to marry her; and possibly he may have fancied that in some rustic retirement, where the parties were unknown, it would be easier than in London to appease the lady's scruples in respect to the sole mode of connection which the law left open to them. The frailty of the will in Mrs Lee was as manifest in this stage of the case as subsequently, when she allowed herself to be over clamoured by Mr Lee and his friends into a capital prosecution of the brothers. After she had once allowed herself to be put into a post-chaise, she was persuaded to believe (and such was her ignorance of English society that possible she *did* believe) herself through the rest of the journey liable at any moment to summary coercion in the case of attempting any resistance. The brothers and herself left London in the evening. Consequently, it was long after midnight when the party halted at a town in Gloucestershire, two stages beyond Oxford. The younger gentleman then persuaded her, but (as she alleged) under the impression on her part that resistance was unavailing, and that the injury to her reputation was by this time irreparable, to allow of his coming to her bedroom. This was perhaps not entirely a fraudulent representation in Mrs Lee. The whole circumstances of the case made it clear that, with any decided opening for deliverance, she would have caught at it; and probably would again, from wavering of mind, have dallied with the danger.

Perhaps at this point, having already in this last paragraph shot ahead by some nine years of the period when she visited Greenhay, allowing myself this license in order to connect my mother's warning through Miss Wesley with the practical sequel of the case, it may be as well for me to pursue the arrears of the story down to its final incident. In 1804, at the Lent Assizes for the county of Oxford, she appeared as principal witness against two brothers, L——t G——n, and L——n G——n, on a capital charge of having forcibly carried her off from her own house in London, and afterwards of having, at some place in Gloucestershire, by collusion with each other and by terror, enabled one of the brothers to offer the last violence to her person. The circumstantial accounts published at the time by the newspapers were of a nature to conciliate the public sympathy altogether to the prisoners; and the general belief accorded with what was, no doubt, the truth— that the lady had been driven into a false accusation by the overpowering remonstrances of her friends, joined, in this instance, by her husband, all of whom were willing to believe, or willing to have it believed by the public, that advantage had been taken of her little acquaintance with English usages. I was present at the trial. The court was opened at eight o'clock in the morning; and such was the interest in the case, that a mob, composed chiefly of gownsmen, besieged the doors for some time before the moment of admission. On this occasion, by the way, I witnessed a remarkable illustration of the profound obedience which Englishmen, under all circumstances, pay to the law. The constables, for what reason I do not know, were very numerous, and very violent. Such of us as happened to have gone in our academic

dress had our caps smashed in two by the constables' staves; *why*, it might
be difficult for the officers to say, as none of us were making any tumult,
nor had any motive for doing so, unless by way of retaliation. Many
of these constables were bargemen or petty tradesmen, who in their ex-
official character had often been engaged in rows with undergraduates,
and usually had had the worst of it. At present, in the service of the
blindfold goddess, these equitable men were no doubt taking out their
vengeance for past favours. But, under all this wanton display of
violence, the gownsmen practised the severest forbearance. The
pressure from behind made it impossible to forbear pressing ahead;
crushed, you were obliged to crush; but, beyond that, there was no
movement or gesture on our part to give any colourable warrant to the
brutality of the officers. For nearly a whole hour, I saw this expression
of reverence to the law triumphant over all provocations. It may be
presumed that, to prompt so much crowding, there must have been
some commensurate interest. There was so, but that interest was not
at all in Mrs Lee. She was entirely unknown; and even by reputation
or rumour, from so vast a wilderness as London, neither her beauty nor
her intellectual pretensions had travelled down to Oxford. Possibly, in
each section of 300 men, there might be one individual whom accident
had brought acquainted, as it had myself, with her extraordinary
endowments. But the general and academic interest belonged exclu-
sively to the accused. They were both Oxonians, one belonging to
University College, and the other, perhaps, to Balliol: and, as they had
severally taken the degree of A.B., which implies a residence of *at least*
three years, they were pretty extensively known. But, known or not
known personally, in virtue of the *esprit de corps*, the accused parties
would have benefited in any case by a general brotherly interest. Over
and above which, there was in this case the interest attached to an
almost unintelligible accusation. A charge of personal violence, under
the roof of a respectable English posting-house, occupied always by a
responsible master and mistress, and within call at every moment of
numerous servants—what could that mean? And again, when it
became understood that this violence was alleged to have realized itself
under a delusion, under a preoccupation of the victim's mind, that
resistance to it was hopeless, how, and under what profound ignorance
of English society, had such a preoccupation been possible? To the
accused, and to the incomprehensible accusation, therefore, belonged
the whole weight of the interest; and it was a very secondary interest,
indeed, and purely as a reflex interest from the main one, which awaited

the prosecutress. And yet, though so little curiosity 'awaited' her, it happened of necessity that, within a few moments after her first coming forward in the witness-box, she had created a separate one for herself— first, through her impressive appearance; secondly, through the appalling coolness of her answers. The trial began, I think, about nine o'clock in the morning; and, as some time was spent on the examination of Mrs Lee's servants, of postillions, ostlers, &c., in pursuing the traces of the affair from London to a place seventy miles north of London, it was probably about eleven in the forenoon before the prosecutress was summoned. My heart throbbed a little as the court lulled suddenly into the deep stillness of expectation, when that summons was heard: 'Rachael Frances Antonina Dashwood Lee' resounded through all the passages; and immediately, in an adjoining anteroom, through which she was led by her attorney, for the purpose of evading the mob that surrounded the public approaches, we heard her advancing steps. Pitiable was the humiliation expressed by her carriage as she entered the witness-box. Pitiable was the change, the world of distance between this faltering and dejected accuser, and that wild leopardess that had once worked her pleasure amongst the sheepfolds of Christianity, and had cuffed my poor guardian so unrelentingly, right and left, front and rear, when he attempted the feeblest of defences. However, she was not long exposed to the searching gaze of the court, and the trying embarrassments of her situation. A single question brought the whole investigation to a close. Mrs Lee had been sworn. After a few questions, she was suddenly asked by the counsel for the defence whether she believed in the Christian religion? Her answer was brief and peremptory, without distinction or circumlocution—*No*. Or, perhaps, not in God? Again she replied, *No*; and again her answer was prompt and *sans phrase*. Upon this the judge declared that he could not permit the trial to proceed. The jury had heard what the witness said: she only could give evidence upon the capital part of the charge; and she had openly incapacitated herself before the whole court. The jury instantly acquitted the prisoners. In the course of the day I left my name at Mrs Lee's lodgings; but her servant assured me that she was too much agitated to see anybody till the evening. At the hour assigned I called again. It was dusk, and a mob had assembled. At the moment I came up to the door, a lady was issuing, muffled up, and in some measure disguised. It was Mrs Lee. At the corner of an adjacent street a post-chaise was drawn up. Towards this, under the protection of the attorney who had managed her case, she made her way as eagerly as possible.

Before she could reach it, however, she was detected; a savage howl was raised; and a rush made to seize her. Fortunately, a body of gownsmen formed round her, so as to secure her from personal assault; they put her rapidly into the carriage; and then, joining the mob in their hootings, sent off the horses at a gallop. Such was the mode of her exit from Oxford.

Subsequently to this painful collision with Mrs Lee at the Oxford Assizes, I heard nothing of her for many years, excepting only this—that she was residing in the family of an English clergyman distinguished for his learning and piety. This account gave great pleasure to my mother—not only as implying some chance that Mrs Lee might be finally reclaimed from her unhappy opinions, but also as a proof that, in submitting to a rustication so mortifying to a woman of her brilliant qualifications, she must have fallen under some influences more promising for her respectability and happiness than those which had surrounded her in London. Finally, we saw by the public journals that she had written and published a book. The title I forget; but by its subject it was connected with political or social philosophy. And one eminent testimony to its merit I myself am able to allege—viz., Wordsworth's. Singular enough it seems, that he who read so very little of modern literature, in fact, next to nothing, should be the sole critic and reporter whom I have happened to meet upon Mrs Lee's work. But so it was: accident had thrown the book in his way during one of his annual visits to London, and a second time at Lowther Castle. He paid to Mrs Lee a compliment which certainly he paid to no other of her contemporaries —viz., that of reading her book very nearly to the end; and he spoke of it repeatedly as distinguished for vigour and originality of thought.

Has my reader forgotten THE BOY JONES? He turns up again in this chronicle, for, on Wednesday, the 2nd of December, the inmates of Buckingham Palace were, shortly after midnight, aroused by an alarm being given that a stranger had been discovered under the sofa in Her Majesty's dressing-room, and the officers of the household were quickly on the alert. It was soon ascertained that the alarm was not without foundation, and the daring intruder was immediately secured, and safely handed over to the tender mercies of the police. The report of the occurrence spread very rapidly, and created the most lively interest in London, as it was feared that the consequent alarm might be attended with the most dangerous effects to the health of the Queen, who had been confined only eleven days previously. Happily, neither mother, nor child suffered in any way.

The facts, as far as can be gathered—the examination being a private one, conducted by the Privy Council—seem to have been as follows: Shortly after midnight, one of Her Majesty's pages, accompanied by other domestics of the Royal household, was summoned into Her Majesty's dressing-room, which adjoined the bed chamber in which Her Majesty's accouchement had taken place, by Mrs Lilly, the nurse, who thought she heard a noise. A strict search was made; and, under the sofa on which Her Majesty had been sitting, only about two hours' previously, they discovered a dirty, ill-looking fellow, who was immediately dragged from his hiding place, and given into custody. The prisoner was searched, but nothing of a dangerous nature was found upon him, and the police, at once, recognized their captive as the Edward Jones, who had, two years previously, entered the palace in such a mysterious way. He is described as being very short for his age, seventeen, and of a most repulsive appearance; but he was, apparently, unconscious of this defect, as he affected an air of great consequence, and repeatedly requested the police to address him in a becoming manner; also behaving with the greatest nonchalance at his examination before the Privy Council, the next day.

His first version of the matter was this: On Monday night, the 30th of November, he scaled the wall of Buckingham Palace, about half-way up Constitution Hill; he then proceeded to the Palace, and gained an entry through one of the windows. He had not, however, been long there, when he considered it unsafe for him to stay, as so many people were moving about; and he left by the same manner as he entered. The next day, Tuesday, about nine o'clock in the evening, he again effected an entrance by the same means as before. He then went on to state that he remained in the Palace the whole of Tuesday night, all Wednesday, and up to one o'clock on Thursday morning, when the inquisitive youth was captured. He was not satisfied with this dull and prosaic account of his entry; but, on the following day, he tried to invent something marvellous, and alleged that he ascended the roof of the Palace, and got down the chimney; but there were no marks of soot on his person, and his first story was doubtless, the correct one.

The greatest mystery attending the affair was, how he could have found his way to the room adjoining that in which Her Majesty slept, without being observed. The delinquent stated that, during the day, he secreted himself under different beds, and in cupboards, until, at length, he gained an entrance into the dressing-room; he, moreover, alleged that he sat upon the throne, that he saw the Queen, and heard the Princess Royal cry, but his story was such a romance, that no reliance could be placed upon it. He was extremely reticent as to the cause of his intrusion into the Palace, the only explanation which he vouchsafed, on being arrested, was, that he wanted to see what was going on in the Palace, that he might write about it, and, if discovered, he should be as well off as Oxford, who fared better in Bedlam, than he, Jones, did out of it. Even the stern discipline of the treadmill, to which he was promptly consigned, failed to extract anything more out of him; his only remark, when interrogated, being that he had got into the scrape, and must do the best he could.

His father stated that, in his belief, his unfortunate son was not of sound mind; but the medical evidence went to show that, though his head was of a most peculiar formation, he was not insane. The Council, therefore, came to the decision that it would be better to inflict summary punishment, and he was committed to the House of Correction for three months, as a rogue and vagabond.

If he is to be believed, he fared remarkably well whilst in his royal residence, as he said he helped himself to soup and other eatables from a room, which he called the 'Cook's Kitchen', but no dependence whatever could be placed on his word.

Prince Albert was taking leave of Her Majesty for the night, when the miscreant was discovered; and the Prince, hearing a noise proceeding from the adjoining apartment, opened the door, and ascertained the cause; but it was not made known to the Queen till the following day, so as to prevent any undue alarm on her part.

It is needless to say that this event excited the greatest interest, and engrossed public attention, nothing else being talked of. The punishment was considered far too light to deter a repetition of the offence, which opinion was subsequently justified. Such an occurrence, of course, was considered fair material for the humourists of the day to exercise their wit upon, and there are many allusions to it in the *Age* and *Satirist* of the period; but, as their remarks are not always conceived in the best taste, they are better left in the obscurity in which they now dwell. Perhaps, however, this little couplet from the *Satirist* may be excepted:

> Now he in chains and in the prison garb is
> Mourning the crime that couples Jones with darbies.

It was Jones's extraordinary powers of finding an entrance into the Palace that caused Samuel Rogers to declare that he must be a descendant of the illustrious In-i-go.

—John Ashton, *Gossip*

WILLIAM BOLITHO

Cagliostro
(and Seraphina)

The man's real name was Guiseppe Balsamo. We are used to the habit of change of name, almost as regular in adventures as in the three other professions that regularly use it, the monastery, the stage, and the streets. We know its almost ceremonial reason: the symbolical abjuration of ties, tasks, duties, those of family preparatory to those of society; its most general motive: ambition in its plainest symptoms, even to the poetry of snobbery. His father was a small store-keeper in Palermo; the date 1743. This Giuseppe, for short Beppo, grew into a stout, blunt-faced Gutter-hero, thievish, daring, calm, the bug-bear of all the house-wives and milk-sops of the neighbourhood. He cut washing lines, incited dog-fights, bullied the timid urchins and led the bold ones to expeditions against street vendors' carts, and added as much confusion as he could to the labyrinthine noise of the hot old city, where at any moment of the day or night there is a quarrel or a bargain being made. At the age of twelve he was sent to the seminary of St Roch to learn his letters, was beaten industriously by the teachers and the porter, and ran away. His father was dead. His mother's brother got him admitted to the Monastery of the Benfratelli—the entrance to the only career for a cleverish boy of his class. Here, after a time, he was sent to work for the apothecary of the establishment; to clean phials, weigh herbs, tend the alembics and sweep the floor, as well as learn the elements of the most sensual and exciting of sciences, Chemistry. Even in its modern austerity, a chemical laboratory is the most fascinating place in the world to those lucky enough to possess strong curiosity and sense of smell. In the eighteenth-century Sicilian monastery, where every bottle looked like a toy and contained a secret, where the materia medica was the Arabian Nights, and every piece of apparatus uncanny folk-lore, Beppo's faculties caught alight. He conceived the idea of magic. He learned so easily and well that his master took a fancy to him, and the queue of beggarly out-patients often had to wait for their potions while the two were lost together in speculatory discussion and operations, in the dark, aromatic crypt. As a spiritual antidote to this exaggeration, the brothers gave Beppo the task of reading to them at mealtime. The book preferred was some interminable martyrology—another potent irritant to his imagination, already alert with desire to commerce with the supernatural. But one day in Lent these stories of devil-worsting bishops, lion-taming virgins, fire-proof fakirs and invulnerable confessors palled on him. Or his nature, which pushed him to practical jokes, suddenly saw the humour of the unkempt solemnity with which the brethren ate their soup; and he began to substitute as he read the names of the most notorious whores of Palermo for the holy ones in his book. For this he was beaten with thongs and then chased from the community.

He must have known more than he should to play this jackanapes trick; no doubt there must be a lost story of unmonastic escapades and encounters before the definite expulsion. It was not then as a lamb that he plunged into the 'loose life' which his only official biographer, the Grand Inquisitor of Rome, now sets down. His next calling was that of a painter; which to him, to his city, and to his country included a shabby, dabbling admixture of marble-counterfeiter, distemperer, sign-writer with the making of those canvas storms at sea, in the distance Vesuvius in eruption, whose manufacture (along with that of plaster casts of sentimental statuary) is the largest artistic product of Italy to this day.

But art was overcrowded, even then. Beppo was forced, or chose, to eke out commissions with another local industry, inseparable as chaperonage from all societies where there is strict seclusion of women, that is, pandering. One of his clients was his pretty cousin's Romeo, whose letters he passed, and whose presents he intercepted. With admirable vitality, he added again to this sort of thing some amount of bespoke forgery; that is, he put his services and his pen at the command of persons in difficulties about a signature. It has been dug up that on one occasion he forged a whole will for the benefit of a religious community, and a pass out for a monk in the name of his Superior in Rome.

With these mean and clever resources he earned enough to eat well. All his life he had an enormous appetite for food, as common an accompaniment of great nervous force as its opposite. The superfluity he worked off in a violent bullying life, he became very muscular, and picked quarrels with sailors, beat the night-watchmen, established his reputation as a ward-terror. All these essays are comically out of proportion, and superficially out of relation to the particular splendour of the destiny before him. Half a hooligan, half a crook: the two commonest and least interesting of human qualities, this is all his peevish biographers, Carlyle and the Inquisitor, make of him who was to become Cagliostro. Deduce that there must have been something that escaped their survey from his last scene in Palermo. This 'obnoxious lout' appears abruptly to have captured the confidence of a goldsmith called Marano, and engaged him on a treasure hunt, in a coast cave, at midnight. In his nagging, prosecuting style, Carlyle presents this as an absurd swindle, an affair (like most events in history to him) of knave and dupe, with an easy laugh in it for Scotch canniness. But we, the jury, must notice that there are facts that do not fit into this view, any more than the Inquisition's Beppo fits into the Cagliostro who has less one-sided chronicles to attest him. There is magic in this affair, not only talk of dowsing, forked hazel rods and the rest, but circles in the moonlight, and burning earth, and the invocation of devils, quite out of character with the loutish Beppo we are told to see. Only in the bare fact that, following a quarrel with the goldsmith, Beppo fled from Palermo, are we satisfied to acquiesce.

His own story of the years that followed must be left to its proper context, the personality Seraphina helped or goaded him to compose. Actually he must have gone East, to that old right wing of the Roman Empire to which all adventurous Italians (as distinguished from honest) still are drawn, to Minor and Hither Asia. Cairo, Bagdad, Smyrna, Aleppo, even Constantinople, may have received him, and fed him in return for his yarns, his daubing, his pandering or his cheating. Like his innumerable compatriots who still drift through all the cities within a week of Suez, he would find himself at home anywhere but out of a crowd. He emerges for certain in Rome, lodging at the Sign of the Sun, poor, and engaged in a messy little business (but which few consider immoral, especially not Carlyle), of selling bad art to the middle class, in species—touched up pen-and-ink drawings of the usual monuments. A precursor of the picture postcard trade.

In this shapeless state, he met his Seraphina, whose real or socially imposed name was Lorenza Feliciani. She was the daughter of a small tradesman, a girdle-maker or glover, and a handsome girl, with, like most others, romantic ideas. Unlike most others, she was prepared to put them into action. In fact she was a born adventuress, and, if there were more recorded about her and her share in the enormous life of her husband, very likely entitled to be called one of the greatest there have ever been. Nevertheless it is true that her own will is so invisible for a long interval or rather separately inaudible in the chord of adventure in which they were both merged, her share so apparently passive, that she is usually forgotten by the writers whom the theme tempts, or, still worse, exhibited as a brave poor thing. The advantage of sentimentality is its short cut through psychology. Nothing in the facts of the case can give us another version of the Griselda legend. Instead, it is probably (though there is not much more than the significant chronology to support me) that the metamorphosis of this obese caterpillar, Beppo Balsamo, into the gorgeous moth, Count Alexander of Cagliostro, Pupil Adored of the sage Althotas, Foster Child of the Scherif of Mecca, putative son of the last King of Trebizond, named Ilso Acharat, and the Unfortunate Child of Nature, Grandmaster Supreme of the Egyptian Free-Masonry of High Science, Grand Cophta of Europe and Asia, was due, effectively, to little Lorenza, his mystical Seraphina. That is, the impetus, the welding of the dual will came, as it came in that other coupling of Lola and Louis, from the female side. Before the joint adventure existed that, single and successful, of Lorenza; the turning of a needy lying lout into—what his nature was capable of becoming.

This, for short, was a charlatan. The greatest charlatan the world has ever possessed. Or suffered. Which does not matter to this enquiry.

The tonic note of her adventure was thus his personality, the education of his will, if the respectable term may be borrowed for a moment. In this she conformed to the tendency which we made out from the case of Lola Montez, that the type adventure of woman is Man. In his ungainliness she perceived dignity, in his loutishness, an undeveloped quality of weight. In his untiring, eager torrent of lies, boasts, about himself and his travels, she detected, not only an uncommonplace imagination, but that rare glint of auto-suggestion, self-belief, which is the radium of imaginative life. Dividing this stage of her adventure into the exploration of Beppo and the invention of Cagliostro, in the first she penetrated the mud-flats and mean deserts of what he was, far into the tropical hinterland of what he might become. This talker might become convincing, because he was half-convinced himself. Even for a little Roman staymaker this insight into the man she loved was not specially remarkable, though audacious. Probably some sort of subconscious quasi-economic appraisement is inherent in the falling in love of all women. But what was extremely rare, in fact original, was the constructive effort with which she gave this intuitive exploration practical value. The education of a personality (as distinguished from that merely mental and physical), though it has had many illustrious exponents—the majority, it is true, no less illustrious bunglers —is still as strictly empirical as dowsing, or mediumship, or political economy.

Learning, which she certainly did not possess, would not have helped her out. In her walks with him through the luminous squares and endless streets of her Rome, sitting on the steps of the Piazza di Spagna where the swallows fly, or on the lip of Baroque fountains, in the vortex of the pilgrim tides of half the world, she must have studied her material and invented her practice. Which for months while they were betrothed, she must have used in an audacious campaign on the citadels and palisades of his essentially barbarous spirit.

Balsamo was evil-tempered, touchy; he must have resisted like a bull-dog the ablation of those vices, those virtues which she decided to drag away out of him; traits like weeds choking the consistent outline of Cagliostro. She had to cure him of his low Sicilian penny-fever; his mongrel habit in time of danger to snap and yelp; his cringe and his strut, both out of place in good society; both his fear and his hatred of the police—and to substitute in their places an unchallengeable indifference. To do all these things was delicate, for the balance of his confidence in himself must not be touched with a feather, or all was lost, both lover and venture. Higher and easier was the twin operation of fortifying what she left; out of his lying to make a visionary; to select a coherent story from his luxuriant brag, and confide him to it; to deflect his bent for pandering, and make him specialize in the trade of commodities more spiritual and also more costly than Eve's flesh; to extract a latent talent for stage management, such as he showed with the Sicilian goldsmith; to collate the coloured scraps of legend and superstition his rag-bag mind was stuffed with; to deepen his fear of devils, and his hopes of supernatural powers and finally to believe in them all herself, and even in him.

In short, she had luck and judgement, but no morals. So she made a personality out of a nonentity, and unravelled the darkest problem in human dynamics, constructing out of a tangle of greedy contradictions a single, sharp will, that could discharge itself upon the world like a bullet, instead of a cartridge of small shot. Whatever her share of the adventure, she was the maker of the adventurer: an operation rarer and more dangerous than any magic Cagliostro ever knew.

The direction of this new force, liberated by the love, vanity, and inspiration of a sharp little shop-assistant, was through the spirit of the times to a personal power that both were content to wish as large as possible, without any limitation or detailed idea. This spirit, since it was the Age of Reason, was love of Mystery. For it cannot be disguised that the prime effect of knowledge of the universe in which we are ship-wrecked is a feeling of despair and disgust, often developing into an energetic desire to escape out of reality altogether. The age of Voltaire is also the age of fairy tales; the vast *Cabinet des Fées*, some volumes of which Marie Antoinette took into her cell to console her, it is said, stood alongside the Encyclopédie. Alice's Adventures in Wonderland belongs to the same age and within seven years of the same date as the Origin of Species. Indeed the beginning of all folk-lore should be postdated to the time when primitive man had lost his brightest illusions. This impression of disgust, and this impulse to escape were naturally very strong in the eighteenth century, which had come to a singularly lucid view of the truth of the laws that govern our existence, the nature of mankind, its passions and instincts, its societies, customs, and possi-bilities, its scope and cosmical setting and the probably length and breadth of its destinies. This escape, since from Truth, can only be into Illusion, the sublime comfort and refuge of that pragmatic fiction we have already praised. There is the usual human poverty of its possible varieties. The shortest way out of Manchester is notoriously a bottle of Gordon's gin; out of any business man's life there is the mirage of Paris; out of Paris, or mediocrity of talent and imagination, there are all the drugs, from subtle, all-conquering opium to cheating, cozening cocaine. There is religion, of course, and music, and gambling: these are the major euphorias. But the queerest and oldest is the sidepath of Magic, where this couple chose to establish themselves, priests, touts, at your choice; a sort of emigration agency for Prospero's Island for those wearied of any too solid Dukedom of Milan. At its deepest, this Magic is concerned with the creative powers of the will; at lowest it is but a barbarous rationalism, the first of all our attempts to force the heavens to be reasonable. Whether there is any truth in this desperate sortie from truth is no matter; it is important in this story to remember that the operations of Cagliostro were entirely dependent on that focusing of the will, that is called belief, not only in the followers, but most of all in the leader himself. There is a smart ignorance that explains men like Cagliostro with the one word 'hypocrite', or 'cheat', a thesis which neither history nor even rudimentary psychology will swallow.

The requirements of this adventure, of will and belief, they had chosen, were an absolutely single will and at any rate a workable and temporary conviction; without a measure of both they could not have sold a gold-brick to an agricultural labourer. Their public was educated, often subtle, fantastic, but as critical as the paying audience at the first night of an opera. Even in the political branch, or spell-binding, the magician must believe in himself, if it is only as long as he is spouting.

But will and belief before they are marketable demand a vehicle; that is, a personality. The substance of a personality is its past. Lorenza—not yet Seraphina—set herself to adapt out of the rich but incoherent yarns of her lover, a *ne varietur* edition of his beginnings. As finally adopted this made a remarkable story. Palermo events were cut out, as she had cut out his Palermo character. He was, they agreed to believe, the unlucky son of the last monarch of Trebizond, disinherited and exiled by the ruin of that distant kingdom. In his flight he fell in with bandits, who sold him in the slave market of Mecca. Whose noble Scherif bought him, and reared him in Cabalistic wisdom. But when he grew, neither the magnanimity nor the favour of the Scherif could keep his ambitions and mission sedentary, so that at last the Mage let him go, bestowing on him the romantic and pitying title of Unfortunate Child of Nature. In his travels he met a sect of whirling Dervishes, also an Osirian fraternity, and a Domdaniel of Alchemists, all of whom received him with honour, initiated him into their mysteries and were reluctantly forced to let him go on his insatiable wandering. At Damascus he found the mahatma of all arcanic wisdoms, the sage Althotas, with whom he embarked for Malta, where the secret remnant of the Gnostic Knights possessed a subterranean laboratory. Here Althotas and he did great works in spiritual chemistry, in every work of the transforming and transmuting irreducibles which is proper to the imagination. They hinted he was obliged to kill Althotas.

As for Lorenza, she contented herself with the name of Seraphina, mystery, and suggestion. She was left to the imagination, which she helped only with such hints as a foreign cut in her dressing, and with a foreign accent in every language.

With this complete equipment of personality, will, and belief, the adventure might begin. But first there was an accident. The couple had taken up their lodging in her parents' house. Cagliostro had never been so comfortable. He knew more of the world than Seraphina and assured her that it was folly to go further. With a basis of three good meals daily, and a feather bed, he felt that his talents had their best chance of development here in Rome. All that they had planned might well be executed without stirring from the base.

Seraphina was at a loss. Fate was obliged to lend her hand; or her foot. For when all seemed spoiled, and the pair seemingly bound to waste their impetus in some hugger-muggery of fortune-telling, palm-reading, horoscoping in this back street, they were kicked out by the father, who came to a decision that he liked neither the face, the stories, nor the pretensions of his son-in-law. So with a sulkiness that unintentionally put the last touch to his make-up, Count Alexander Cagliostro put on his Prussian Colonel's uniform, to buy which, practically new, his mysterious Seraphina had spent a twelfth of her savings, and, accompanied by a hooded velvet figure, took the coach for Milan.

We have no precise knowledge of their adventures for the next years. Even a bald account would have been better reading than all the poems of the time. Only the statement of the Inquisition-biographer who sets down instead a descriptive catalogue of their dupes—official synonym for the converts of a heretic. This contains a full set of personages for an historical drama: Italian Counts, French Envoys, Spanish Marquises, Dukes and masked ladies of fashion. The couple appear at Venice, Milan, Marseilles, Madrid, Cadiz, Lisbon, and Brussels. They travelled in a japanned black coach, with sober heraldry in gold on the doors, with six armed attendants in dark livery, and a great deal of luggage.

Everywhere they stopped they had the same introductory technique, which was probably that of their poor and doubtful beginning. The romantic coach would draw up at the best Inn of the city. They ordered their meal in a private room, asking for strange dishes in a grave voice and a strong yet indefinable foreign accent. At first they must then have staged some little comedy of appearances at the window by Seraphina, looking unutterably sad and sweet, or chance collisions on the stairs and long, impressive, old-fashioned apologies by the Count, to attract the right curiosity. But as soon as they had servants, to be bribed and pumped, the introductions must have been much easier.

The profession of magician, in which our wandering couple were thus rising to inaccessible heights, is one of the most perilous and arduous specializations of the imagination. On the one hand there is the hostility of God and the police to be guarded against; on the other it is as difficult as music, as deep as poetry, as ingenious as stagecraft, as nervous as the manufacture of high explosives, and as delicate as the trade in narcotics. Technically in its upper atmospheres where Cagliostro and

Seraphina flew, it is social. For it aims to satisfy the deepest wishes of the human heart, which are rarely individual; and its tools are secret societies. The fear of death, crypto-sexual longings for supernatural terrors and beauties and all the rest of the complex motive that sends men to Mahomet, Beethoven, or Cagliostro, cannot be satisfied adequately except by a church, an orchestra, or a free-masonry. In occultism this apparatus must be secret, for it is not a salvation, but an escape; an escape from the prison of reality, into another world, without birth or death, outside the organic flux, with another rhythm than the eternal Out and In, conception and corruption, eating and excretion. The inscription over the little side door, where Cagliostro dangled the key is.

OSER
VOULOIR
SE TAIRE[1]

So a better idea of the skeleton of their doings, while the couple were posting over Europe, is not at all a plotless succession of coups, like Gil Blas, or Eulenspeigel, but in the venerable records of missionaries, propagating a faith and building a church. Their work was not the making of a blacklist, but a cult. Their captures were converts, to be preserved, not dupes to be fled from, disciples to be put on the registers of the initiated members of the Egyptian Freemasonry of High Science. President: a great Unknown, living in the unknown recesses of the mountains of the moon. Grand Cophta for Europe and Asia: Count Alexander Cagliostro; Grand Mistress: the disincarcerated Seraphina.

This reticulated organism that spread its threads before it was done over a thousand miles of Europe did not itself, in the magical way, spring full grown out of the night. The first contacts between the couple and their adepts, those meetings in close-shuttered sitting-rooms in the inns of the route, must have been rather masterpieces of suggestion and allusion than definite propaganda for the huge machine of which not a cog-wheel yet existed. The curious inquirer who paid for the first dinner of the adventure must have been the beneficiary of a performance, of unusual artistic value; some virtuosic confidence trick worked with only the talk of the man, and the silence of Seraphina, as distinct from the elaborate later exercise of the Egyptian Rite as lyric from dramatic. Still, even without apparatus, the couple must have traded

---

[1] DARE, WILL, KEEP SILENCE

substantially the same commodity: mystery, and the invisible. That is, spiritual romance.

From this artistically penurious embryo, their adventure developed and branched rapidly. In their second town they were able to offer a materialization of the devil. In their third a range of those transformations which are the first object of necromancy, hemp into silk, pearls out of pebbles, roses out of powder. They had a crystal ball, and could produce in it the little iridescent scenes, bed-room interiors, inexplicable nostalgic landscapes, concentrated perspectives where figures of the past and future walk out and in that are the recompense of long staring. Cagliostro could for a consideration show you a mandragore, those little earthly creatures who cry at night out of the earth at the foot of trees, and are born of the 'voluptuous and ambiguous tears' of a hanged man. He had like Descartes in the legend a satin-lined chest with him that contained a sylph six inches high, of the most perfect beauty and life. He reproduced the secret of Count Kueffstein, who knew how to fabricate homunculi by rare distillation and fermentations, who answered questions, and lived in bottles, carefully sealed because they were quarrelsome.

But all these curiosities were represented as preliminaries, instalments of incommensurably greater mysteries he had in store. He showed them as a travelling circus puts a juggler and a clown on the platform in front of the ticket office, to advertise the main show inside. Those who wished to go further were set on the first initiations of his Egyptian Freemasonry, and as it grew in his mind and in numbers, promoted through successive grades. The only details that remain of this organization are unfortunately mutilated and deformed. They give no fuller idea of the reality than a hostile detective could of the secret performance of a new opera, if he had only heard the chatter of sceneshifters. The music is not there, in these malignant accounts in the Inquisition records which is all we possess, nor the plot, nor even the glitter.

'The men elevated to the rank of Master take the names of early prophets; the women those of Sibyls.

'The Grand Mistress Seraphina blows on the faces of the female initiates, all along from brow to chin, and says: "I give you this breath to germinate and become alive in your heart the spirit of truth, which we possess by the names of Helios, Mene, Tetragrammaton."

'The recipient is led by a dark path into an immense hall, the ceiling, the walls, the floor of which are covered by a black cloth, embroidered with serpents. Three sepulchre lights glimmer there showing from time to time certain wrecks of humanity suspended by funereal cloths. A heap of skeletons makes an altar. On both sides of it are piled books. Some of these contain threats against the perjured. Others contain accounts of the working of the invisible revenging spirit. Eight hours pass. Then phantoms slowly cross the hall and sink, without noise of trapdoors.

'The novice spends twenty-four hours here in the midst of silence. A strict fast has already weakened his thinking faculties. Liquors with which he is provided wear out his resolution and make him sleepy.

'Three cups are at his feet. At last three men appear. These put a pale-coloured ribbon round his forehead dipped in blood and covered with silvery characters, some of them Christian. Copper amulets, among them a crucifix of copper, are tied round his neck. He is stripped naked; signs are traced on his body with blood. In that state of humiliation five phantoms stride towards him, armed with swords and dripping with blood. They spread a carpet on the floor to kneel on. The pyre is lit. In the smoke is seen a gigantic transparent figure who repeats the terms of the oath, etc.'

The stuff, as it is, is probably no worse than the current hocus pocus of any secret society in the world. But in these vestigial, mangled remains of what was, quite likely, part pasteboard when new, it is vain to look for the most faded fragment of the high excitement it once stirred in souls that were neither simple nor trivial. It is a charred leaf of a score written in a mode and for instruments that are irremediably lost.

However there is something else to be found in rummaging this junk: a clue to the hidden progress of their adventure. For this rigmarole is a religious, not a magical rite. Its purpose, that is to say, is obviously the same as that of all Mysteries, an initiation into a method of gaining immortality for the soul. The couple have been turned clean off their first course by the gulf tide of the human mind, that rises in the depths of its profound constitution—the fear of death. Instead of their first offer, an escape from the cosmos, they have come down to offer merely escape from the grave. Their magic peep-show has turned into a religious circus. Instead of sylphs, they trade in ghosts. Instead of an anodyne against disgust of human life, an elixir for prolonging it in *soecula soeculorum*.

Following the glistening japanned coach of their destiny to and fro on the trunk roads of Europe there are other similar changes of horses to be observed. The Unfortunate Child of Nature progresses if not in the science of the supernatural, in the science of men. He has discovered that drugs against life are infinitely more desired even than drugs against death, and he supplies them. He is as flexible as Casanova to the hints of his destiny. When he finds that Seraphina's body pleases even more than her aura, he was willing, says the Inquisitor, to supply even that. Seraphina too. And with impetus he descends (since the road leads downwards) to the vulgar branches of the black art, quite deserting its subtilties. He makes love-philtres, he has the secret of turning copper into gold. He asks his Ariel no longer for aerial music, but for cures for the gout. The noble and refined despairs that came to him turned out in the end to be only desires, and common desires, for health, for women, for survival, and above all for money. And it is curious to see how the pharmacopoeia of tricks of Cagliostro shrinks, as he grows in wisdom, to the single chapter of alchemy, the single nostrum for the single elemental desire of man, Gold. The difficult therapeutics of *Weltschmerz* can be resolved, in his experience, into prescriptions for unrequited love, unsatisfactory health, unappeased fear of death: all these with scientific economy, in turn superfluous if he can only teach the secret of quick and easy riches. So following the well-beaten road, he turned from magic to doctoring, from doctoring to psychology.

Seraphina his companion pursued her private parallel to knowledge, by his side. She learnt with irritation that all men want mystery in woman; but more than mystery, poetry; more than poetry, love; more than love; the urgent satisfaction of desire. After desire, comes satiety; then use, the use to which Cagliostro put her—to get him money, which brought her out after an uncomfortable excursion to the summit of his own discovery.

Come together to this much more venerable than Egypt's science of the human heart, their joint course leaves the mists and proceeds for a time in strict prose. They became a business partnership; in the immortality, love-philtering and alchemist trade, that had its regular booms and depressions. Very likely it is true that Cagliostro was willing to oblige the widespread demand for a dependable and quick poison, often needed in the tangled affairs of great families such as formed the most esteemed part of his clientèle: to simplify a succession, or solve a domestic estrangement. It was not for this, in the age of La Voisin and the Marquise de Brinvilliers, that his troubles with the high police of the whole continent progressively increased, nor because of the complaints of those dissatisfied with his expensive recipes for making gold cheaply. Alchemy like Astrology breeds no sceptics. It was the religious and political penumbra of his doings that fascinated Society's bull-dogs and foxes; the infringement of the Christian monopoly in his Egyptian Lodges, the odd twigs of democratic doctrine this eclectic jack-daw had built into his ritual.

Cagliostro himself clearly saw how things stood, and desired to exercise the cause by abandoning, or at any rate reducing what displeased his persecutors, the Egyptian Scientific branch, and confining himself to the more paying pursuit of practical sorcery. But Seraphina had not come out for mere gain. With true womanly idealism, she loved the things that money can buy; especially the meals (she shared Cagliostro's enthusiastic appetite), the dresses, the comforts, but despised and misunderstood the materialism of earning it. She assisted him in his imaginative chemistry against her will; except perhaps in the matter of love potions; and never ceased to nag him for his neglect of the pure though less profitable supernatural. So their unitary will showed signs of disintegration. Cagliostro turned his head irritably towards his national and hereditary ambition; the status of a retired millionaire. Seraphina gazed constantly towards power and rank; some joint Papacy of a vast underground religion, where in the becoming majesty of the robes he had invented for her, she would share in an Empire over the minds of all the romantics in Europe, shake governments, shape lives, receive homages, in the combined principles of hope and a little blackmail.

Restated constructively, the end of the adventure already drags the course of the man; he is in love with satiety. But she is in love with adventure. Her pitch is higher.

This is the moment of the Palermo catastrophe. Every day Cagliostro grew more sullen. Frequent quarrels were heard; questions of money to those that listened; underneath, the profound discord of their projects. The heavier prevailed. They travelled to Palermo, where Cagliostro wished to round off his fortune and retire. We have seen what happened to Mahomet, when he too tried to step off his adventure in full motion, the merciless recoil of the past that shot him forward with accelerated velocity and higher trajectory than ever. So now with Cagliostro. His invented past had obliterated the real in himself, but not in his enemies, who were waiting for him with a vengeance matured to over-proof by the long wait. He was recognized and clapped into jail for forgery (in the matter of the monastery will) and fraud, or sorcery (in that of the goldsmith).

Seraphina saved him with the greatest devotion and difficulty. There was a Lodge of Egyptian High Science in Palermo. Its president, or Cophta, was the son of a great Sicilian noble.

Seraphina knew how to settle the doubts that had come to this personage, from the revelation of Cagliostro's real name and history; and not only aroused his interest in the prisoner (who stood in some danger of a capital sentence) but his fanatical zeal. To such an extent that failing in peaceful manoeuvrings to get the case stopped, the adept came into the court with his followers, seized hold of the prosecuting advocate and beat half the life out of him, until he agreed to abandon his brief. The judges themselves, never eager about the case after they learned what powerful friends now stood behind Cagliostro, consented readily to have seen nothing and forgotten everything, and our Count was set free.

For a long way from this, the duad is again perfect; its interior forces composed. Consequently this is the period of their magnificence. The ritual gateway of the Invisible Kingdom is enriched by the full resources of their joint imagination. The Egyptian Lodge creeps into every reserved part of the society of Europe. Its adepts grow to thousands, with a fine proportion of princes, millionaires and court ladies among them. Everyone capable of curiosity has heard Cagliostro's name, even if they do not hope anything from him. He and Seraphina and their coach became a sign of the times. Sometimes in honestly untidy anti-quarian shops you can still come across one of the busts that were made and sold of him, in plaster or biscuit or porcelain, 'a most portentous face of scoundrelism, dew-lapped, flat-nosed, greasy, full of greediness, sensuality, ox-like obstinacy, a forehead impudent, refusing to be ashamed, and then two eyes turned up seraphically languishing, a touch of quiz too, the most perfect quack face . . .' Of Seraphina there remains, as far as I know, nothing material on which to base even such a manifestly prejudiced portrait as this of Carlyle; but intuitionally we know that her eyes must have been more intense than his, her pose less rhetorical, less explanatory.

The besetting disfigurement of his personality, thrift, has for now quite vanished. They spend money splendidly, are never caught making it, so that mere speculation on their fortune is a pleasure to all imaginations. In conscious or unconscious mimicry of their only serious rival in history, Apollonius of Tyana, Cagliostro gave a bonus to his personality, by giving the hospitals and the poor the preferential benefit of his science. The rich often failed in their first or second attempts to consult him; and he would visit in pageant the local infirmary as soon as he arrived in a city, dispensing to all the patients his Extract of Saturn, the most famous and genuine panacea of those times.

In 1780 he was in St Petersburg, and had more persecution there, notably from the Court Physician who was a Scotsman, and reported to the Emperor that Cagliostro's 'Spagiric Food', intended to increase the life span of its eaters to two centuries, was 'unfit for a dog'. The German Ambassador, entering into the cabal with a complaint against the Count about the unauthorized use of a Prussian uniform, was expelled.

He lost more than he could afford on this spoilt voyage, and in Warsaw he botched an experiment in gold-making, was denounced by a rationalist courtier and again forwarded out of the country. But at Berlin, Frankfurt, Vienna, he recovered his balance. So that when they arrived in Strassburg in 1783, the couple had arrived at the very altitude of their adventure.

In that rich city, where the roofs are superstitious, and the pavements cobbled like the contradictory character of the Alsatians, the great man was that most distinguished ass of history, The Prince Cardinal de Rohan, of the blood royal of Brittany. This de Rohan was immense in every way, in his person, his wealth, his importance, his vanity, his good nature, and in the unexampled mess into which these magnitudes were destined to lead him, the court of France, the institution of monarchy, and derivatively the general history of Europe itself.

Into the centre of this mess, the affair of the Diamond Necklace, the first epicentre of the universal upheaval, the French Revolution, whose time was now near, the line of the duad adventure led as straight as the pull of gravitation. Rohan wrote to Cagliostro as soon as he arrived to say he wished to meet him. The Count replied, with his unvarying technique, 'If Monseigneur the Cardinal is sick, let him come to me and I will cure him; if he is well, he has no need of me, I none of him.' The Abbé Georgel, the Prince-Cardinal's memorialist, describes the further course of their relations:

'Admitted at length to Cagliostro's sanctuary, the Prince saw, according his own account to me, in the incommunicative man's physiognomy, something so dignified, so imposing, that he felt a religious awe, and spoke to him reverently. Their interview, which was brief, excited more keenly than ever his desire of further acquaintance. This he finally attained, and the empiric gained the Prince's entire confidence without appearing to court it, and mastery over his will. "Your soul," he said one day to the Prince, "is worthy of mine; you deserve to be made participator of all my secrets." This captivated the whole faculties of a man who always hunted after secrets of alchemy and botany. Their interviews became long and frequent. I remember once having learnt, by a sure way, that there were frequent most expensive orgies in the Archiepiscopal Palace at Strassburg, where Tokay wine ran like water to regale Cagliostro and Seraphina ...'

From another testimony of the same period, by one Meiners, professor at Göttingen, we have a fact of importance. 'The darkness which this Cagliostro has spread over the sources of his necessarily immense income and outlay contributes even more than his munificence and miraculous cures to the notion that he is a divine extraordinary man, who has watched Nature in her deepest operations, and stolen the secret of Gold-Making from her ...' Gold-making again ... He had also fallen into what was, for him, bad company. This was one Jeanne de St Remy de Valois, a poor relation of the Royal House of France, a sharp, bird-voiced creature who lived just over the border that divides adventure from resolute swindling. She was as attached to de Rohan as Cagliostro himself, but without any other apparatus than her wits, her tiny body, and her knowledge of court scandals. One of the juiciest of these was the long standing bitterness between de Rohan, who had suffered quasi-exile in Strassburg through it, and Marie Antoinette, the Queen. Jeanne also knew about the Diamond Necklace, the treasure and the ruin of the court goldsmiths, Boehmer and Bassenge, who had locked up the value of a warship in it, hoping and hitherto failing to find a purchaser. It was known at court and to de Rohan that the Queen had been dreadfully tempted to acquire it. But the chronic bankruptcy of the royal exchequer, the king, or her own reasonableness, had dissuaded her from this. Jeanne had interrupted Cagliostro's mystical tête-a-tête with de Rohan with her plan, which the Grand Cophta, after much resentment and hesitation agreed to share in and assist. Cagliostro was anxious to get to his dessert; to make in one coup enough to transmute his supernatural adventure into the solid, material castle in Sicily we have spoken of before—the natural breaking-point of his single fate, from which hitherto the underpinning of Seraphina's had saved him.

There was to be a great deal to share: exactly, the value of the Diamond Necklace. The Queen wanted it. De Rohan, the only man in France who could afford it. But Jeanne had something better than this bare coincidence, for the bare truth is not bait for fools. She knew de Rohan, and she told him the Queen had fallen in love with him; deeply; to the extent that she longed for *him* to give her the Necklace.

There is a library of conjecture on the quality of Jeanne's authority for this request, the sum and point of her obvious lies. We know that she was a liar, but also that Marie Antoinette loved to exercise the rights of a pretty woman to be treacherous and imprudent; also that the Queen hated de Rohan very much. Our part of the story is that de Rohan fell into whoever's trap it was, and that Cagliostro brought up all his ghosts, sciences, predictions, and supernatural counsels to help him into it. The magnificent ass bought the Necklace, and sent it through Jeanne to the Queen; since when it has never authentically been heard of.

But human stupidity, the source these two experts were tapping, is as ultimately treacherous and incalculable as any other elemental force, wind, water, fire. Here, it betrayed them disastrously. If de Rohan had had a grain of sense, the plot would have succeeded. Instead the booby must needs go to the jewellers, Boehmer and Bassenge, enjoy their thanks, and indulge himself in the nobility of telling them to thank, not him, but the Queen, for the transaction. Which they did.

There are moments in history when the mind, with surprise and excitement rather than consternation, becomes suddenly aware that the general train of events it has been watching is only a prelude. So at the Bridge of Sarajevo in 1914, so with the visit of Boehmer and Bassenge to Versailles to Marie Antoinette. It is as if we were startled by the rap of a conductor's baton, and the following crash of the drums of the major orchestra of Fate, whose invisible existence we had clean forgotten.

The curtain rattles up on the first scene of the Revolution. As if they had been carefully coached in foolery, without making a single error of sense, all these personages we have collected together played out their parts. The Queen with perfect naturalness had de Rohan arrested at the one moment when it would cause most noise and damage to her reputation: when the whole Court was present to hear him say the Mass of the Assumption, the 15th August, 1785. Her police, to make certain that the affair should do its maximum of damage by remaining a mystery, allowed de Rohan to destroy his papers. Cagliostro's arrest that followed made triply certain that the remotest curiosity of the whole of Europe should follow this public examination of the virtue of the Queen and the prestige of a whole régime by her enemies, the Parlement de Paris. Folly built on folly, in the true farcical style in which all the tragic chapters of human history are written.

The steeple of this edifice was the verdict; ambiguous, mysterious, exonerating the condemned Jeanne de Valois by the acquittal of Cagliostro, whose complicity was a necessary part of the case against her; branding de Rohan as a fool by denying he was a knave; leaving on the Queen's reputation the fatal marks of an officious discretion.

So Cagliostro totters out of History, his glamour torn, his mysteries in rags, and worst of all, hopelessly unfashionable. He took refuge in England, the sanctuary of the out-of-date. If he had been alone, there he would have ended, in some seedy City debt-jail, or in some legend of begging or guzzling hung round one of the unauthentic taverns in the tourist trade, that are the fortune of the purlieus of Fleet Street.

But in the imaginative silence that conceals him in London for months, there is at least a commotion, the track of his lost and heroic duad, Seraphina, to the rescue. And following on the reconstitution of the atom, which his will had disastrously split in Strassburg, there follows a sudden, painful emergence of the old Cagliostro, starting into our view again as a drowned man bobs up to the surface out of the mud. 'One de Morande, Editor of a Courier de l'Europe published in London, had for some time made it his distinction to be the foremost of Cagliostro's enemies. Cagliostro enduring much in silence, happens once, in some public audience to mention a practice he had witnessed in Arabia the Stony: the people there, it seems, are in the habit of fattening a few pigs annually, on provender mixed with arsenic, whereby the whole pig carcase by and by becomes, so to speak, arsenical; the arsenical pigs are then let loose into the woods, eaten by lions, leopards and other ferocious creatures; which latter naturally all die in consequence, and so the woods are cleared of them. This adroit practice the Sieur Morande thought a proper subject for banter; and accordingly in his seventeenth and two following numbers, made merry enough with it. Whereupon Count Front-of-Brass writes an advertisement in the Public Advertizer (under date September 3rd, 1786) challenging the witty Sieur to breakfast with him for the 9th of November next, in the face of the world, on an actual sucking pig, fattened by Cagliostro, but cooked and carved by the Sieur Morande— under bet of Five Thousand Guineas sterling that, next morning after, he, the Sieur Morande, shall be dead, and Count Cagliostro be alive. The poor Sieur durst not cry, Done; and backed out of the transaction making wry faces. Thus does a king of red coppery splendour encircle our Arch-Quack's decline; thus with brow of brass, grim smiling, does he meet his destiny.'

Or rather, so, feebly, but inimitably, the reconstructed adventure lifts itself from the mud into which its fragments had fallen and essays to drive the old course. The inflexible, unadaptable course of Seraphina, which passed across all practical materiality, like the base line of an astronomer through space. Her adventure could be broken off short, as it was when he gadded with Jeanne in Strassburg. But it could not be bent. Now that she had triumphantly regained her man, she had and could have no new plan; nothing but to begin all over again the parabolic graph of her fate.

The two set out therefore from London, on the same course they had laid, twenty years before, from Rome, to make a fresh start. There was nothing left of her but her eyes; Cagliostro had grown into a piece of unwieldy luggage. It was 1789; the grand days of terror and excitement. The two rolled like dismasted caravels in strange seas, through Basel, Aix in Savoy, Turin, at every stopping place presented by the police with an order of instant expulsion. Nowhere was any trace of Egyptian adepts, the temples of unreality were all vanished; they were hopelessly lost. The only thing Seraphina could think of to pick up her bearings was to go back to Rome. Cagliostro no longer counted; so from frontier to frontier they drifted heavily along to their starting point.

Destination, rather, for there on the 29th December, 1789, 'the Holy Inquisition detects them founding some feeble moneyless ghost of an Egyptian Lodge, picks them off, and locks them hard and fast in the Castle of St Angelo.'

No; Adventure does not end her stories in that style, with slick cues for pity or yawns. You must wait a moment for the end; until the inevitable has revenged itself, in its obscenest manner on the dowdy, battered couple who had so long complotted against it. Both the Unfortunate Child of Nature, and the Grand Mistress of the Fixed Idea are now finished by any human dramatic rules. The zagging course and the soaring have both come to term, and the audience wait only to be released by a solemn curtain. Even some sort of a happy ending was possible, in matter of fact, for the Inquisition hesitated about letting them go. After a while Cagliostro might have become Old Beppo, one of the curiosities of back-alley commerce in Rome, with a dignified, slightly cracked old wife, whose eyes were fascinating as long as she lived. Instead of that we have the meaningless, unprofitable wickedness of the truth. When the accusation of impiety and 'liberalism' was on the point of dropping for lack of evidence, Seraphina began to talk. Venomously, treacherously, disastrously, blurting out the whole truth, and much more than the truth against her life's companion and meaning, supplying much more than the judges hoped for. She even told them the final secret, the one which Cagliostro cherished most—the details of his real name and unromantic birth. The sort of frenzy that makes women round on their lovers in the dock beside them, to their common doom? Some specific weakness of the sex under the torture of justice, court rooms, police, cells, which they can no more resist than tickling on the soles of their feet? But Cagliostro talked too. Between them they made a horrible duet across the prison of betrayal. They spent nights of concentration, when they had emptied their stock of memories before the police, devising cunning charges to down each other still deeper.

Even the inquisitors at last tired of listening to them. Long before they died in the old prison, nobody paid any more attention to the two queer old dodderers.

HAROLD DEARDEN

Dan Graham

It is an excellent thing to have a certain amount of self-confidence, but like most other good things in life it is possible to have too much of it. Dan Graham suffered severely from this disability. He was born in New York. His father had been attached for a great many years to one of the wealthy families on Fifth Avenue, first as a coachman and later on as one of those elderly chauffeurs who commonly contrive to look so embarrassingly more distinguished than the occupant of the vehicle they are driving.

Dan's parents had been married for some years before he made his appearance, and they naturally adored him; but indeed from the outset he seemed to be no less a favourite of the gods. He was a sturdy little boy, with a gay and affectionate disposition and such perfection of features that he was an easy winner in a beauty contest for which his parents entered him when he was still in short trousers. Intellectually he was no less richly endowed. He was consistently at the top of his form at school, and since he was a first-class athlete in addition he inevitably became a hero to his school-fellows. He had, one would have thought, every qualification for a successful and entirely desirable citizen. But he had one very serious flaw in his outlook. He attributed these gifts for fortune to some special merit in himself.

Time after time, as a small boy, when his charm of manner and exceptional good looks enabled him to evade punishment for some childish escapade or other, he ascribed these escapes to his own cleverness. He believed himself to be a super-man of sorts. He interpreted the benefits derived from his personality, in fact, as the result of some peculiar immunity to the normal sequence of cause and effect which was enjoyed by himself alone. Anyone who is guilty of such an error of reasoning is clearly heading for trouble.

But it is only fair to say, that for quite a number of years Dan had every excuse for entertaining this attractive but disastrous notion. His love affairs among the young ladies in the neighbourhood of his home became a sort of legend in the district. It seemed that no woman could resist him, and no error of tactics caused him the smallest inconvenience. Over and over again he emerged with enviable ease from situations commonly associated with the most uncomfortable results. And, having smiled his way gaily through an interview with the infuriated parents of one incautious maiden, he had thereafter only to flash his black eyes in the direction of another to be assured of a no less easy success.

But it was not only his achievements as a roving lover which tended to augment Dan's confidence in his own ability to be a law unto himself. He did pretty much as he liked in almost every form of activity. At the age of about nineteen his father's influence secured him an excellent job as a chauffeur, and young Dan proceeded at once to take the fullest advantage of the opportunities afforded him by the situation. If his employer did not happen to be using the car, Dan just naturally used it himself. On one such occasion an incident occurred, typical of many which helped continuously to stimulate his already flourishing egotism.

Dan had driven the young lady of the moment out into the country for the evening, and on his way home the exhilaration natural in the circumstances culminated in a head-on crash with another vehicle. His employer's car was irreparably damaged. Even Dan looked forward with a certain amount of misgiving to the interview with that gentleman next morning. But even in this crisis his personality pulled him through. Where nine men out of ten would assuredly have been dismissed without a reference, young Dan not only retained his situation but considerably increased his prestige with his employer.

In reporting what had happened, he gave a perfectly irresistible account of the events which had led up to the accident. He was frank, boyishly contrite, and at the same time mischievously conscious of the atmosphere of illicit romance which had surrounded the whole affair, and his employer appears to have been enchanted by the recital. Possibly he found Dan's description of some of his activities during the earlier part of the evening to be so infinitely superior to anything which he himself had achieved in his youth, that he had no room in his heart for anything but envy. At all events he administered only the mildest rebuke. Dan continued to enjoy his patronage, and doubtless his motor-car also, for some time to come.

After his triumph, Dan's self-confidence justifiably increased in leaps and bounds; and it was about this time that he began deliberately to seek opportunities for the pleasurable demonstration of his apparently unlimited capacity to impose his personality and his desires on others. He was now about twenty-two, a superbly-built young fellow with slim hips and a magnificent pair of shoulders which his uniform admirably displayed. He had clearly a unique employer, and one would have expected him therefore to be entirely contented. But a chauffeur's livery is undeniably not suggestive of any high degree of authority. It may have been with the object of rectifying this deficiency that Dan now joined the New York police.

Here, from the very first, he had a superb time. His gifts as an athlete made him a very welcome recruit. He was immensely popular with his brother officers, while the nature of his duties provided him with almost unlimited facilities for ordering his fellow citizens about and generally enjoying himself. But it is clear that in the few years interval between his schooldays and his manhood Dan had lost some, at any rate, of the genuine kindliness and desire to please which had hitherto been his most characteristic attributes. He had always wanted his own way in everything, and he had invariably got it. But where formerly he had been prepared to gain his ends by persuasion and sheer charm of manner, he now demanded the subservience of others as a right. This somewhat sinister change in his outlook is admirably illustrated by an incident that occurred shortly after he joined the police.

He was in a bar one evening, and for the edification of a crowd of his old admirers he was displaying a few of the juggling tricks with his baton and revolver which he had picked up from his colleagues in the canteen. One young gentleman in the audience unaccountably failed to be impressed by the performance, and it doubtless seemed to Dan that something must be done to stimulate so indifferent an observer. Lounging back in his chair he made an airy but unmistakable gesture with his revolver.

'You want waking up,' he said genially. 'Get busy now. Dance.'

It must be presumed that the other took no more interest in dancing than he did in juggling. He turned his back on Dan and leaned up against the bar without a word. Clearly this sort of thing could not be tolerated for a moment. It was a direct challenge to Dan's self-esteem, and he acted without a moment's hesitation. He continued to smile. But when he spoke next, there was that in his voice and the expression of his eyes which brought a sudden hush over the crowded bar.

'I told you to dance,' he said. When this produced nothing but a somewhat sickly smile, Dan put a couple of bullets into the boards within an inch or two of the feet of the young gentleman, who presumably danced thereafter with abandon.

Incidents, more or less of this nature, occurred with increasing frequency during the next year or two. They inevitably lost Dan a few friends; but at the same time they were a most agreeable and efficacious stimulant to his egotism and, since he was intelligent enough to restrict these exhibitions of his powers to comparatively unimportant civilians, his popularity among the rank and file of his colleagues was, if anything, thereby increased. It was not long before he was the hero of the force.

He was just as well liked by his superiors. It was common knowledge, by the end of his third year of service, that Dan was marked down for promotion. That this was so, must still further have increased his belief that he was completely immune from the consequences of his acts, for his conduct as a patrolman had by no means been exemplary. On the contrary, ever since he had joined the force he had been guilty of a series of breaches of the official regulations, any one of which would undoubtedly have resulted in the instant dismissal of a less fortunate individual.

Dan had a habit when on point duty, for instance, of leaving his post for an hour or two to take a stroll with a lady or a drink with a friend; and even in that atmosphere of freedom of thought and action which is so happily a characteristic feature of the American conception of discipline, this sort of thing is looked upon with a certain amount of disfavour. Dan had several times been taken to task on account of his indulgence in this practice, but apparently his superiors had never been able to bring themselves to do more than administer a mild rebuke. It is clear, at any rate, that these incidents in no way diminished their appreciation of Dan's merits.

Then, one day, when Dan announced that he was engaged to be married, the whole section joined in an effort to celebrate the tidings. A subscription was unanimously organized to present the Sheikh, as Dan was invariably called, with some token of their universal esteem. And as a special mark of favour on the part of his superiors, he was appointed to one of those official sinecures which it was occasionally in their power to bestow.

A firm of building contractors were engaged in the construction of a new apartment-house in the district. One of their engineers, a young man of the name of Pratt, was in the habit of going down from the headquarters of the firm every Saturday with the employees' wages. On these occasions he would carry as much as two thousand pounds in cash on his person, and since in this year of 1927 hold-ups were of almost daily occurrence in New York, this routine procedure was obviously not devoid of risk. The firm had applied for police protection for Mr Pratt. Dan Graham was appointed to undertake the duty.

It proved to be a perfectly delightful job. It involved no more than a comfortable trip in Mr Pratt's motor-car from the head office to the apartment-house, and an hour or two of pleasurable lounging, during which time Mr Pratt dispersed the wages and Dan collected an eminently satisfactory amount of admiration from the civilian population in the neighbourhood.

But Dan was within a few days of his wedding, and it must be supposed that this fact diminished to some extent the enjoyment to be derived from the admiration of strange young ladies. After the novelty of his official task had worn off, he began to find himself more and more preoccupied with the contents of the satchel which Mr Pratt on these occasions placed on the seat beside him with such impressive unconcern.

Dan's fine eyes glowed as he looked at it. He knew what it contained: fat wads of notes with which a young married man could do a lot. To an individual of his peculiar gifts in the way of immunity, any unpleasantness normally associated with the forcible acquisition of such aids to happiness might surely be evaded with the utmost simplicity.

It is true that up to this point in his career Dan had never undertaken any activity whatever of a definitely anti-social nature. He had been a braggart and a bully, but that was all. He had no grounds whatever for visualizing himself as a master criminal. But his belief in the Divine Right of Dan Graham, fostered by so many minor successes, had grown by now into an unshakable conviction. He appears to have embarked on the slaughter of Mr Pratt with almost unbelievable unconcern.

It must be supposed that it was entirely out of consideration for his friends in the police force that he decided to take even one elementary precaution. To drive away from the Police Station with a live Mr Pratt and return later with a dead one, would undeniably be tactless. There was no object in putting his friends to too much trouble. Dan decided that on the following Saturday morning he would adopt a procedure which should obviate entirely any chance of unpleasantness. He had very little difficulty in doing so. On a plea of sickness he was excused from duty for the day, and another officer was told off to accompany Mr Pratt in his stead.

Dan and Mr Pratt, however, were by now close friends; and the notion entertained by the former appears to have been that while this official deviation from routine was essential in theory, for the purpose of safeguarding himself and his colleagues from embarrassing complications, there was no need whatever to take the slightest notice of it in practice. If he simply arranged for Mr Pratt to pick him up at his own house, instead of going round to the Police Station in accordance with what was obviously nothing but a formality, the rest of the enterprise would proceed like clockwork. He would still be able to slaughter Mr Pratt with a minimum of inconvenience, while at the same time, from an official point of view, no one would have the least idea that he had anything to do with the affair at all. It was a splendid scheme and it worked admirably.

Mr Pratt called for Dan as arranged, and while the other officer who had been detailed for the duty waited anxiously at the Police Station for the arrival of his charge, Dan and Mr Pratt drove round to the Bank and collected the money. Thereafter, smoking two of Mr Pratt's excellent cigars, they proceeded happily on their way, just as though this was an ordinary morning instead of the most momentous in both their lives.

Dan was in superb spirits. On the previous afternoon he and his fiancée had paid the first instalment on a much more charming little house than that young lady had ever hoped for; and Dan knew that in a few minutes he would have two thousand pounds in his pocket wherewith to pay the balance. It was hard lines in a way on poor old Pratt, of course; but that couldn't be helped. As far as Dan Graham was concerned the future looked as rosy as could be.

But Mr Pratt was in pretty good form at the time too. He was unaware of the precise extent to which he was interested in the subject, but he responded to Dan's description of his future home with the utmost sympathy and enthusiasm. He had always liked Dan, and this glimpse into the healthy simplicity of his nature made him now seem all the more attractive. When Dan suddenly put a revolver to his ear and pulled the trigger, Mr Pratt was literally too surprised for words.

This absence of any outcry on the part of Mr Pratt was eminently convenient. They were driving down one of the main streets at the moment, and any demonstration, vocal or otherwise, with regard to Dan's activity with his revolver might quite easily have spoiled the whole thing. Dan himself had foreseen this. When he pulled the trigger of his revolver with his right hand, he had taken over the steering wheel from Mr Pratt with his left and, having thus drawn the coupé gracefully up to the kerb, it was simply a matter of getting out in an entirely orthodox manner and attending to Mr Pratt at his leisure.

It might admittedly have been surmised by a more apprehensive slaughterer, that the firing off of a revolver in the main street of a city at eleven o'clock in the morning would arouse a certain amount of curiosity on the part of the bystanders, in spite of what might otherwise be the most decorous behaviour. But there was nothing timorous or imaginative about Dan. He appears to have decided that details of this sort might safely be left to take care of themselves. It is only fair to say that, up to a point, he was eminently justified in this assumption.

Many people undoubtedly heard the sound of the shot, but they subsequently explained that they thought the coupé from which the noise clearly came, had backfired or something. If it had not been for the presence of two small boys on the footpath, Dan's future might well have fulfilled his rosiest anticipations. But unfortunately these two small boys had cause to know Dan. On this particular morning they had wandered for some reason or other far away from their customary haunts. The street in which they usually played was on Dan's beat; and on one or two occasions Dan had interfered with their ligitimate pursuits, such as cat-stoning and football, to an extent which seemed to them excessive.

When, therefore, they saw him get out of the coupé and, pushing the driver from behind the wheel, take his place and drive rapidly down the street, they recognized him immediately in spite of his civilian clothes. The incident was thus impressed upon their youthful memories to an extent much greater than would otherwise have been the case.

As far as Dan was concerned, however, everything seemed to be going on as well as possible, for he had entirely overlooked the two small boys. This in itself was regrettable enough. But he had failed, in addition, to appreciate in sufficient detail the effect of his bullet on Mr Pratt.

The general effect on Mr Pratt's head had, of course, by no means escaped him. But on the top of that head there had been a smart straw hat with a neat black bow attached; and it was the behaviour of this bow, unobserved by Dan at the time, which was to have such really disastrous consequences. For the bow, together with a small but essential part of Mr Pratt's person, was carried into the roadway by the flight of the bullet, and it is just these trifles in life which cause trouble.

But happily Dan knew nothing of all this, and with a mind unclouded by either small boys or bows he drove Mr Pratt about two miles down the street till he came to a conveniently deserted spot under some railway arches. Here he parted company with both Mr Pratt and his coupé and, with his own pockets comfortably bulging with notes, he hurried eagerly back to town to keep a luncheon engagement with his fiancée.

This young lady testified later that she had never seen Dan so gay, boyish, and altogether adorable as he was during that meal. He showed her the notes and announced that they represented a legacy from an aunt. They had an excellent lunch on the strength of it, and subsequently paid the first instalments on, among other things, a charming little motor car, a diamond necklace, and a most attractive summer outfit which the young lady had coveted for some time. Dan drove her about the town for an hour or two in their new car; and finally, after a wholly delightful afternoon, he saw her home. It was then about six o'clock.

Thereafter Dan drove out to Coney Island with a man friend. He had a marvellous evening and left for home about twelve o'clock. It must have been perfectly heartbreaking, after a day of such unbroken success and happiness, to be arrested on his arrival by three of his colleagues, who had been waiting outside his front door, with a cast iron charge against him in their hands, since four o'clock in the afternoon.

But Dan was not the man to make mountains out of molehills. Admittedly the evidence of the bow and the two small boys, to say nothing of a number of elderly ladies who appeared to have nothing whatever to do but scrutinize from their windows the behaviour of total strangers in the street, was likely on the face of it to be somewhat embarrassing. But that couldn't be helped. Dan's confidence as to the upshot of the matter was entirely unimpaired. Something or other would happen to disperse these clouds as it always had done in the past; and after one, or possibly two, unpleasant interviews with his superiors, the affair would doubtless blow over. It would then simply be a matter of making up to his friends for the trouble they would undoubtedly be put to on his behalf.

In this attitude of mind he cheerfully submitted to the boredom of a few months in prison, and when he came up for trial he was just as jaunty, handsome and self-confident as ever. But the evidence for the Prosecution depressed him slightly. He could not but realize that this incident in connection with Mr Pratt looked like developing into a bit of a bother. After a talk with his counsel on this point, he was so far prepared to take the matter seriously as to accede to the latter's suggestion that he should enter a plea of insanity as being the simplest method of avoiding any further unpleasantness. He probably felt that not to do so might, in the circumstances, have seemed somewhat flippant and ungenerous.

Having entered this plea it must be admitted in common justice that he did his very best to live up to it. That night, in the privacy of his cell, he tore his clothes and smeared his face with dirt, and on making his appearance in court next morning he stared wildly around him and muttered continuously. He gave, in fact, as convincing an imperson-ation of a lunatic as it was reasonable to expect in view of the fact that he had never in his life seen one.

It was regrettable that such whole-hearted efforts to make his acquit-tal as easy for the jury as possible should have been received by those gentlemen in so unhelpful a spirit; but Dan accepted their verdict of guilty in the most generous manner. The sentence, of course, sounded most unfriendly too. However, Dan was still sustained by his life-long assumption that no one in the end would have the heart to do anything really drastic or unpleasant. It would all work out somehow. Meanwhile there was no further need for this lunatic stunt. That was one good thing anyhow.

His first act on returning to his cell after the verdict was to call for the services of a tailor, a manicurist and a hairdresser. He had always been proud of his appearance. When at length, dapper and handsome as ever, he surveyed himself in the glass, his sole recorded comment is an almost staggering tribute to his unassailable conviction that he had nothing in the world to worry about. He turned to his guards with all his accustomed irresistible geniality.

'Well, boys,' he said, 'I'm the same old Sheikh again. You wait a while and you'll see something.'

Precisely what type of miraculous intervention he anticipated was never made clear by him to anyone, but he was still referring to it with his habitual assurance when he was walking cheerily to the place of execution. What he must have thought when they actually electrocuted him, it is impossible to imagine.

LYTTON STRACHEY

Florence Nightingale

I

Every one knows the popular conception of Florence Nightingale. The saintly, self-sacrificing woman, the delicate maiden of high degree who threw aside the pleasures of a life of ease to succour the afflicted, the Lady with the Lamp, gliding through the horrors of the hospital at Scutari, and consecrating with the radiance of her goodness the dying soldier's couch—the vision is familiar to all. But the truth was different. The Miss Nightingale of fact was not as facile fancy painted her. She worked in another fashion, and towards another end; she moved under the stress of an impetus which finds no place in the popular imagination. A Demon possessed her. Now demons, whatever else they may be, are full of interest. And so it happens that in the real Miss Nightingale there was more that was interesting than in the legendary one; there was also less that was agreeable.

Her family was extremely well-to-do, and connected by marriage with a spreading circle of other well-to-do families. There was a large country house in Derbyshire; there was another in the New Forest; there were Mayfair rooms for the London season and all its finest parties; there were tours on the Continent with even more than the usual number of Italian operas and of glimpses at the celebrities of Paris. Brought up among such advantages, it was only natural to suppose that Florence would show a proper appreciation of them by doing her duty in that state of life unto which it had pleased God to call her—in other words, by marrying, after a fitting number of dances and dinner-parties, an eligible gentleman, and living happily ever afterwards. Her sister, her cousins, all the young ladies of her acquaintance, were either getting ready to do this or had already done it. It was inconceivable that Florence should dream of anything else; yet dream she did. Ah! To do her duty in that state of life unto which it had pleased God to call her! Assuredly she would not be behindhand in doing her duty; but unto what state of life *had* it pleased God to call her? That was the question. God's calls are many, and they are strange. Unto what state of life had it pleased Him to call Charlotte Corday, or Elizabeth of Hungary? What was that secret voice in her ear, if it was not a call? Why had she felt, from her earliest years, those mysterious promptings towards . . . she hardly knew what, but certainly towards something very different from anything around her? Why, as a child in the nursery, when her sister had shown a healthy pleasure in tearing her dolls to pieces, had *she* shown an almost morbid one in sewing them up again? Why was she driven now to minister to the poor in their cottages, to watch by sick-beds, to put her dog's wounded paw into elaborate splints as if it was a human being? Why was her head filled with queer imaginations of the country house at Embley turned, by some enchantment, into a hospital, with herself as matron moving about among the beds? Why was even her vision of heaven itself filled with suffering patients to whom she was being useful? So she dreamed and wondered, and, taking out her diary, she poured into it the agitations of her soul. And then the bell rang, and it was time to go and dress for dinner.

As the years passed, a restlessness began to grow upon her. She was unhappy, and at last she knew it. Mrs Nightingale, too, began to notice that there was something wrong. It was very odd; what could be the matter with dear Flo? Mr Nightingale suggested that a husband might be advisable; but the curious thing was that she seemed to take no interest in husbands. And with her attractions, and her accomplishments, too! There was nothing in the world to prevent her making a really brilliant match. But no! She would think of nothing but how to satisfy that singular craving of hers to be *doing* something. As if there was not plenty to do in any case, in the ordinary way, at home. There was the china to look after, and there was her father to be read to after dinner. Mrs Nightingale could not understand it; and then one day her perplexity was changed to consternation and alarm. Florence announced an extreme desire to go to Salisbury Hospital for several months as a nurse; and she confessed to some visionary plan of eventually setting up in a house of her own in a neighbouring village, and there founding 'something like a Protestant sisterhood, without vows, for women of educated feelings'. The whole scheme was summarily brushed aside as preposterous; and Mrs Nightingale, after the first shock of terror, was able to settle down again more or less comfortably to her embroidery. But Florence, who was now twenty-five and

felt that the dream of her life had been shattered, came near to desperation.

And, indeed, the difficulties in her path were great. For not only was
it an almost unimaginable thing in those days for a woman of means
to make her own way in the world and to live in independence, but
the particular profession for which Florence was clearly marked out
both by her instincts and her capacities was at that time a peculiarly
disreputable one. A 'nurse' meant then a coarse old woman, always
ignorant, usually dirty, often brutal, a Mrs Gamp, in bunched-up
sordid garments, tippling at the brandy-bottle or indulging in worse
irregularities. The nurses in the hospitals were especially notorious for
immoral conduct; sobriety was almost unknown among them; and they
could hardly be trusted to carry out the simplest medical duties.
Certainly, things have changed since those days; and that they *have*
changed is due, far more than to any other human being, to Miss
Nightingale herself. It is not to be wondered at that her parents should
have shuddered at the notion of their daughter devoting her life to such
an occupation. 'It was as if,' she herself said afterwards, 'I had wanted
to be a kitchen-maid.' Yet the want, absurd, impracticable as it was,
not only remained fixed immovably in her heart, but grew in intensity
day by day. Her wretchedness deepened into a morbid melancholy.
Everything about her was vile, and she herself, it was clear, to have
deserved such misery, was even viler than her surroundings. Yes, she
had sinned—'standing before God's judgment seat.' 'No one,' she
declared, 'has so grieved the Holy Spirit'; of that she was quite certain.
It was in vain that she prayed to be delivered from vanity and hypocrisy, and she could not bear to smile or to be gay, 'because she hated
God to hear her laugh, as if she had not repented of her sin.'

A weaker spirit would have been overwhelmed by the load of such
distresses—would have yielded or snapped. But this extraordinary
young woman held firm, and fought her way to victory. With an
amazing persistency, during the eight years that followed her rebuff
over Salisbury Hospital, she struggled and worked and planned. While
superficially she was carrying on the life of a brilliant girl in high society,
while internally she was a prey to the tortures of regret and of remorse,
she yet possessed the energy to collect the knowledge and to undergo
the experience which alone could enable her to do what she had determined she would do in the end. In secret she devoured the reports of
medical commissions, the pamphlets of sanitary authorities, the his-
tories of hospitals and homes. She spent the intervals of the London

season in ragged schools and workhouses. When she went abroad with her family, she used her spare time so well that there was hardly a great hospital in Europe with which she was not acquainted, hardly a great city whose slums she had not passed through. She managed to spend some days in a convent school in Rome, and some weeks as a 'Soeur de Charité' in Paris. Then, while her mother and sister were taking the waters at Carlsbad, she succeeded in slipping off to a nursing institution at Kaiserswerth, where she remained for more than three months. This was the critical event of her life. The experience which she gained as a nurse at Kaiserswerth formed the foundation of all her future action and finally fixed her in her career.

But one other trial awaited her. The allurements of the world she had brushed aside with disdain and loathing; she had resisted the subtler temptation which, in her weariness, had sometimes come upon her, of devoting her baffled energies to art or literature; the last ordeal appeared in the shape of a desirable young man. Hitherto, her lovers had been nothing to her but an added burden and a mockery; but now—. For a moment, she wavered. A new feeling swept over her—a feeling which she had never known before, which she was never to know again. The most powerful and the profoundest of all the instincts of humanity laid claim upon her. But it rose before her, that instinct, arrayed—how could it be otherwise?—in the inevitable habiliments of a Victorian marriage; and she had the strength to stamp it underfoot. 'I have an intellectual nature which requires satisfaction,' she noted, 'and that would find it in him. I have a passional nature which requires satisfaction, and that would find it in him. I have a moral, an active nature which requires satisfaction, and that would not find it in his life. Sometimes I think that I will satisfy my passional nature of all events ...' But no, she knew in her heart that it could not be. 'To be nailed to a continuation and exaggeration of my present life ... to put it out of my power ever to be able to seize the chance of forming for myself a true and rich life'—that would be a suicide. She made her choice, and refused what was at least a certain happiness for a visionary good which might never come to her at all. And so she returned to her old life of waiting and bitterness. 'The thoughts and feelings that I have now,' she wrote, 'I can remember since I was six years old. A profession, a trade, a necessary occupation, something to fill and employ all my faculties, I have always felt essential to me, I have always longed for. The first thought I can remember, and the last, was nursing work; and in the absence of this, education work, but more the education of the bad than of the young … everything has been tried, foreign travel, kind friends, everything. My God! What is to become of me?' A desirable young man? Dust and ashes! What was there desirable in such a thing as that? 'In my thirty-first year,' she notes in her diary, 'I see nothing desirable but death.'

Three more years passed, and then at last the pressure of time told; her family seemed to realize that she was old enough and strong enough to have her way; and she became the superintendent of a charitable nursing home in Harley Street. She had gained her independence, though it was in a meagre sphere enough; and her mother was still not quite resigned: surely Florence might at least spend the summer in the country. At times, indeed, among her intimates, Mrs Nightingale almost wept. 'We are ducks,' she said with tears in her eyes, 'who have hatched a wild swan.' But the poor lady was wrong; it was not a swan that they had hatched; it was an eagle.

II

Miss Nightingale had been a year in her nursing-home in Harley Street, when Fate knocked at the door. The Crimean War broke out; the battle of the Alma was fought; and the terrible condition of our military hospitals at Scutari began to be known in England. It sometimes happens that the plans of Providence are a little difficult to follow, but on this occasion all was plain; there was a perfect co-ordination of events. For years Miss Nightingale had been getting ready; at last she was prepared—experienced, free, mature, yet still young—she was thirty-four—desirous to serve, accustomed to command: at that precise moment the desperate need of a great nation came, and she was there to satisfy it. If the war had fallen a few years earlier, she would have lacked the knowledge, perhaps even the power, for such a work; a few years later and she would, no doubt, have been fixed in the routine of some absorbing task, and moreover, she would have been growing old. Nor was it only the coincidence of Time that was remarkable. It so fell out that Sidney Herbert was at the War Office and in the Cabinet; and Sidney Herbert was an intimate friend of Miss Nightingale's, convinced, from personal experience in charitable work, of her supreme capacity. After such premises, it seems hardly more than a matter of course that her letter, in which she offered her services for the East, and Sidney Herbert's letter, in which he asked for them, should actually have crossed in the post. Thus it all happened, without a hitch.

The appointment was made, and even Mrs Nightingale, overawed by the magnitude of the venture, could only approve. A pair of faithful friends offered themselves as personal attendants; thirty-eight nurses were collected; and within a week of a crossing of the letters Miss Nightingale, amid a great burst of popular enthusiasm, left for Constantinople.

Among the numerous letters which she received on her departure was one from Dr Manning, who at that time was working in comparative obscurity as a Catholic priest in Bayswater. 'God will keep you,' he wrote, 'and my prayer for you will be that your one object of Worship, Pattern of Imitation, and source of consolation and strength may be the Sacred Heart of our Divine Lord.'

To what extent Dr Manning's prayer was answered must remain a matter of doubt; but this much is certain, that, if ever a prayer was needed, it was needed then for Florence Nightingale. For dark as had been the picture of the state of affairs at Scutari, revealed to the English public in the despatches of the *Times* correspondent and in a multitude of private letters, yet the reality turned out to be darker still. What had occurred was, in brief, the complete break-down of our medical arrangements at the seat of war. The origins of this awful failure were complex and manifold; they stretched back through long years of peace and carelessness in England; they could be traced through endless ramifications of administrative incapacity—from the inherent faults of confused systems to the petty bunglings of minor officials, from the inevitable ignorance of Cabinet Ministers to the fatal exactitudes of narrow routine. In the inquiries which followed it was clearly shown that the evil was in reality that worst of all evils—one which has been caused by nothing in particular and for which no one in particular is to blame. The whole organization of the war machine was incompetent and out of date. The old Duke had sat for a generation at the Horse Guards repressing innovations with an iron hand. There was an extraordinary overlapping of authorities, an almost incredible shifting of responsibilities to and fro. As for such a notion as the creation and the maintenance of a really adequate medical service for the army—in that atmosphere of aged chaos, how could it have entered anybody's head? Before the war, the easy-going officials at Westminster were naturally persuaded that all was well—or at least as well as could be expected; when some one, for instance, actually had the temerity to suggest the formation of a corps of army nurses, he was at once laughed out of court. When the war had begun, the gallant British officers in control of affairs had other things to think about than the petty details of medical organization. Who had bothered with such trifles in the Peninsula? And surely, on that occasion, we had done pretty well. Thus the most obvious precautions were neglected, the most necessary preparations put off from day to day. The principal medical officer of the army, Dr Hall, was summoned from India at a moment's notice, and was unable to visit England before taking up his duties at the front. And it was not until after the battle of the Alma, when we had been at war for many months, that we acquired hospital accommodation at Scutari for more than a thousand men. Errors, follies, and vices on the part of individuals there doubtless were; but, in the general reckoning, they were of small account—insignificant symptoms of the deep disease of the body politic—the enormous calamity of administrative collapse.

Miss Nightingale arrived at Scutari—a suburb of Constantinople, on the Asiatic side of the Bosphorus—on November 4th, 1854; it was ten days after the battle of Balaclava, and the day before the battle of Inkerman. The organization of the hospitals, which had already given way under the stress of the battle of the Alma, was now to be subjected to the further pressure which these two desperate and bloody engagements implied. Great detachments of wounded were already beginning to pour in. The men, after receiving such summary treatment as could be given them at the smaller hospitals in the Crimea itself, were forthwith shipped in batches of two hundred across the Black Sea to Scutari. This voyage was in normal times one of four days and a half; but the times were no longer normal, and now the transit often lasted for a fortnight or three weeks. It received, not without reason, the name of 'the middle passage'. Between, and sometimes on the decks, the wounded, the sick, and the dying were crowded—men who had just undergone the amputation of limbs, men in the clutches of fever or of frostbite, men in the last stages of dysentery and cholera—without beds, sometimes without blankets, often hardly clothed. The one or two surgeons on board did what they could; but medical stores were lacking, and the only form of nursing available was that provided by a handful of invalid soldiers, who were usually themselves prostrate by the end of the voyage. There was no other food beside the ordinary salt rations of ship diet; and even the water was sometimes so stored that it was out of reach of the weak. For many months, the average of deaths during these voyages was 74 in the thousand; the corpses were shot out into the waters; and who shall say that they were the most unfortunate? At Scutari, the landing-stage, constructed with all the perverseness of

Oriental ingenuity, could only be approached with great difficulty, and, in rough weather, not at all. When it was reached, what remained of the men in the ships had first to be disembarked, and then conveyed up a steep slope of a quarter of a mile to the nearest of the hospitals. The most serious cases might be put upon stretchers—for there were far too few for all; the rest were carried or dragged up the hill by such convalescent soldiers as could be got together, who were not too obviously infirm for the work. At last the journey was accomplished; slowly, one by one, living or dying, the wounded were carried up into the hospital. And in the hospital what did they find?

Lasciate ogni speranza, voi ch'entrate: the delusive doors bore no such inscription; and yet behind them Hell yawned. Want, neglect, confusion, misery—in every shape and in every degree of intensity—filled the endless corridors and the vast apartments of the gigantic barrack-house, which, without forethought or preparation, had been hurriedly set aside as the chief shelter for the victims of the war. The very building itself was radically defective. Huge sewers underlay it, and cesspools loaded with filth wafted their poison into the upper rooms. The floors were in so rotten a condition that many of them could not be scrubbed; the walls were thick with dirt; incredible multitudes of vermin swarmed everywhere. And, enormous as the building was, it was yet too small. It contained four miles of beds, crushed together so close that there was but just room to pass between them. Under such conditions, the most elaborate system of ventilation might well have been at fault; but here there was no ventilation. The stench was indescribable. 'I have been well acquainted,' said Miss Nightingale, 'with the dwellings of the worst parts of most of the great cities in Europe, but have never been in any atmosphere which I could compare with that of the Barrack Hospital at night.' The structural defects were equalled by the deficiencies in the commonest objects of hospital use. There were not enough bedsteads; the sheets were of canvas, and so coarse that the wounded men recoiled from them, begging to be left in their blankets; there was no bedroom furniture of any kind, and empty beer-bottles were used for candlesticks. There were no basins, no towels, no soap, no brooms, no mops, no trays, no plates; there were neither slippers nor scissors, neither shoebrushes nor blacking; there were no knives or forks or spoons. The supply of fuel was constantly deficient. The cooking arrangements were preposterously inadequate, and the laundry was a farce. As for purely medical materials, the tale was no better. Stretchers, splints, bandages—all were lacking; and so were the most ordinary drugs.

To replace such wants, to struggle against such difficulties, there was a handful of men overburdened by the strain of ceaseless work, bound down by the traditions of official routine, and enfeebled either by old age or inexperience or sheer incompetence. They had proved utterly unequal to their task. The principal doctor was lost in the imbecilities of a senile optimism. The wretched official whose business it was to provide for the wants of the hospital was tied fast hand and foot by red tape. A few of the younger doctors struggled valiantly, but what could they do? Unprepared, disorganized, with such help only as they could find among the miserable band of convalescent soldiers drafted off to tend their sick comrades, they were faced with disease, mutilation, and death in all their most appalling forms, crowded multitudinously about them in an ever increasing mass. They were like men in a shipwreck, fighting, not for safety, but for the next moment's bare existence—to gain, by yet another frenzied effort, some brief respite from the waters of destruction.

In these surroundings, those who had been long inured to scenes of human suffering—surgeons with a world-wide knowledge of agonies, soldiers familiar with fields of carnage, missionaries with remembrances of famine and of plague—yet found a depth of horror which they had never known before. There were moments, there were places, in the Barrack Hospital at Scutari, where the strongest hand was struck with trembling, and the boldest eye would turn away its gaze.

Miss Nightingale came, and she at any rate, in that Inferno, did not abandon hope. For one thing, she brought material succour. Before she left London she had consulted Dr Andrew Smith, the head of the Army Medical Board, as to whether it would be useful to take out stores of any kind to Scutari; and Dr Andrew Smith had told her that 'nothing was needed.' Even Sidney Herbert had given her similar assurances; possibly, owing to an oversight, there might have been some delay in the delivery of the medical stores, which, he said, had been sent out from England 'in profusion,' but 'four days would have remedied this.' She preferred to trust her own instincts, and at Marseilles purchased a large quantity of miscellaneous provisions, which were of the utmost use at Scutari. She came, too, amply provided with money—in all, during her stay in the east, about £7000 reached her from private sources; and, in addition, she was able to avail herself of another valuable means of help. At the same time as herself, Mr Macdonald, of the *Times*, had arrived at Scutari, charged with the duty of administering the large sums of money collected through the agency of that newspaper in aid of the sick and wounded; and Mr Macdonald had the sense to see that the best use he could make of the *Times* Fund was to put it at the disposal of Miss Nightingale. 'I cannot conceive,' wrote an eye-witness, 'as I now calmly look back on the first three weeks after the arrival of the wounded from Inkerman, how it could have been possible to have avoided a state of things too disastrous to contemplate, had not Miss Nightingale been there, with the means placed at her disposal by Mr Macdonald.' But the official view was different. What! Was the public service to admit, by accepting outside charity, that it was unable to discharge its own duties without the assistance of private and irregular benevolence? Never! And accordingly when Lord Stratford de Redcliffe, our ambassador at Constantinople, was asked by Mr Macdonald to indicate how the *Times* Fund could best be employed, he answered that there was indeed one object to which it might very well be devoted—the building of an English Protestant Church at Pera.

Mr Macdonald did not waste further time with Lord Stratford, and immediately joined forces with Miss Nightingale. But, with such a frame of mind in the highest quarters, it is easy to imagine the kind of disgust and alarm with which the sudden intrusion of a band of amateurs and females must have filled the minds of the ordinary officer and the ordinary military surgeon. They could not understand it; what had women to do with war? Honest Colonels relieved their spleen by the cracking of heavy jokes about 'the Bird'; while poor Dr Hall, a rough terrier of a man, who had worried his way to the top of his profession, was struck speechless with astonishment, and at last observed that Miss Nightingale's appointment was extremely droll.

Her position was, indeed, an official one, but it was hardly the easier for that. In the hospitals it was her duty to provide the services of herself and her nurses when they were asked for by the doctors, and not until then. At first some of the surgeons would have nothing to say to her, and, though she was welcomed by others, the majority were hostile and suspicious. But gradually she gained ground. Her good will could not be denied, and her capacity could not be disregarded. With consummate tact, with all the gentleness of supreme strength, she managed at last to impose her personality upon the susceptible, overwrought, discouraged, and helpless group of men in authority who surrounded her. She stood firm; she was a rock in the angry ocean; with her alone was safety, comfort, life. And so it was that hope dawned at Scutari. The reign of chaos and old night began to dwindle; order came upon the scene, and common sense, and forethought, and decision, radiating out from the little room off the great gallery in the Barrack Hospital where, day and night, the Lady Superintendent was at her task. Progress might be slow, but it was sure. The first sign of a great change came with the appearance of some of those necessary objects with which the hospitals had been unprovided for months. The sick men began to enjoy the use of towels and soap, knives and forks, combs and tooth-brushes. Dr Hall might snort when he heard of it, asking, with a growl, what a soldier wanted with a tooth-brush; but the good work went on. Eventually the whole business of purveying to the hospitals was, in effect, carried out by Miss Nightingale. She alone, it seemed, whatever the contingency, knew where to lay her hands on what was wanted; she alone could dispense her stores with readiness; above all she alone possessed the art of circumventing the pernicious influences of official etiquette. This was her greatest enemy, and sometimes even she was baffled by it. On one occasion 27,000 shirts, sent out at her instance by the Home Government, arrived, were landed, and were only waiting to be un-packed. But the official 'Purveyor' intervened; 'he could not unpack them, he said, 'without a Board.' Miss Nightingale pleaded in vain; the sick and wounded lay half-naked shivering for want of clothing; and three weeks elapsed before the Board released the shirts. A little later, however, on a similar occasion, Miss Nightingale felt that she could assert her own authority. She ordered a Government consignment to be forcibly opened, while the miserable 'Purveyor' stood by, wringing his hands in departmental agony.

Vast quantities of valuable stores sent from England lay, she found, engulfed in the bottomless abyss of the Turkish Custom House. Other ship-loads, buried beneath munitions of war destined for Balaclava, passed Scutari without a sign, and thus hospital materials were some-times carried to and fro three times over the Black Sea, before they reached their destination. The whole system was clearly at fault, and Miss Nightingale suggested to the home authorities that a Government Store House should be instituted at Scutari for the reception and distribution of the consignments. Six months after her arrival this was done.

In the meantime she had reorganized the kitchens and the laundries in the hospitals. The ill-cooked hunks of meat, vilely served at irregular intervals, which had hitherto been the only diet for the sick men were replaced by punctual meals, well-prepared and appetizing, while strengthening extra foods—soups and wines and jellies ('preposterous luxuries,' snarled Dr Hall)—were distributed to those who needed them. One thing, however, she could not effect. The separation of the bones from the meat was no part of official cookery: the rule was that the food must be divided into equal portions, and if some of the portions were all bone—well, every man must take his chance. The rule, perhaps, was not a very good one; but there it was. 'It would require a new Regulation of the Service,' she was told, 'to bone the meat.' As for the washing arrangements, they were revolutionized. Up to the time of Miss Nightingale's arrival the number of shirts the authorities had succeeded in washing was seven. The hospital bedding, she found, was 'washed' in cold water. She took a Turkish house, had boilers installed, and employed soldiers' wives to do the laundry work. The expenses were defrayed from her own funds and that of the *Times*; and henceforward the sick and wounded had the comfort of clean linen.

Then she turned her attention to their clothing. Owing to military exigencies the greater number of the men had abandoned their kit; their knapsacks were lost for ever; they possessed nothing but what was on their persons, and that was usually only fit for speedy destruction. The 'Purveyor', of course, pointed out that, according to the regulations, all soldiers should bring with them into hospital an adequate supply of clothing, and he declared that it was no business of his to make good their deficiencies. Apparently, it was the business of Miss Nightingale. She procured socks, boots, and shirts in enormous quantities; she had trousers made, she rigged up dressing-gowns. 'The fact is,' she told Sidney Herbert, 'I am now clothing the British Army.'

All at once, word came from the Crimea that a great new contingent of sick and wounded might shortly be expected. Where were they to go? Every available inch in the wards was occupied; the affair was serious and pressing, and the authorities stood aghast. There were some dilapidated rooms in the Barrack Hospital, unfit for human habitation, but Miss Nightingale believed that if measures were promptly taken they might be made capable of accommodating several hundred beds. One of the doctors agreed with her; the rest of the officials were irresolute: it would be a very expensive job, they said; it would involve building; and who could take the responsibility? The proper course was that a representation should be made to the Director-General of the Army Medical Department in London; then the Director-General would apply to the Horse Guards, the Horse Guards would move the Ordnance, the Ordnance would lay the matter before the Treasury, and, if the Treasury gave its consent, the work might be correctly carried through, several months after the necessity for it had disappeared. Miss Nightingale, however, had made up her mind, and she persuaded Lord Stratford—or thought she had persuaded him—to give his sanction to the required expenditure. A hundred and twenty-five workmen were immediately engaged, and the work was begun. The workmen struck; whereupon Lord Stratford washed his hands of the whole business. Miss Nightingale engaged two hundred other workmen on her own authority, and paid the bill out of her own resources. The wards were ready by the required date; five hundred sick men were received in them; and all the utensils, including knives, forks, spoons, cans and towels, were supplied by Miss Nightingale.

This remarkable woman was in truth performing the function of an administrative chief. How had this come about? Was she not in reality merely a nurse? Was it not her duty simply to tend the sick? And indeed, was it not as a ministering angel, a gentle 'lady with a lamp' that she actually impressed the minds of her contemporaries? No doubt that was so; and yet it is no less certain that, as she herself said, the specific business of nursing was 'the least important of the functions into which she had been forced.' It was clear that in the state of disorganization into which the hospitals at Scutari had fallen the most pressing, the really vital, need was for something more than nursing; it was for the necessary elements of civilized life—the commonest material objects, the most ordinary cleanliness, the rudimentary habits of order and authority. 'Oh, dear Miss Nightingale,' said one of her party as they were approaching Constantinople, 'when we land, let there be no delays, let us get straight to nursing the poor fellows!' 'The strongest will be wanted at the wash-tub,' was Miss Nightingale's answer. And it was upon the wash-tub, and all that the wash-tub stood for, that she expended her greatest energies. Yet to say that is perhaps to say too much. For to those who watched her at work among the sick, moving day and night from bed to bed, with that unflinching courage, with that indefatigable vigilance, it seemed as if the concentrated force of an undivided and unparalleled devotion could hardly suffice for that portion of her task alone. Wherever, in those vast wards, suffering was at its worst and the need for help was greatest, there, as if by magic, was Miss Nightingale. Her super-human equanimity would, at the moment of some ghastly operation, nerve the victim to endure and almost to hope. Her sympathy would assuage the pangs of dying and bring back to those still living something of the forgotten charm of life. Over and over again her untiring efforts rescued those whom the surgeons had abandoned as beyond the possibility of cure. Her mere presence brought with it a strange influence. A passionate idolatry spread among the men: they kissed her shadow as it passed. They did more. 'Before she came,' said a soldier, 'there was cussin' and swearin', but after that it was as 'oly as a church.' The most cherished privilege of the fighting man was abandoned for the sake of Miss Nightingale. In those 'lowest sinks of human misery,' as she herself put it, she never heard the use of one expression 'which could distress a gentlewoman.'

She was heroic; and these were the humble tributes paid by those of grosser mould to that high quality. Certainly, she was heroic. Yet her heroism was not of that simple sort so dear to the readers of novels and the compilers of hagiologies—the romantic sentimental heroism with which mankind loves to invest its chosen darlings: it was made of sterner stuff. To the wounded soldier on his couch of agony she might well appear in the guise of a gracious angel of mercy; but the military surgeons, and the orderlies, and her own nurses, and the 'Purveyor,' and Dr Hall, and even Lord Stratford himself could tell a different story. It was not by gentle sweetness and womanly self-abnegation that she had brought order out of chaos in the Scutari Hospitals, that, from her own resources, she had clothed the British Army, that she had spread her dominion over the serried and reluctant powers of the official world; it was by strict method, by stern discipline, by rigid attention to detail, by ceaseless labour, by the fixed determination of an indomitable will. Beneath her cool and calm demeanour lurked fierce and passionate fires. As she passed through the wards in her plain dress, so quiet, so unassuming, she struck the casual observer simply as the pattern of a perfect lady; but the keener eye perceived something more than that—the serenity of high deliberation in the scope of the capacious brow, the sign of power in the dominating curve of the thin nose, and the traces of a harsh and dangerous temper—something peevish, something mocking, and yet something precise—in the small and delicate mouth. There was humour in the face; but the curious watcher might wonder whether it was humour of a very pleasant kind; might ask himself, even as he heard the laughter and marked the jokes with which she cheered· the spirits of her patients, what sort of sardonic merriment this same lady might not give vent to, in the privacy of her chamber. As for her voice, it was true of it, even more than of her countenance, that it 'had that in it one must fain call master'. Those clear tones were in no need of emphasis: 'I never heard her raise her voice,' said one of her companions. Only, when she had spoken, it seemed as if nothing could follow but obedience. Once, when she had given some direction, a doctor ventured to remark that the thing could not be done. 'But it must be done,' said Miss Nightingale. A chance bystander, who heard the words, never forgot through all his life the irresistible authority of them. And they were spoken quietly—very quietly indeed.

Late at night, when the long miles of beds lay wrapped in darkness, Miss Nightingale would sit at work in her little room, over her correspondence. It was one of the most formidable of all her duties. There were hundreds of letters to be written to the friends and relations of soldiers; there was the enormous mass of official documents to be dealt with; there were her own private letters to be answered; and, most important of all, there was the composition of her long and confidential reports to Sidney Herbert. These were by no means official communications. Her soul, pent up all day in the restraint and reserve of a vast responsibility, now at last poured itself out in these letters with all its natural vehemence, like a swollen torrent through an open sluice. Here, at least, she did not mince matters. Here she painted in her darkest colours the hideous scenes which surrounded her; here she tore away remorselessly the last veils still shrouding the abominable truth. Then she would fill pages with recommendations and suggestions, with criticisms of the minutest details of organization, with elaborate calculations of contingencies, with exhaustive analyses and statistical statements piled up in breathless eagerness one on the top of the other. And then her pen, in the virulence of its volubility, would rush on to the discussion of individuals, to the denunciation of an incompetent surgeon or the ridicule of a self-sufficient nurse. Her sarcasm searched the ranks of the officials with the deadly and unsparing precision of a machine-gun. Her nick-names were terrible. She respected no one: Lord Stratford, Lord Raglan, Lady Stratford, Dr Andrew Smith, Dr Hall, the Commissary-General, the Purveyor—she fulminated against them all. The intolerable futility of mankind obsessed her like a nightmare, and she gnashed her teeth against it. 'I do well to be angry,' was the burden of her cry. How many just men were there at Scutari? How many who cared at all for the sick, or had done anything for their relief Were there ten? Were there five? Was there even one? She could not be sure.

At one time, during several weeks, her vituperations descended upon the head of Sidney Herbert himself. He had misinterpreted her wishes, he had traversed her positive instructions, and it was not until he had admitted his error and apologized in abject terms that he was allowed again into favour. While this misunderstanding was at its height an aristocratic young gentleman arrived at Scutari with a recommendation from the Minister. He had come out from England filled with a romantic desire to render homage to the angelic heroine of his dreams. He had, he said, cast aside his life of ease and luxury; he would devote his days and nights to the service of that gentle lady; he would perform the most menial offices, he would 'fag' for her, he would be her footman—and feel requited by a single smile. A single smile, indeed, he had, but it was of an unexpected kind. Miss Nightingale at first refused to see him, and then, when she consented, believing that he was an emissary sent by Sidney Herbert to put her in the wrong over their dispute, she took notes of her conversation with him, and insisted on his signing them at the end of it. The young gentleman returned to England by the next ship.

This quarrel with Sidney Herbert was, however, an exceptional incident. Alike by him, and by Lord Panmure, his successor at the War Office, she was firmly supported; and the fact that during the whole of her stay at Scutari she had the Home Government at her back, was her trump card in her dealings with the hospital authorities. Nor was it only the Government that was behind her: public opinion in England early recognized the high importance of her mission, and its enthusiastic appreciation of her work soon reached an extraordinary height. The Queen herself was deeply moved. She made repeated inquiries as to the welfare of Miss Nightingale; she asked to see her accounts of the wounded, and made her the intermediary between the throne and the troops. 'Let Mrs Herbert know,' she wrote to the War Minister, 'that I wish Miss Nightingale and the ladies would tell these poor noble, wounded, and sick men that *no one* takes a warmer interest or feels *more* for their sufferings or admires their courage and heroism *more* than their Queen. Day and night she thinks of her beloved troops. So does the Prince. Beg Mrs Herbert to communicate these my words to those ladies, as I know that *our* sympathy is much valued by these noble fellows.' The letter was read aloud in the wards by the Chaplain. 'It is a very feeling letter,' said the men.

And so the months passed, and that fell winter which had begun with Inkerman and had dragged itself out through the long agony of the investment of Sebastopol, at last was over. In May, 1855, after six months of labour, Miss Nightingale could look with something like satisfaction at the condition of the Scutari hospitals. Had they done nothing more than survive the terrible strain which had been put upon them, it would have been a matter for congratulation; but they had done much more than that; they had marvellously improved. The confusion and the pressure in the wards had come to an end; order reigned in them, and cleanliness; the supplies were bountiful and prompt; important sanitary works had been carried out. One simple comparison of figures was enough to reveal the extraordinary change: the rate of mortality among the cases treated had fallen from 42 per cent. to 22 per thousand. But still the indefatigable lady was not satisfied. The main problem had been solved—the physical needs of the men had been provided for; their mental and spiritual needs remained. She set up and furnished reading-rooms and recreation-rooms. She started classes and lectures. Officers were amazed to see her treating their men as if they were human beings, and assured her that she would only end by 'spoiling the brutes'. But that was not Miss Nightingale's opinion, and she was justified. The private soldier began to drink less, and even—though that seemed impossible—to save his pay. Miss Nightingale became a banker for the army, receiving and sending home large sums of money every month. At last, reluctantly, the Government followed suit, and established machinery of its own for the remission of money. Lord Panmure, however, remained sceptical; 'it will do no good,' he pronounced; 'the British soldier is not a remitting animal.' But, in fact, during the next six months, £71,000 was sent home.

Amid all these activities, Miss Nightingale took up the further task of inspecting the hospitals in the Crimea itself. The labour was extreme, and the conditions of life were almost intolerable. She spent whole days in the saddle, or was driven over those bleak and rocky heights in a baggage cart. Sometimes she stood for hours in the heavily falling snow, and would only reach her hut at dead of night after walking for miles through perilous ravines. Her powers of resistance seemed incredible, but at last they were exhausted. She was attacked by fever, and for a moment came very near to death. Yet she worked on; if she could not move, she could at least write; and write she did until her mind had left her; and after it had left her, in what seemed the delirious trance of death itself, she still wrote. When, after many weeks, she was strong enough to travel, she was implored to return to England, but she utterly refused. She would not go back, she said, before the last of the soldiers had left Scutari.

This happy moment had almost arrived, when suddenly the smouldering hostilities of the medical authorities burst out into a flame. Dr Hall's labours had been rewarded by a K.C.B.—letters which, as Miss Nightingale told Sidney Herbert, she could only suppose to mean

'Knight of the Crimean Burial-grounds'—and the honour had turned his head. He was Sir John, and he would be thwarted no longer. Disputes had lately arisen between Miss Nightingale and some of the nurses in the Crimean hospitals. The situation had been embittered by rumours of religious dissensions, for, while the Crimean nurses were Roman Catholics, many of those at Scutari were suspected of a regrettable propensity towards the tenets of Dr Pusey. Miss Nightingale was by no means disturbed by these sectarian differences, but any suggestion that her supreme authority over all the nurses with the Army was in doubt was enough to rouse her to fury; and it appeared that Mrs Bridgeman, the Reverend Mother in the Crimea, had ventured to call that authority in question. Sir John Hall thought that his opportunity had come, and strongly supported Mrs Bridgeman—or, as Miss Nightingale preferred to call her, the 'Reverend Brickbat'. There was a violent struggle; Miss Nightingale's rage was terrible. Dr Hall, she declared, was doing his best to 'root her out of the Crimea'. She would bear it no longer; the War Office was playing her false; there was only one thing to be done—Sidney Herbert must move for the production of papers in the House of Commons, so that the public might be able to judge between her and her enemies. Sidney Herbert with great difficulty calmed her down. Orders were immediately despatched putting her supremacy beyond doubt, and the Reverend Brickbat withdrew from the scene. Sir John, however, was more tenacious. A few weeks later, Miss Nightingale and her nurses visited the Crimea for the last time, and the brilliant idea occurred to him that he could crush her by a very simple expedient—he would starve her into submission; and he actually ordered that no rations of any kind should be supplied to her. He had already tried this plan with great effect upon an unfortunate medical man whose presence in the Crimea he had considered an intrusion; but he was now to learn that such tricks were thrown away upon Miss Nightingale. With extraordinary foresight, she had brought with her a great supply of food; she succeeded in obtaining more at her own expense and by her own exertions; and thus for ten days, in that inhospitable country, she was able to feed herself and twenty-four nurses. Eventually the military authorities intervened in her favour, and Sir John had to confess that he was beaten.

It was not until July, 1856—four months after the Declaration of Peace—that Miss Nightingale left Scutari for England. Her reputation was now enormous, and the enthusiasm of the public was unbounded. The royal approbation was expressed by the gift of a brooch, accompanied by a private letter. 'You are, I know, well aware,' wrote Her Majesty, 'of the high sense I entertain of the Christian devotion which you have displayed during this great and bloody war, and I need hardly repeat to you how warm my admiration is for your services, which are fully equal to those of my dear and brave soldiers, whose sufferings you have had the *privilege* of alleviating in so merciful a manner. I am, however anxious of marking my feelings in a manner which I trust will be agreeable to you, and therefore send you with this letter a brooch, the form and emblems of which commemorate your great and blessed work, and which I hope you will wear as a mark of the high approbation of your Sovereign!'

'It will be a very great satisfaction to me,' Her Majesty added, 'to make the acquaintance of one who has set so bright an example to our sex.'

The brooch, which was designed by the Prince Consort, bore a St George's cross in red enamel, and the Royal cypher surmounted by diamonds. The whole was encircled by the inscription 'Blessed are the Merciful'.

III

The name of Florence Nightingale lives in the memory of the world by virtue of the lurid and heroic adventure of the Crimea. Had she died—as she nearly did—upon her return to England, her reputation would hardly have been different; her legend would have come down to us almost as we know it to-day—that gentle vision of female virtue which first took shape before the adoring eyes of the sick soldiers at Scutari. Yet, as a matter of fact, she lived for more than half a century after the Crimean War; and during the greater part of that long period all the energy and all the devotion of her extraordinary nature were working at their highest pitch. What she accomplished in those years of unknown labour could, indeed, hardly have been more glorious than her Crimean triumphs; but it was certainly more important. The true history was far stranger even than the myth. In Miss Nightingale's own eyes the adventure of the Crimea was a mere incident—scarcely more than a useful stepping-stone in her career. It was the fulcrum with which she hoped to move the world; but it was only the fulcrum. For more than a generation she was to sit in secret, working her lever: and her real life began at the very moment when, in the popular imagination, it had ended.

She arrived in England in a shattered state of health. The hard-ships and the ceaseless effort of the last two years had undermined her nervous system; her heart was pronounced to be affected; she suffered constantly from fainting-fits and terrible attacks of utter physical prostration. The doctors declared that one thing alone would save her—a complete and prolonged rest. But that was also the one thing with which she would have nothing to do. She had never been in the habit of resting; why should she begin now? Now, when her opportunity had come at last; now, when the iron was hot, and it was time to strike? No; she had work to do; and, come what might, she would do it. The doctors protested in vain; in vain her family lamented and entreated, in vain her friends pointed out to her the madness of such a course. Madness? Mad—possessed—perhaps she was. A demoniac frenzy had seized upon her. As she lay upon her sofa, gasping, she devoured blue-books, dictated letters, and, in the intervals of her palpitations, cracked her febrile jokes. For months at a stretch she never left her bed. For years she was in daily ex-pectation of death. But she would not rest. At this rate, the doctors assured her, even if she did not die, she would become an invalid for life. She could not help that; there was the work to be done; and, as for rest, very likely she might rest ... when she had done it.

Wherever she went, in London or in the country, in the hills of Derbyshire, or among the rhododendrons at Embley, she was haunted by a ghost. It was the spectre of Scutari—the hideous vision of the organization of a military hospital. She would lay that phantom, or she would perish. The whole system of the Army Medical Department, the education of the Medical Officer, the regulations of hospital procedure ... *rest?* How could she rest while these things were as they were, while, if the like necessity were to arise again, the like results would follow? And, even in peace and at home, what was the sanitary condition of the Army? The mortality in the barracks was, she found, nearly double the mortality in civil life. 'You might as well take 1100 men every year out upon Salisbury Plain and shoot them,' she said. After inspecting the hospitals at Chatham, she smiled grimly. 'Yes, this is one more symptom of the system which, in the Crimea, put to death 16,000 men.' Scutari had given her knowledge; and it had given her power too: her enormous reputation was at her back—an incalculable force. Other work, other duties, might lie before her; but the most urgent, the most obvious, of all was to look to the health of the Army.

One of her very first steps was to take advantage of the invitation which Queen Victoria had sent her to the Crimea, together with the commemorative brooch. Within a few weeks of her return she visited Balmoral, and had several interviews with both the Queen and the Prince Consort. 'She put before us,' wrote the Prince in his diary, 'all the defects of our present military hospital system, and the reforms that are needed.' She related 'the whole story' of her experiences in the East; and, in addition, she managed to have some long and confidential talks with His Royal Highness on metaphysics and religion. The impression which she created was excellent. 'Sie gefällt uns sehr,' noted the Prince, 'ist sehr bescheiden.' Her Majesty's comment was different—'Such a *head*! I wish we had her at the War Office.'

But Miss Nightingale was not at the War Office, and for a very simple reason: she was a woman. Lord Panmure, however, *was* (though indeed the reason for that was not quite so simple); and it was upon Lord Panmure that the issue of Miss Nightingale's efforts for reform must primarily depend. That burly Scottish nobleman had not, in spite of his most earnest endeavours, had a very easy time of it as Secretary of State for War. He had come into office in the middle of the Sebastopol campaign, and had felt himself very well fitted for the position, since he had acquired in former days an inside knowledge of the Army—as a Captain of Hussars. It was this inside knowledge which had enabled him to inform Miss Nightingale with such authority that 'the British soldier is not a remitting animal.' And perhaps it was this same consciousness of a command of his subject which had impelled him to write a dispatch to Lord Raglan, blandly informing the Commander-in-Chief in the Field just how he was neglecting his duties, and pointing out to him that if he would only try he really might do a little better next time. Lord Raglan's reply, calculated as it was to make its recipient sink into the earth, did not quite have that effect upon Lord Panmure, who, whatever might have been his faults, had never been accused of being supersensitive. However, he allowed the matter to drop; and a little later Lord Raglan died—worn out, some people said, by work and anxiety. He was succeeded by an excellent red-nosed old gentleman, General Simpson, whom nobody has ever heard of, and who took Sebastopol. But Lord Panmure's relations with him were hardly more satisfactory than his relations with Lord Raglan; for, while Lord Raglan had been too independent, poor General Simpson erred in the opposite direction, perpetually asked advice, suffered from lumbago, doubted, his nose growing daily redder and redder, whether he was fit for his post, and, by alternate mails, sent in and withdrew his resignation. Then, too, both the General and the Minister suffered acutely from that distressingly useful new invention, the electric telegraph. On one occasion General Simpson felt obliged actually to expostulate. 'I think, my Lord,' he wrote, 'that some telegraphic messages reach us that cannot be sent under due authority, and are perhaps unknown to you, although under the protection of your Lordship's name. For instance, I was called up last night, a dragoon having come express with a telegraphic message in these words, "Lord Panmure to General Simpson—Captain Jarvis has been bitten by a centipede. How is he now?"' General Simpson might have put up with this, though to be sure it did seem 'rather too trifling an affair to call for a dragoon to ride a couple of miles in the dark that he may knock up the Commander of the Army out of the very small allowance of sleep permitted him'; but what was really more than he could bear was to find 'upon sending in the morning another mounted dragoon to inquire after Captain Jarvis, four miles off, that he never has been bitten at all, but has had a boil, from which he is fast recovering.' But Lord Panmure had troubles of his own. His favourite nephew, Captain Dowbiggin, was at the front, and to one of his telegrams to the Commander-in-Chief the Minister had taken occasion to append the following carefully qualified sentence—'I recommend Dowbiggin to your notice, should you have a vacancy, and if he is fit.' Unfortunately, in those early days, it was left to the discretion of the telegraphist to compress the messages which passed through his hands; so that the result was that Lord Panmure's delicate appeal reached its destination in the laconic form of 'Look after Dowb.' The Headquarters Staff were at first extremely puzzled; they were at last extremely amused. The story spread; and 'Look after Dowb' remained for many years the familiar formula for describing official hints in favour of deserving nephews.

And now that all this was over, now that Sebastopol had been, somehow or another, taken, now that peace was, somehow or another, made, now that the troubles of office might surely be expected to be at an end at last—here was Miss Nightingale breaking in upon the scene, with her talk about the state of the hospitals and the necessity for sanitary reform. It was most irksome; and Lord Panmure almost began to wish that he was engaged upon some more congenial occupation—discussing, perhaps, the constitution of the Free Church of Scotland—a question in which he was profoundly interested. But no; duty was paramount; and he set himself, with a sigh of resignation, to the task of doing as little of it as he possibly could.

'The Bison' his friends called him; and the name fitted both his physical demeanour and his habit of mind. That large low head seemed to have been created for butting rather than for anything else. There he stood, four-square and menacing, in the doorway of reform and it remained to be seen whether the bulky mass, upon whose solid hide even the barbed arrows of Lord Raglan's scorn had made no mark, would prove amenable to the pressure of Miss Nightingale. Nor was he alone in the doorway. There loomed behind him the whole phalanx of professional conservatism, the stubborn supporters of the out-of-date, the worshippers and the victims of War Office routine. Among these it was only natural that Dr Andrew Smith, the head of the Army Medical Department, should have been pre-eminent—Dr Andrew Smith, who had assured Miss Nightingale before she left England that 'nothing was wanted at Scutari'. Such were her opponents; but she too was not without allies. She had gained the ear of Royalty—which was something; at any moment that she pleased she could gain the ear of the public—which was a great deal. She had a host of admirers and friends; and—to say nothing of her personal qualities—her knowledge, her tenacity, her tact—she possessed, too, one advantage which then, far more even than now, carried an immense weight—she belonged to the highest circle of society. She moved naturally among Peers and Cabinet Ministers—she was one of their own set; and in those days their set was a very narrow one. What kind of attention would such persons have paid to some middle-class woman with whom they were not acquainted, who possessed great experience of army nursing and had decided views upon hospital reform? They would have politely ignored her; but it was impossible to ignore Flo Nightingale. When she spoke, they were obliged to listen; and, when they had once begun to do that—what might not follow? She knew her power, and she used it. She supported her weightiest minutes with familiar witty little notes. The Bison began to look grave. It might be difficult—it might be damned difficult—to put down one's head against the white hand of a lady.

Of Miss Nightingale's friends, the most important was Sidney Herbert. He was a man upon whom the good fairies seemed to have showered, as he lay in his cradle, all their most enviable goods. Well born, handsome, rich, the master of Wilton—one of those great country-houses, clothed with the glamour of a historic past, which are the peculiar glory of England—he possessed, besides all these advantages, so charming, so lively, so gentle a disposition that no one who had once come near him could ever be his enemy. He was, in fact, a man of whom it was difficult not to say that he was a perfect English gentleman. For his virtues were equal even to his good fortune. He was religious—deeply religious: 'I am more and more convinced every day,' he wrote, when he had been for some years a Cabinet Minister, 'that in politics, as in everything else, nothing can be right which is not in accordance with the spirit of the Gospel.' No one was more unselfish; he was charitable and benevolent to a remarkable degree; and he devoted the whole of his life with an unwavering conscientiousness to the public service. With such a character, with such opportunities, what high hopes must have danced before him, what radiant visions of accomplished duties, of ever-increasing usefulness, of beneficent power, of the consciousness of disinterested success! Some of those hopes and visions were, indeed, realized; but, in the end, the career of Sidney Herbert seemed to show that, with all their generosity, there was some gift or other—what was it?—some essential gift—which the good fairies had withheld, and that even the qualities of a perfect English gentleman may be no safeguard against anguish, humiliation, and defeat.

That career would certainly have been very different if he had never known Miss Nightingale. The alliance between them which had begun with her appointment to Scutari, which had grown closer and closer while the war lasted, developed, after her return, into one of the most extraordinary of friendships. It was the friendship of a man and a woman intimately bound together by their devotion to a public cause; mutual affection, of course, played a part in it, but it was an incidental part; the whole soul of the relationship was a community of work. Perhaps out of England such an intimacy could hardly have existed—an intimacy so utterly untinctured not only by passion itself but by the suspicion of it. For years Sidney Herbert saw Miss Nightingale almost daily, for long hours together, corresponding with her incessantly when they were apart; and the tongue of scandal was silent; and one of the most devoted of her admirers was his wife. But what made the connection still more remarkable was the way in which the parts that were played in it were divided between the two. The man who acts, decides, and achieves; the woman who encourages, applauds, and—from a distance—inspires:—the combination is common enough; but Miss Nightingale was neither an Aspasia nor an Egeria. In her case it is almost true to say that the rôles were reversed; the qualities of pliancy and sympathy fell to the man, those of command and initiative to the woman. There was one thing only which Miss Nightingale lacked in her equipment for public life; she had not—she never could have—the public power and authority which belong to the successful politician. That power and authority Sidney Herbert possessed; the fact was obvious, and the conclusions no less so: it was through the man that the woman must work her will. She took hold of him, taught him, shaped him, absorbed him, dominated him through and through. He did not resist—he did not wish to resist; his natural inclination lay along the same path as hers; only that terrific personality swept him forward at her own fierce pace and with her own relentless stride. Swept him—where to? Ah! Why had he ever known Miss Nightingale? If Lord Panmure was a bison, Sidney Herbert, no doubt, was a stag—a comely, gallant creature springing through the forest; but the forest is a dangerous place. One has the image of those wide eyes fascinated suddenly by something feline, something strong; there is a pause; and then the tigress has her claws in the quivering haunches; and then—!

Besides Sidney Herbert, she had other friends who, in a more restricted sphere, were hardly less essential to her. If, in her condition of bodily collapse, she were to accomplish what she was determined that she should accomplish, the attentions and the services of others would be absolutely indispensable. Helpers and servers she must have; and accordingly there was soon formed about her a little group of devoted disciples upon whose affections and energies she could implicitly rely. Devoted, indeed, these disciples were, in no ordinary sense of the term; for certainly she was no light task-mistress, and he who set out to be of use to Miss Nightingale was apt to find, before he had gone very far, that he was in truth being made use of in good earnest—to the very limit of his endurance and his capacity. Perhaps, even beyond those limits; why not? Was she asking of others more than she was giving herself? Let them look at her lying there pale and breathless on the couch; could it be said that she spared herself? Why, then, should she spare others? And it was not for her own sake that she made these claims. For her own sake, indeed! No! They all knew it! it was for the sake of the work. And so the little band, bound body and soul in that strange servitude, laboured on ungrudgingly. Among the most faithful was her 'Aunt Mai,' her father's sister, who from the earliest days had stood beside her, who had helped her to escape from the thraldom of family life, who had been with her at Scutari, and who now acted almost the part of a mother to her, watching over her with infinite care in all the movements and uncertainties which her state of health involved. Another constant attendant was her brother-in-law, Sir Harry Verney, whom she found particularly valuable in parliamentary affairs. Arthur Clough, the poet, also a connection by marriage, she used in other ways. Ever since he had lost his faith at the time of the Oxford Movement, Clough had passed his life in a condition of considerable uneasiness, which was increased rather than diminished by the practice of poetry. Unable to decide upon the purpose of an existence whose savour had fled together with his belief in the Resurrection, his spirits lowered still further by ill-health, and his income not all that it should be, he had determined to seek the solution of his difficulties in the United States of America. But, even there, the solution was not forthcoming; and when, a little later, he was offered a post in a government department at home, he accepted it, came to live in London, and immediately fell under the influence of Miss Nightingale. Though the purpose of existence might be still uncertain and its nature still unsavoury, here, at any rate, under the eye of this inspired woman, was something real, something earnest: his only doubt was—could he be of any use? Certainly he could. There were a great number of miscellaneous little jobs which there was nobody handy to do. For instance, when Miss Nightingale was travelling, there were the railway-tickets to be taken; and there were proof-sheets to be corrected; and then there were parcels to be done up in brown paper, and carried to the post. Certainly he could be useful. And so, upon such occupations as these, Arthur Clough was set to work. 'This that I see, is not all,' he comforted himself by reflecting, 'and this that I do is but little; nevertheless it is good, though there is better than it.'

As time went on, her 'Cabinet', as she called it, grew larger. Officials with whom her work brought her into touch and who sympathized with her objects, were pressed into her service; and old friends of the Crimean days gathered round her when they returned to England. Among these the most indefatigable was Dr Sutherland, a sanitary expert, who for more than thirty years acted as her confidential private secretary, and surrendered to her purposes literally the whole of his life. Thus sustained and assisted, thus slaved for and adored, she prepared to beard the Bison.

Two facts soon emerged, and all that followed turned upon them. It became clear, in the first place, that that imposing mass was not immovable, and, in the second, that its movement, when it did move, would be exceeding slow. The Bison was no match for the Lady. It was in vain that he put down his head and planted his feet in the earth; he could not withstand her; the white hand forced him back. But the process was an extraordinarily gradual one. Dr Andrew Smith and all his War Office phalanx stood behind, blocking the way; the poor Bison groaned inwardly, and cast a wistful eye towards the happy pastures of the Free Church of Scotland; then slowly, with infinite reluctance, step by step, he retreated, disputing every inch of the ground.

The first great measure, which, supported as it was by the Queen, the Cabinet, and the united opinion of the country, it was impossible to resist, was the appointment of a Royal Commission to report upon the health of the Army. The question of the composition of the Commission then immediately arose; and it was over this matter that the first hand-to-hand encounter between Lord Panmure and Miss Nightingale took place. They met, and Miss Nightingale was victorious; Sidney Herbert was appointed Chairman; and, in the end, the only member of the Commission opposed to her views was Dr Andrew Smith. During the interview, Miss Nightingale made an important discovery: she found that 'the Bison was bullyable'—the hide was the hide of a Mexican buffalo, but the spirit was the spirit of an Alderney calf. And there was one thing above all others which the huge creature dreaded—an appeal to public opinion. The faintest hint of such a terrible eventuality made his heart dissolve within him; he would agree to anything—he would cut short his grouse-shooting—he would make a speech in the House of Lords—he would even overrule Dr Andrew Smith—rather than that. Miss Nightingale held the fearful threat in reserve—she would speak out what she knew; she would publish the truth to the whole world, and let the whole world judge between them. With supreme skill, she kept this sword of Damocles poised above the Bison's head, and more than once she was actually on the point of really dropping it. For his recalcitrancy grew and grew. The *personnel* of the Commission once determined upon, there was a struggle, which lasted for six months, over the nature of its powers. Was it to be an efficient body, armed with the right of full inquiry and wide examination, or was it to be a polite official contrivance for exonerating Dr Andrew Smith? The War Office phalanx closed its ranks, and fought tooth and nail; but it was defeated: the Bison was bullyable. 'Three months from this day,' Miss Nightingale had written at last, 'I publish my experience of the Crimean Campaign, and my suggestions for improvement, unless there has been a fair and tangible pledge by that time for reform.' Who could face that?

And, if the need came, she meant to be as good as her word. For she had now determined, whatever might be the fate of the Commission, to draw up her own report upon the questions at issue. The labour involved was enormous; her health was almost desperate; but she did not flinch, and after six months of incredible industry she had put together and written with her own hand her 'Notes affecting the Health, Efficiency, and Hospital Administration of the British Army.' This extraordinary composition, filling more than eight hundred closely printed pages, laying down vast principles of far-reaching reform, discussing the minutest details of a multitude of controversial subjects, containing an enormous mass of information of the most varied kinds—military, statistical, sanitary, architectural—was never given to the public, for the need never came; but it formed the basis of the Report of the Royal Commission; and it remains to this day the leading authority on the medical administration of armies.

Before it had been completed the struggle over the powers of the Commission had been brought to a victorious close. Lord Panmure had given way once more; he had immediately hurried to the Queen to obtain her consent; and only then, when her Majesty's initials had been irrevocably affixed to the fatal document, did he dare to tell Dr Andrew Smith what he had done. The Commission met, and another immense load fell upon Miss Nightingale's shoulders. To-day she would, of course, have been one of the Commission herself; but at that time the idea of a woman appearing in such a capacity was unheard of; and no one even suggested the possibility of Miss Nightingale's doing so. The result was that she was obliged to remain behind the scenes throughout, to coach Sidney Herbert in private at every important juncture, and to convey to him and to her other friends upon the Commission the vast funds of her expert knowledge—so essential in the examination of witnesses—by means of innumerable consultations, letters, and memoranda. It was even doubtful whether the proprieties would admit of her giving evidence; and at last, as a compromise, her modesty only allowed her to do so in the form of written answers to written questions. At length the grand affair was finished. The Commission's Report, embodying almost word for word the suggestions of Miss Nightingale, was drawn up by Sidney Herbert. Only one question remained to be answered—would anything, after all, be done? Or would the Royal Commission, like so many other Royal Commissions before and since, turn out to have achieved nothing but the concoction of a very fat blue-book on a very high shelf?

And so the last and the deadliest struggle with the Bison began. Six months had been spent in coercing him into granting the Commission effective powers; six more months were occupied by the work of the Commission; and now yet another six were to pass in extorting from him the means whereby the recommendations of the Commission might be actually carried out. But, in the end, the thing was done. Miss Nightingale seemed indeed, during these months, to be upon the very brink of death. Accompanied by the faithful Aunt Mai, she moved from place to place—to Hampstead, to Highgate, to Derbyshire, to Malvern—in what appeared to be a last desperate effort to find health somewhere; but she carried that with her which made health impossible. Her desire for work could now scarcely be distinguished from mania. At one moment she was writing a 'last letter' to Sidney Herbert; at the next she was offering to go out to India to nurse the sufferers in the Mutiny. When Dr Sutherland wrote, imploring her to take a holiday, she raved. Rest!—'I am lying without my head, without my claws, and you all peck at me. It is *de rigueur, d'obligation*, like the saying something to one's hat, when one goes into church, to say to me all that has been said to me 110 times a day during the last three months. It is the *obbligato* on the violin, and the twelve violins all practise it together, like the clocks striking 12 o'clock at night all over London, till I say like Xavier de Maistre, *Assez, je le sais, je ne le sais que trop*. I am not a penitent; but you are like the R.C. confessor, who says what is *de rigueur* ...' Her wits began to turn, and there was no holding her. She worked like a slave in a mine. She began to believe, as she had begun to believe at Scutari, that none of her fellow-workers had their hearts in the business; if they had, why did they not work as she did? She could only see slackness and stupidity around her. Dr Sutherland, of course, was grotesquely muddle-headed; and Arthur Clough incurably lazy. Even Sidney Herbert ... oh yes, he had simplicity and candour and quickness of perception, no doubt; but he was an eclectic; and what could one hope for from a man who went away to fish in Ireland just when the Bison most needed bullying? As for the Bison himself he had fled to Scotland, where he remained buried for many months. The fate of the vital recommendation in the Commission's Report—the appointment of four Sub-Commissions charged with the duty of determining upon the details of the proposed reforms and of putting them into execution—still hung in the balance. The Bison consented to everything; and then, on a flying visit to London, withdrew his consent and hastily returned to Scotland. Then for many weeks all business was suspended; he had gout—gout in the hands, so that he could not write. 'His gout was always handy,' remarked Miss Nightingale. But eventually it was clear even to the Bison that the game was up, and the inevitable surrender came.

There was, however, one point in which he triumphed over Miss Nightingale. The building of Netley Hospital had been begun, under his orders, before her return to England. Soon after her arrival she examined the plans, and found that they reproduced all the worst faults of an out-of-date and mischievous system of hospital construction. She therefore urged that the matter should be reconsidered, and in the meantime the building stopped. But the Bison was obdurate; it would be very expensive, and in any case it was too late. Unable to make any impression on him, and convinced of the extreme importance of the question, she determined to appeal to a higher authority. Lord Palmerston was Prime Minister; she had known him from her childhood; he was a near neighbour of her father's in the New Forest. She went down to the New Forest, armed with the plans of the proposed hospital and all the relevant information, stayed the night at Lord Palmerston's house, and convinced him of the necessity of rebuilding Netley. 'It seems to me,' Lord Palmerston wrote to Lord Panmure, 'that at Netley all consideration of what would best tend to the comfort and recovery of the patients has been sacrificed to the vanity of the architect, whose sole object has been to make a building which cut a dash when looked at from the Southampton river ... Pray, therefore, stop all further progress in the work until the matter can be duly considered.' But the Bison was not to be moved by one peremptory letter, even if it was from the Prime Minister. He put forth all his powers of procrastination, Lord Palmerston lost interest in the subject, and so the chief military hospital in England was triumphantly completed on unsanitary principles, with unventilated rooms, and with all the patients' windows facing north-east.

But now the time had come when the Bison was to trouble and to be troubled no more. A vote in the House of Commons brought about the fall of Lord Palmerston's Government, and Lord Panmure found himself at liberty to devote the rest of his life to the Free Church of Scotland. After a brief interval, Sidney Herbert became Secretary of State for War. Great was the jubilation in the Nightingale Cabinet: the day of achievement had dawned at last. The next two and a half years (1859–61) saw the introduction of the whole system of reforms for which Miss Nightingale had been struggling so fiercely— reforms which make Sidney Herbert's tenure of power at the War Office an important epoch in the history of the British Army. The four Sub-Commissions, firmly established under the immediate control of the minister, and urged forward by the relentless perseverance of Miss Nightingale, set to work with a will. The barracks and the hospitals were remodelled; they were properly ventilated and warmed and lighted for the first time; they were given a water supply which actually supplied water, and kitchens where, strange to say, it was possible to cook. Then the great question of the Purveyor—that portentous functionary whose powers and whose lack of powers had weighed like a nightmare upon Scutari—was taken in hand, and new regulations were laid down, accurately defining his responsibilities and his duties. One Sub-Commission reorganized the medical statistics of the Army. Another established—in spite of the last convulsive efforts of the Department—an Army Medical School. Finally the Army Medical Department itself was completely reorganized; an administrative code was drawn up; and the great and novel principle was established that it was as much a part of the duty of the authorities to look after the soldier's health as to look after his sickness. Besides this, it was at last officially admitted that he had a moral and intellectual side. Coffee-rooms and reading-rooms, gymnasiums and workshops were instituted. A new era did in truth appear to have begun. Already by 1861 the mortality in the Army had decreased by one half since the days of the Crimea. It was no wonder that even vaster possibilities began now to open out before Miss Nightingale. One thing was still needed to complete and to assure her triumphs. The Army Medical Department was indeed reorganized; but the great central machine was still untouched. The War Office itself—!—If she could remould *that* nearer to her heart's desire—there indeed would be a victory! And until that final act was accomplished, how could she be certain that all the rest of her achievements might not, by some capricious turn of Fortune's wheel—a change of Ministry, perhaps, replacing Sidney Herbert by some puppet of the permanent official gang—be swept to limbo in a moment?

Meanwhile, still ravenous for more and yet more work, her activities had branched out into new directions. The army in India claimed her attention. A Sanitary Commission, appointed at her suggestion, and working under her auspices, did for our troops there what the four Sub-Commissions were doing for those at home. At the same time, these very years which saw her laying the foundations of the whole modern system of medical work in the army, saw her also beginning to bring her knowledge, her influence, and her activity into the service of the country at large. Her *Notes on Hospitals* (1859) revolutionized the theory of hospital construction and hospital management. She was immediately recognized as the leading expert upon all the questions involved; her advice flowed unceasingly and in all directions, so that there is no great hospital to-day which does not bear upon it the impress of her mind. Nor was this all. With the opening of the Nightingale Training School for Nurses at St Thomas's Hospital (1860), she became the founder of modern nursing.

But a terrible crisis was now fast approaching. Sidney Herbert had consented to undertake the root and branch reform of the War Office. He had sallied forth into that tropical jungle of festooned obstructiveness, of inter-twisted irresponsibilities, of crouching prejudices, of abuses grown stiff and rigid with antiquity, which for so many years to come was destined to lure reforming ministers to their doom. 'The War Office,' said Miss Nightingale, 'is a very slow office, an enormously expensive office, and one in which the Minister's intentions can be entirely negatived by all his sub-departments, and those of each of the sub-departments by every other.' It was true; and, of course, at the first rumour of a change, the old phalanx of reaction was bristling with its accustomed spears. At its head stood no longer Dr Andrew Smith, who, some time since, had followed the Bison into outer darkness, but a yet more formidable figure, the permanent Under Secretary himself, Sir Benjamin Hawes—Ben Hawes the Nightingale cabinet irreverently dubbed him—a man remarkable even among civil servants for adroitness in baffling inconvenient inquiries, resource in raising false issues, and, in short, a consummate command of all the arts of officially sticking in the mud. 'Our scheme will probably result in Ben Hawes's resignation,' Miss Nightingale said; 'and that is another of its advantages.' Ben Hawes himself, however, did not quite see it in that light. He set himself to resist the wishes of the Minister by every means in his power. The struggle was long and desperate; and, as it proceeded, it gradually became evident to Miss Nightingale that something was the matter with Sidney Herbert. What was it? His health, never strong, was, he said, in danger of collapsing under the strain of his work. But, after all, what is illness, when there is a War Office to be reorganized? Then he began to talk of retiring altogether from public life. The doctors were consulted, and declared that, above all things, what was necessary was rest. Rest! She grew seriously alarmed. Was it possible that, at the last moment, the crowning wreath of victory was to be snatched from her grasp? She was not to be put aside by doctors; they were talking nonsense; the necessary thing was not rest but the reform of the War Office; and, besides, she knew very well from her own case what one could do even when one was on the point of death. She expostulated vehemently, passionately; the goal was so near, so very near; he could not turn back now! At any rate, he could not resist Miss Nightingale. A compromise was arranged. Very reluctantly, he exchanged the turmoil of the House of Commons for the dignity of the House of Lords, and he remained at the War Office. She was delighted. 'One fight more, the best and the last,' she said.

For several more months the fight did indeed go on. But the strain upon him was greater even than she perhaps could realize. Besides the intestine war in his office, he had to face a constant battle in the Cabinet with Mr Gladstone—a more redoubtable antagonist even than Ben Hawes—over the estimates. His health grew worse and worse. He was attacked by fainting-fits; and there were some days when he could only just keep himself going by gulps of brandy. Miss Nightingale spurred him forward with her encouragements and her admonitions, her zeal and her example. But at last his spirit began to sink as well as his body. He could no longer hope; he could no longer desire; it was useless, all useless; it was utterly impossible. He had failed. The dreadful moment came when the truth was forced upon him: he would never be able to reform the War Office. But a yet more dreadful moment lay behind; he must go to Miss Nightingale and tell her that he was a failure, a beaten man.

'Blessed are the merciful!' What strange ironic prescience had led Prince Albert, in the simplicity of his heart, to choose that motto for the Crimean brooch? The words hold a double lesson; and, alas! when she brought herself to realize at length what was indeed the fact and what there was no helping, it was not in mercy that she turned upon her old friend. 'Beaten!' she exclaimed. 'Can't you see that you've simply thrown away the game? And so noble a game! Sidney Herbert beaten! And beaten by Ben Hawes! It is a worse disgrace ...' her full rage burst out at last, '... a worse disgrace than the hospitals at Scutari.'

He dragged himself away from her, dragged himself to Spa, hoping vainly for a return to health, and then, despairing, back again to England to Wilton, to the majestic house standing there resplendent in the summer sunshine, among the great cedars which had lent their shade to Sir Philip Sidney, and all those familiar, darling haunts of beauty which he loved, each one of them, 'as if they were persons'; and at Wilton he died. After having received the Eucharist, he had become perfectly calm; then, almost unconscious, his lips were seen to be moving. Those about him bent down. 'Poor Florence! Poor Florence!' they just caught. '... Our joint work ... unfinished ... tried to do ...' and they could hear no more.

When the onward rush of a powerful spirit sweeps a weaker one to its destruction, the commonplaces of the moral judgment are better left unmade. If Miss Nightingale had been less ruthless, Sidney Herbert would not have perished; but then, she would not have been Miss Nightingale. The force that created was the force that destroyed. It was her Demon that was responsible. When the fatal news reached her, she was overcome by agony. In the revulsion of her feelings, she made a worship of the dead man's memory; and the facile instrument which had broken in her hand she spoke of for ever after as her 'Master'. Then, almost at the same moment, another blow fell on her. Arthur Clough, worn out by labours very different from those of Sidney Herbert, died too: never more would he tie up her parcels. And yet a third disaster followed. The faithful Aunt Mai did not, to be sure, die; no, she did something almost worse: she left Miss Nightingale. She was growing old, and she felt that she had closer and more imperative duties with her own family. Her niece could hardly forgive her. She poured out, in one of her enormous letters, a passionate diatribe upon the faithlessness, the lack of sympathy, the stupidity, the ineptitude of women. Her doctrines had taken no hold among them; she had never known one who had *appris à apprendre*; she could not even get a woman secretary; 'they don't know the names of the Cabinet Ministers—they don't know which of the Churches has Bishops and which not.' As for the spirit of self-sacrifice, well—Sidney Herbert and Arthur Clough were men, and they indeed had shown their devotion; but women—! She would mount three widow's caps 'for a sign'. The first two would be for Clough and for her Master; but the third, 'the biggest widow's cap of all'—would be for Aunt Mai. She did well to be angry; she was deserted in her hour of need; and, after all, could she be sure that even the male sex was so impeccable? There was Dr Sutherland, bungling as usual. Perhaps even he intended to go off, one of these days, too? She gave him a look, and he shivered in his shoes. No!—she grinned sardonically; she would always have Dr Sutherland. And then she reflected that there was one thing more that she would always have—her work.

IV

Sidney Herbert's death finally put an end to Miss Nightingale's dream of a reformed War Office. For a moment, indeed, in the first agony of her disappointment, she had wildly clutched at a straw; she had written to Mr Gladstone to beg him to take up the burden of Sidney Herbert's work. And Mr Gladstone had replied with a sympathetic account of the funeral.

Succeeding Secretaries of State managed between them to undo a good deal of what had been accomplished, but they could not undo it all; and for ten years more (1862–72) Miss Nightingale remained a potent influence at the War Office. After that, her direct connection with the army came to an end, and her energies began to turn more and more completely towards more general objects. Her work upon hospital reform assumed enormous proportions; she was able to improve the conditions in infirmaries and workhouses; and one of her most remarkable papers forestalls the recommendations of the Poor Law Commission of 1909. Her training school for nurses, with all that it involved in initiative, control, responsibility, and combat, would have been enough in itself to have absorbed the whole efforts of at least two lives of ordinary vigour. And at the same time her work in connection with India, which had begun with the Sanitary Commission on the Indian Army, spread and ramified in a multitude of directions. Her tentacles reached the India Office and succeeded in establishing a hold even upon those slippery high places. For many years it was *de rigueur* for the newly appointed Viceroy, before he left England, to pay a visit to Miss Nightingale.

After much hesitation, she had settled down in a small house in South Street, where she remained for the rest of her life. That life was a very long one; the dying woman reached her ninety-first year. Her ill-health gradually diminished; the crises of extreme danger became less frequent, and at last altogether ceased; she remained an invalid, but an invalid of a curious character—an invalid who was too weak to walk downstairs and who worked far harder than most Cabinet Ministers. Her illness, whatever it may have been, was certainly not inconvenient. It involved seclusion; and an extraordinary, an unparalleled seclusion was, it might almost have been said, the mainspring of Miss Nightingale's life. Lying on her sofa in the little upper room in South Street, she combined the intense vitality of a dominating woman of the world with the mysterious and romantic quality of a myth. She was a legend in her lifetime, and she knew it. She tasted the joys of power, like those Eastern Emperors whose autocratic rule was based upon invisibility, with the mingled satisfactions of obscurity and fame. And she found the machinery of illness hardly less effective as a barrier against the eyes of men than the ceremonial of a palace. Great statesmen and renowned generals were obliged to beg for audiences; admiring princesses from foreign countries found that they must see her at her own time, or not at all; and the ordinary mortal had no hope of ever getting beyond the downstairs sitting-room and Dr Sutherland. For that indefatigable disciple did, indeed, never desert her. He might be impatient, he might be restless, but he remained. His 'incurable looseness of thought', for so she termed it, continued at her service to the end. Once, it is true, he had actually ventured to take a holiday; but he was recalled, and he did not repeat the experiment. He was wanted downstairs. There he sat, transacting business, answering correspondence, interviewing callers, and exchanging innumerable notes with the unseen power above. Sometimes word came down that Miss Nightingale was just well enough to see one of her visitors. The fortunate man was led up, was ushered, trembling, into the shaded chamber, and, of course, could never afterwards forget the interview. Very rarely, indeed, once or twice a year, perhaps, but nobody could be quite certain, in deadly secrecy, Miss Nightingale went out for a drive in the Park. Unrecognized, the living legend flitted for a moment before the common gaze. And the precaution was necessary; for there were times when, at some public function, the rumour of her presence was spread abroad; and ladies, mistaken by the crowd for Miss Nightingale, were followed, pressed upon, and vehemently supplicated— 'Let me touch your shawl,'—'Let me stroke your arm'; such was the strange adoration in the hearts of the people. That vast reserve of force lay there behind her; she could use it, if she would. But she preferred never to use it. On occasions, she might hint or threaten; she might balance the sword of Damocles over the head of the Bison; she might, by a word, by a glance, remind some refractory minister, some unpersuadable viceroy, sitting in audience with her in the little upper room, that she was something more than a mere sick woman, that she had only, so to speak, to go to the window and wave her handkerchief, for ... dreadful things to follow. But that was enough; they understood; the myth was there—obvious, portentous, impalpable; and so it remained to the last.

With statesmen and governors at her beck and call, with her hands on a hundred strings, with mighty provinces at her feet, with foreign governments agog for her counsel, building hospitals, training nurses—she still felt that she had not enough to do. She sighed for more worlds to conquer—more, and yet more. She looked about her— what was there left? Of course! Philosophy! After the world of action, the world of thought. Having set right the health of the British Army, she would now do the same good service for the religious convictions of mankind. She had long noticed—with regret—the growing tendency towards free-thinking among artisans. With regret, but not altogether with surprise: the current teaching of Christianity was sadly to seek; nay, Christianity itself was not without its defects. She would rectify these errors. She would correct the mistakes of the Churches; she would point out just where Christianity was wrong; and she would explain to the artisans what the facts of the case really were. Before her departure for the Crimea, she had begun this work; and now, in the interval of her other labours, she completed it. Her 'Suggestions for Thought to the Searchers after Truth among the Artisans of England' (1860), unravels, in the course of three portly volumes, the difficulties—hitherto, curiously enough, unsolved—connected with such matters as Belief in God, the Plan of Creation, the Origin of Evil, the Future Life, Necessity and Free Will, Law, and the Nature of Morality. The Origin of Evil, in particular, held no perplexities for Miss Nightingale. 'We cannot conceive,' she remarks, 'that Omnipotent Righteousness would find satisfaction in *solitary existence.*' This being so, the only question remaining to be asked is, 'What beings should we then conceive that God would create?' Now, He cannot create perfect beings, 'since, essentially, perfection is one'; if He did so, He would only be adding to Himself. Thus the conclusion is obvious: He *must* create *im*perfect ones. Omnipotent Righteousness, faced by the intolerable *impasse* of a solitary existence, finds itself bound, by the very nature of the case, to create the hospitals at Scutari.

Whether this argument would have satisfied the artisans, was never discovered, for only a very few copies of the book were printed for private circulation. One copy was sent to Mr Mill, who acknowledged it in an extremely polite letter. He felt himself obliged, however, to confess that he had not been altogether convinced by Miss Nightingale's proof of the existence of God. Miss Nightingale was surprised and mortified; she had thought better of Mr Mill; for surely her proof of the existence of God could hardly be improved upon. 'A law,' she had pointed out, 'implies a lawgiver.' Now the Universe is full of laws—the law of gravitation, the law of the excluded middle, and many others; hence it follows that the Universe has a lawgiver—and what would Mr Mill be satisfied with, if he was not satisfied with that?

Perhaps Mr Mill might have asked why the argument had not been pushed to its logical conclusion. Clearly, if we are to trust the analogy of human institutions, we must remember that laws are, as a matter of fact, not dispensed by lawgivers, but passed by Act of Parliament. Miss Nightingale, however, with all her experience of public life, never stopped to consider the question whether God might not be a Limited Monarchy.

Yet her conception of God was certainly not orthodox. She felt towards Him as she might have felt towards a glorified sanitary engineer; and in some of her speculations she seems hardly to distinguish between the Deity and the Drains. As one turns over these singular pages, one has the impression that Miss Nightingale has got the Almighty too into her clutches, and that, if He is not careful, she will kill Him with overwork.

Then, suddenly, in the very midst of the ramifying generalities of her metaphysical disquisitions there is an unexpected turn, and the reader is plunged all at once into something particular, something personal, something impregnated with intense experience—a virulent invective upon the position of women in the upper ranks of society. Forgetful alike of her high argument and of the artisans, the bitter creature rails through a hundred pages of close print at the falsities of family life, the ineptitudes of marriage, the emptinesses of convention, in the spirit of an Ibsen or a Samuel Butler. Her fierce pen, shaking with intimate anger, depicts in biting sentences the fearful fate of an unmarried girl in a wealthy household. It is a *cri du cœur*; and then, as suddenly, she returns once more to instruct the artisans upon the nature of Omnipotent Righteousness.

Her mind was, indeed, better qualified to dissect the concrete and distasteful fruits of actual life than to construct a coherent system of abstract philosophy. In spite of her respect for Law, she was never at home with a generalization. Thus, though the great achievement of her life lay in the immense impetus which she gave to the scientific treatment of sickness, a true comprehension of the scientific method itself was alien to her spirit. Like most great men of action – perhaps like all – she was simply an empiricist. She believed in what she saw, and she acted accordingly; beyond that she would not go. She had found in Scutari that fresh air and light played an effective part in the prevention of the maladies with which she had to deal; and that was enough for her; she would not inquire further; what were the general principles underlying that fact—or even whether there were any—she refused to consider. Years after the discoveries of Pasteur and Lister, she laughed at what she called the 'germ-fetish'. There was no such thing as 'infection'; she had never seen it, therefore it did not exist. But she *had* seen the good effects of fresh air; therefore there could be no doubt about them; and therefore it was essential that the bedrooms of patients should be well ventilated. Such was her doctrine; and in those days of hermetically sealed windows it was a very valuable one. But it was a purely empirical doctrine, and thus it led to some unfortunate results. When, for instance, her influence in India was at its height, she issued orders that all hospital windows should be invariably kept open. The authorities, who knew what an open window in the hot weather meant, protested, but in vain; Miss Nightingale was incredulous. She knew nothing of the hot weather, but she did know the value of fresh air—from personal experience; the authorities were talking nonsense; and the windows must be kept open all the year round. There was a great outcry from all the doctors in India, but she was firm; and for a moment it seemed possible that her terrible commands would have to be put into execution. Lord Lawrence, however, was Viceroy, and he was able to intimate to Miss Nightingale, with sufficient authority, that he himself had decided upon the question, and that his decision must stand, even against her own. Upon that, she gave way, but reluctantly and quite unconvinced; she was only puzzled by the unexpected weakness of Lord Lawrence. No doubt, if she had lived to-day, and if her experience had lain, not among cholera cases at Scutari, but among yellow-fever cases in Panama, she would have declared fresh air a fetish, and would have maintained to her dying day that the only really effective way of dealing with disease was by the destruction of mosquitoes.

Yet her mind, so positive, so realistic, so ultra-practical, had its singular revulsions, its mysterious moods of mysticism and of doubt. At times, lying sleepless in the early hours, she fell into long strange agonized meditations, and then, seizing a pencil, she would commit to paper the confessions of her soul. The morbid longings of her pre-Crimean days came over her once more; she filled page after page with self-examination, self-criticism, self-surrender. 'O Father,' she wrote, 'I submit, I resign myself, I accept with all my heart this stretching out of Thy hand to save me ... O how vain it is, the vanity of vanities, to live in men's thoughts instead of God's!' She was lonely, she was miserable. 'Thou knowest that through all these horrible twenty years, I have been supported by the belief that I was working with Thee who wert bringing every one, even our poor nurses, to perfection,'—and yet, after all, what was the result? Had not even she been an unprofitable servant? One night, waking suddenly, she saw, in the dim light of the nightlamp, tenebrous shapes upon the wall. The past rushed back upon her. 'Am I she who once stood on that Crimean height?' she wildly asked—' "The Lady with a lamp shall stand ..." The lamp shows me only my utter shipwreck.'

She sought consolation in the writings of the Mystics and in a correspondence with Mr Jowett. For many years the Master of Balliol acted as her spiritual adviser. He discussed with her in a series of enormous letters the problems of religion and philosophy; he criticized her writings on those subjects with the tactful sympathy of a cleric who was also a man of the world; and he even ventured to attempt at times to instil into her rebellious nature some of his own peculiar suavity. 'I sometimes think,' he told her, 'that you ought seriously to consider how your work may be carried on, not with less energy, but in a calmer spirit. I am not blaming the past ... But I want the peace of God to settle on the future.' He recommended her to spend her time no longer in 'conflicts with Government offices,' and to take up some literary work. He urged her to 'work out her notion of Divine Perfection,' in a series of essays for *Frazer's Magazine*. She did so; and the result was submitted to Mr Froude, who pronounced the second essay to be 'even more pregnant than the first. I cannot tell,' he said, 'how sanitary, with disordered intellects, the effects of such papers will be.' Mr Carlyle, indeed, used different language, and some remarks of his about a lost lamb bleating on the mountains having been unfortunately repeated to Miss Nightingale, all Mr Jowett's suavity was required to keep the peace. In a letter of fourteen sheets, he turned her attention from this painful topic towards a discussion of Quietism. 'I don't see why,' said the Master of Balliol, 'active life might not become a sort of passive life too.' And then, he added, 'I sometimes fancy there are possibilities of human character much greater than have been realized.' She found such sentiments helpful, underlining them in blue pencil; and, in return, she assisted her friend with a long series of elaborate comments upon the Dialogues of Plato, most of which he embodied in the second edition of his translation. Gradually her interest became more personal; she told him never to work again after midnight, and he obeyed her. Then she helped him to draw up a special form of daily service for the College Chapel, with selections from the Psalms under the heads of 'God the Lord, God the Judge, God the Father, and God the Friend,'—though, indeed, this project was never realized; for the Bishop of Oxford disallowed the alterations, exercising his legal powers, on the advice of Sir Travers Twiss.

Their relations became intimate. 'The spirit of the twenty-third psalm and the spirit of the nineteenth psalm should be united in our lives,' Mr Jowett said. Eventually, she asked him to do her a singular favour. Would he, knowing what he did of her religious views, come to London and administer to her the Holy Sacrament? He did not hesitate, and afterwards declared that he would always regard the occasion as a solemn event in his life. He was devoted to her; though the precise nature of his feelings towards her never quite transpired. Her feelings towards him were more mixed. At first, he was 'that great and good man,'—'that true saint, Mr Jowett'; but, as time went on, some gall was mingled with the balm; the acrimony of her nature asserted itself. She felt that she gave more sympathy than she received; she was exhausted, she was annoyed, by his conversation. Her tongue, one day, could not refrain from shooting out at him. 'He comes to me, and he talks to me,' she said, 'as if I were someone else.'

V

At one time she had almost decided to end her life in retirement, as a patient at St Thomas's Hospital. But partly owing to the persuasions of Mr Jowett, she changed her mind; for forty-five years she remained in South Street; and in South Street she died. As old age approached, though her influence with the official world gradually diminished, her activities seemed to remain as intense and widespread as before. When hospitals were to be built, when schemes of sanitary reform were in agitation, when wars broke out, she was still the adviser of all Europe. Still, with a characteristic self-assurance, she watched from her Mayfair bedroom over the welfare of India. Still, with an indefatigable enthusiasm, she pushed forward the work, which, perhaps, was nearer to her heart, more completely her own, than all the rest—the training of nurses. In her moments of deepest depression, when her greatest achievements seemed to lose their lustre, she thought of her nurses, and was comforted. The ways of God, she found, were strange indeed. 'How inefficient I was in the Crimea,' she noted. 'Yet He has raised up from it trained nursing.'

At other times she was better satisfied. Looking back, she was amazed by the enormous change which, since her early days, had come over the whole treatment of illness, the whole conception of public and domestic health—a change in which, she knew, she had played her part. One of her Indian admirers, the Aga Khan, came to visit her. She expatiated on the marvellous advances she had lived to see in the management of hospitals, in drainage, in ventilation, in sanitary work of every kind. There was a pause; and then, 'Do you think you are improving?' asked the Aga Khan. She was a little taken aback, and said, 'What do you mean by "improving"?' He replied, 'Believing more in God.' She saw that he had a view of God which was different from hers. 'A most interesting man,' she noted after the interview; 'but you could never teach him sanitation.'

When old age actually came, something curious happened. Destiny, having waited very patiently, played a queer trick on Miss Nightingale. The benevolence and public spirit of that long life had only been equalled by its acerbity. Her virtue had dwelt in hardness, and she had poured forth her unstinted usefulness with a bitter smile upon her lips. And now the sarcastic years brought the proud woman her punishment. She was not to die as she had lived. The sting was to be taken out of her: she was to be made soft; she was to be reduced to compliance and complacency. The change came gradually, but at last it was unmistakable. The terrible commander who had driven Sidney Herbert to his death, to whom Mr Jowett had applied the words of Homer, ἄμστον μεμανῖα—raging insatiably—now accepted small compliments with gratitude, and indulged in sentimental friendships with young girls. The author of 'Notes on Nursing'—that classical compendium of the besetting sins of the sisterhood, drawn up with the detailed acrimony, the vindictive relish,

of a Swift—now spent long hours in composing sympathetic Addresses
to Probationers, whom she petted and wept over in turn. And, at
the same time, there appeared a corresponding alteration in her
physical mould. The thin, angular woman, with her haughty eye
and her acrid mouth, had vanished; and in her place was the rounded
bulky form of a fat old lady, smiling all day long. Then something
else became visible. The brain which had been steeled at Scutari
was indeed, literally, growing soft. Senility—an ever more and more
amiable senility—descended. Towards the end, consciousness itself
grew lost in a roseate haze, and melted into nothingness. It was just
then, three years before her death, when she was eighty-seven years
old (1907), that those in authority bethought them that the opportune
moment had come for bestowing a public honour on Florence Nightingale. She was offered the Order of Merit. That Order, whose roll
contains, among other distinguished names, those of Sir Laurence
Alma Tadema and Sir Edward Elgar, is remarkable chiefly for the
fact that, as its title indicates, it is bestowed because its recipient
deserves it, and for no other reason. Miss Nightingale's representatives
accepted the honour, and her name, after a lapse of many years,
once more appeared in the Press. Congratulations from all sides came
pouring in. There was a universal burst of enthusiasm—a final
revivification of the ancient myth. Among her other admirers, the
German Emperor took this opportunity of expressing his feelings towards her. 'His Majesty,' wrote the German Ambassador, 'having
just brought to a close a most enjoyable stay in the beautiful
neighbourhood of your old home near Romsey, has commanded me
to present you with some flowers as a token of his esteem.' Then,
by Royal command, the Order of Merit was brought to South Street,
and there was a little ceremony of presentation. Sir Douglas Daw-
son, after a short speech, stepped forward, and handed the insignia
of the Order to Miss Nightingale. Propped up by pillows, she dimly
recognized that some compliment was being paid her. 'Too kind—too
kind,' she murmured; and she was not ironical.

S. N. BEHRMAN

The Red and
The Blue

Like his self-avowed prototype, Casanova, and like Marcel Proust, Avraam Elia Kazan sits in a room writing down his remembrance of things past. He has already published two books, *Life of a Kazanova* and *Sixty Minutes Experience*, and he has the material for several more. Kazan, who signs his works and all his letters 'A. E. (Joe) Kazan' and frequently refers to himself in conversation as A.E., is a little younger than the Venetian was when he finally got around to remembering at Dux: Casanova was seventy-two; Kazan is sixty-eight. The small hotel room on West Fifty-eight Street where, for the past few years, Kazan has sat pouring out his recollections is not cork-lined, like Proust's, but the intensity of his preoccupation with what he has lost is the same. Like Proust again, he has had to pay for the publication of his memoirs himself. The books he has either published or only partly completed have various titles, but, like the worldly recluse of the Boulevard Haussmann, he has really written only one work; it is an endless statement of what he has enjoyed and endured. Spiritually, of course—and he would be the first to acknowledge it— this latter-day A.E., who is of Greek descent, is much nearer the Italian than the Frenchman; his life is an astonishing span of the modern picaresque—from rags to riches, and beyond that to disillusion and moralizing. A seven-dollar-a-week messenger boy on the streets of New York at twenty, Kazan became a millionaire before he was thirty. However, the Algeric analogy will lead you astray in any summary of the career of A. E. (Joe) Kazan. Virtue was not its terminal, or idealism its motive power. You will be on firmer ground if you stick, as A.E. does, to Casanova. If he has regrets, it is because he has not always done the expedient thing. The conscience that hurts him is economic; the only guilt he feels is for not having held on to his money. Toward his lapses from strict rectitude, he is tolerant. What he cannot forgive is his poverty, for which he holds himself directly responsible. Like George Bernard Shaw, he looks upon poverty as a sin, and, in a rather ducal way, he is contrite about having committed it. His detachment about himself and his contempt for his major failure are symbolized in his invention of the name by which he is known in the circles he frequents—Flat Tire Joe. 'It's a good name, don't you think?' he will inquire, without wistfulness. A.E. is never wistful. He is stern, he is sardonic, he is zestful, and he has reached old age without mellowness. This endows his personality with a kind of clean jauntiness. You can take him or leave him, but you don't have to be sorry for him.

In his appearance, Kazan sharply contradicts his self-applied pseudonym of Flat Tire Joe. He looks like a Morgan partner of the nineteen-hundreds (probably far more so than the Morgan partners ever looked) on the way to lunch on the Corsair with the head of the firm. His manner of dress is invariable and impeccable: a somewhat outmoded but impressive double-breasted black coat, very square and long, gray-striped trousers, gray spats, stiff-winged collar, and dark-blue bow tie with tiny white polka dots. His shirt front is dazzling white and stiffly starched. He carries a silver-headed cane. He wears a black bowler with an old-fashioned square crown. He is tall, square, white-faced, and bald, with snapping eyes and a somewhat bleak and rugged aspect. His usual expression is austere. It takes a lifetime of self-indulgence to produce a look so ascetic. Kazan sits in his hotel room mornings and early afternoons writing. About four, he usually walks to his favorite haunt, the Café de la Paix, at the Hotel St Moritz, where he has a regular table. He is a striking figure on the street. If you passed him on his way to the Café de la Paix, moving slowly along, encased in his boxlike garments, tapping the sidewalk with his walking stick, his expression tense and unrevealing, his mind polishing up submerged facets of his past, you would think that he was the diplomatic representative of some strange country and that his avocation was abstract philosophy, which, indeed, it is.

Unless you have read his two published works, it is very difficult to have a sustained conversation with A. E. (Joe) Kazan. The full title of his first book is, somewhat after the ample eighteenth-century manner, *Sixty Minutes Experience: Modern Philosophy and Psychology: Joe Kazan's 50 Years' Experience*. This one, which he wrote for children, is bound in bright red. The second book is called, in full, *Life of a Kazanova: I Lived, Loved, and Learned: Joe Kazan's 50 Years'*

Experience, and is bound in bright blue. It is necessary to be up on both these volumes. If, undocumented, you ask him about some period of his past, he will answer, with a benign testiness, 'That's in the blue.' Should your question be in the realm of the philosophical, the speculative, or the psychological, he will say, 'That's in the red.' He is like the master of some esoteric science who will not discuss it with you until you have learned at least the fundamentals. If you ask him, for example, how he got his start in America, he will simply say, 'It's in the blue.' Illiterates just cannot converse with A.E.

The juvenile, *Sixty Minutes Experience: Modern Philosophy and Psychology*, is on sale in the philosophical section of Macy's book department. Macy's would not stock *Kazanova*. Presumably the buyers were afraid of the effect of this intimate autobiography on their customers. *Sixty Minutes Experience* is prefaced, again in the eighteenth-century manner, with a prospectus which says:

> Father tells his experience to young ones—they do not like it—and they
> do not take advantage. In later years they wish they had. This applies
> also to sixty minutes experience paragraphs.

This book is published by the Capano Press of New York. *Kazanova* is published by the Alexander Press of New York. On the first page of each volume is a ruled square, in which appears 'Compliments of', followed by a blank line. *Sixty Minutes Experience* goes even farther than *Kazanova* in its implications of generosity. The second inside page is headed 'To My Good Friend', below which is a blank line for the name. The next line, waiting, like a blank check, for a signature, has the word 'Author' at the end. The modesty of this is ingratiating; it is as if A.E. could not imagine that anyone but himself would make a present of this volume. The Capano Press offers a further convenience for the careful reader of *Sixty Minutes Experience*, the last page is ruled and is headed INDEX FOR PARAGRAPHS YOU LIKE.

The two books differ in intent; *Sixty Minutes Experience* is didactic, whereas *Kazanova* is sensationally confessional. It is interesting, however, to note that the author has numbered the pages of the two books as if they were one outpouring. Thus, *Sixty Minutes*, or the red, ends on Page 120, and *Kazanova* begins on Page 121. It would undoubtedly seem odd, if you innocently picked up *Kazanova* in someone's library and found yourself, at the very start, already on Page

121. Perhaps, in a shy way, Kazan is merely trying to anticipate those hard critics of even more prolific writers—of Somerset Maugham, for example—who say that no matter how much these authors turn out, they really write only one book. This is especially true of Kazan, because he is a behavioristic rather than an imaginative writer. He embosses what he knows, has seen, and has lived through; he is materialistic and factual. Although nothing could be farther from the child's world of *Sixty Minutes Experience* than the livid realism of *Kazanova*, there is internal evidence that the two books are webbed together in the obscure caverns of Kazan's unconscious. Thus *Kazanova*, while not overtly a juvenile, is a long apostrophe to a generic nephew named Bob; it is an avuncular fireside chat from a sophisticated older man to a guileless boy. Almost every admonition in the book is addressed to this imaginary Bob. And it is not unusual, when Bob asks his uncle a question, to find such a brusque answer as 'Read paragraph 127 of *Sixty Minutes Experience*.' A.E. won't talk even to Bob unless he is up on the red. It should here be noted that in the juvenile *Sixty Minutes Experience* there are no cross references to *Kazanova*. Obviously, Kazan belongs to the rather old-fashioned school of pedagogy that does not believe in pushing children too far beyond their depth.

On the title and facing pages of *Sixty Minutes Experience*, Kazan, following Fielding and Richardson, permits himself to revel in creative anticipation, as follows:

WISDOM OF EXPERIENCE

IF YOU WOULD BENEFIT

FROM THE EXPERIENCE OF THE

AUTHOR, AGED 67, READ THIS BOOK

SIXTY MINUTES EXPERIENCE

FULL OF TRUTH

ALSO

FOUNDATION FOR GROWN CHILDREN

THIS BOOK IS DICTIONARY OF

THE PROBLEMS OF LIFE ANYTHING

HAPPENS WILL HAPPEN:

READ IT AGAIN AND YOU WILL FIND

THE ANSWER AND THE REMEDY

Following is experience
(not advice)

Underneath this introduction is a box with the legend 'This Book is obtainable at:—' The promise of the colon is not fulfilled; the emptiness that follows leaves you dangling in an irritated suspense, unless you happen to find out about Macy's.

Kazan urges anyone he meets to feed *Sixty Minutes Experience* to the children. 'If they cannot read,' he will say, 'read to them.' The book is written in the manner of *Also Sprach Zarathustra*, in chased aphorisms. Some of the epigrams suggest that the children for whom Kazan intended them must be not only grown but even precocious.

The aphorisms are all numbered. Aphorism 3 indicates that A.E. has at least something in common with the progressive school of educators: 'Do not do anything you do not want to do. Ignore forcing.'

Aphorism 85 is evidently for incipient politicians: 'Question. What benefit does bribing bring in this world? Answer. Plenty. Very few persons refuse bribes if they are big enough and legal.'

Aphorism 121 must be intended for children who are about to go into business: 'Any proposition comes to you, say "No" first, easy to change it to "Yes", not easy to change it to "No". This will protect you from better trader than yourself in business.'

Similarly, Aphorism 25: 'If you write nasty letters, mail them next day; you may change them. Mail all important letters yourself.'

Kazan seldom makes the concessions usually demanded of the writers of juvenilia; he expects the tots to supplement their experience with imagination, to fill in the void of the present with the fullness of anticipation. Probably on no other basis, for example, could he counsel: 'The right time to propose marriage to a lady is at a wedding. The poor lady's heart is soft and trembling.'

But occasionally A.E. forgets Chesterfield and remembers Polonius, as in Aphorism 39: 'Do not swear and do not use vulgar language. Your tongue will get used to it. You might call your family names.'

For girl babies, A.E. has special advice: 'Ladies, do not fight with your man in the morning; he cannot attend to his business and you will not have luxuries or automobiles.'

Again: 'Ladies and sweethearts, save your money, because for no reason your man may switch his affection to another woman with 50% less charm than yourself.'

He can be hard: 'Do not trust anyone until you find him otherwise; an agreeable surprise. This means you are protecting yourself.'

There are echoes of Aesop: 'Story: An old farmer's wife was very fond of pigeons and erected a pigeon house in back yard, and watched them every day. Neighbors asked her why she was so fond of pigeons. She said, "I like the billing and cooing of the male pigeon and his love".'

And echoes of La Rochefoucald: 'Definition of partner—prays his partner will become extravagant so that he can own the business himself.'

And of King Lear: 'Father spends thousands and lots of trouble to bring up the youngsters; when father, mother, or sister gets poor and the children get rich they do not look after father, sister, or mother; they are beasts in human clothes.'

And of Cicero: 'Before 50, if you just happen to be in some risky business and accumulated a fortune, quit at 50 and become 98% honest. Otherwise, you will be caught doing wrong. It requires youth, nerve, technique to do wrong. You haven't got it after 50.'

And of Montaigne: 'Careless remark: Bill: "Since when are you taking all birds to a night club?" James: "The blonde is my wife." Bill: "Oh, I meant the brunette." James: "She is my sister." (You have embarrassed yourself.) Diplomat says, "I saw you with two charming ladies at the club", as ladies are charming at any age.'

And of Wilde: 'What is the easiest thing in life to do? Wrong.'

Sometimes one suspects—and it is true of so many books for children—that the inner message of *Sixty Minutes Experience* is intended for adults, as when the author ruminates, in Aphorism 259: 'What is alibi of Philosopher? When he becomes poor, he says to himself, "Too much money is no good anyhow!"'

Perhaps the most poignant moment in the book is the author's final paragraph, in which he reflects on the advantages contemporary children have that he lacked as a child. This is his envoi to his wandering in the child's world: 'THE AUTHOR SAYS: I wish this book had been printed 50 years ago so that I might have read it and gotten the benefit.'

The blue, or *Life of a Kazanova: I Lived, Loved, and Learned: Joe Kazan's 50 Years' Experience*, most of which is written in numbered episodes, is surely one of the frankest self-exposures in the long history of confessional literature. In Kazan's millionaire period, he maintained apartments in New York and in Paris and sported Rolls-Royces and Isotta-Fraschinis on two continents. Essentially (like so many bachelors) a homebody, he had sweethearts in various capitals so that while he was travelling he could enjoy the illusion the Statler hotels have always striven to achieve of a 'home away from home'. He also helped to make himself feel at home by taking with him, wherever he went, his most prized possession, a custom-built brown velvet sofa, on which he slept. He has clung to this sofa; it is all that is left of his former opulence. It stands now in his hotel room. A vanished and fascinating world is opened for you in *Kazanova*, a world of uninhibited enterprise, of mighty fortunes made in selling rugs, of $64,000 staked on one hand in *chemin de fer*, of flying trips between Constantinople and New York, of international business amalgamations, of sybaritism in New York, Paris, Madrid, Vienna, Budapest, and Cairo.

Under the statement 'This Book Is a Lesson for Adults', A.E. begins his autobiography with his birth:

> Bob, I was born in the city of Cesaria in Turkey in Asia Minor. There were three of us children. My mother passed away when I was six years old. I don't remember anything about her except that when I approached to her for a kiss (she was sick in bed) they pulled me away from her.

What effect this earliest remembered trauma has had on the career of A.E. it will remain for the psychologists to expound. There is certainly no indication in *Kazanova* that it made an introvert of him. Of the childhood incidents he relates, the following is perhaps the matrix of what was to come:

> Bob, at the age of nine when I was going to school, the best my family could do was to give me Turkish bologna sandwiches for my lunch almost every day. Then I became a racketeer, at the age of nine. (Compulsory.) A rich parents' son (sissy) at school. His lunch contained cheese, chicken sandwiches, cake, candy. One day I asked him to give me some of his lunch. He said no. The next day at noon I said to the rich boy, 'Let us go on the roof and have our lunch in the sun.' (Only the two of us were alone on the roof.) I grabbed his lunch box and ate half of his lunch, and I gave him half of my bologna. I also gave him a couple of slaps. I told him: 'If you don't get me extra lunch every day you will be licked by me.' The sissy obeyed me from fear. I had a delicious luncheon every day for a year. He told his mother he got awfully hungry at 3 o'clock and wanted more lunch. Years after, returning to Constantinople from America (having money) I met a young man at the Tokatlian restaurant. From his name I recognized him as the boy whose lunch I robbed every day at school. For days and days I treated him, dining him, champagne, girls, etc.—never allowing him to spend money. He never guessed who I was.

The free-lunch racket waned (perhaps the sissy became virile), but A.E. supplanted it with another. The boys in Cesaria used to play a game called *ashik*, with marbles that were made out of the little bones in the knee joints of lambs. The young Kazan put lead in one of these marbles, and with this he could, at a distance of ten feet, easily break through a row of normal ones. For a season he had a steady income of what came to two American cents a week. But he was too consistent a winner, the device was discovered, and, at the age of ten, he was expelled from school. A.E. has never fought the temptation to gamble, no matter how much it has cost him; he feels that the instinct is both congenital and insurmountable. He does not believe, he says, in fighting nature.

The young Kazan went to work, at the age of eleven, as a messenger boy, carrying rugs around from one establishment to another, but, after four years of it, Kazan, Sr., felt that the boy was too smart for Cesaria and sent him off to Constantinople, a four-day journey by carriage, to live with an uncle and aunt and their children. There A.E. got a job in a drugstore, at eighty cents a week. He noticed that apparently no matter what the ailment, the doctors prescribed the same medicines, so he took to filling prescriptions himself, with an admirable uniformity. But the atmosphere in his uncle's house was unfriendly. The family slept together in one room, on wool beds—layers of matted wool piled one on top of another. A.E. had brought a wool bed with him from Cesaria, a parting gift from his father. Gradually he became aware of a diminishing altitude in his bed; he slept lower and lower, and finally he reached the floor. He could only conclude that the layers had been removed one at a time by his relatives while he was at work—whether for mere gain or as a delicate hint that he was unwelcome, he was not sure. In any case, he took to sleeping in the drugstore. Avraam had grown up in the rug business, and he soon felt the call to return to it. It was in his bones. 'I know the business so well,' he says, 'that rugs are afraid of me.' He got a tryout for a job with a leading rug merchant in Constantinople, spreading out the rugs and helping to show them, at a dollar a week. On his first day, he saw a coin on the floor—a coin worth a quarter. He picked it up and gave it to the boss. The evidence of honesty clinched the job for him. He had been forewarned that this dropped coin was a stratagem of the boss's, and he survived this first test of his probity.

A.E. calls the years from 1887 to 1897, when he left Turkey for

America, his 'chiselling days'. It was while working in the rug establishment in Constantinople that there came to the Avraam the first impulse to go to America. Tersely, he describes, in *Kazanova*, this turning point in his young life:

> Bob, one day a friend of my father's got me a job in a rug store in Constantinople (my father's trade) at a dollar a week. I slept in his warehouse. Every Saturday, lots of Armenian merchants visited his office to talk over business and gossip about America with my boss. I used to listen. They would say: This man became a millionaire in America. This man bought a chateau. This one is wealthy. I said to myself: me for America. I went to my rich uncle to get some money to go to America. (No dice.) What next? My boss was paying loads of money to have his rugs repaired. What could I do? I learned how to repair rugs and I worked at night for three years to save enough money to come to America.

Kazan was twenty when at last he sailed, by freighter. The journey from Constantinople to Marseille took nine days. He was quartered on the steerage deck, but as it was summer, this was no great hardship. His capital was forty-two dollars and several silk rugs he was to deliver to a brother of his Constantinople boss who was in the rug business in New York. The blandishments of Marseille were too much for the young adventurer. He left the freighter, squandered his capital, and then sold one of the silk rugs for forty-five dollars. When at last he got on a ship for America, he had five dollars left. He gambled four-ninety-five of this away. From a fellow-passenger, a lady, he borrowed a quarter to wire his boss's brother from Ellis Island. For two days he slept on benches there until the boss's brother appeared and rescued him.

Kazan considers the time between 1897 and 1904 the happiest of his life, because it was the only period of his business career when he had no overhead. His faculty for cleaning, repairing, showing, and selling rugs stood him in good stead. He went to work for his boss's brother in his establishment at Broadway and Seventeenth Street, and he earned extra money repairing rugs at night. He lived in a boarding house near Wanamaker's and got himself a girl. This girl the boss coveted. The boss seemed to have been something of a Biblical student, for he sent A.E. on the road to sell so that he could woo the girl with an easier conscience. With A.E., he sent along another young member of his staff, who had been stealing from him. The boss told A.E. that he was sending him, A.E., along to watch the other fellow, but the maneuver was transparent to A.E. However, not counting the world lost for love, A.E. consented to go on tour. The two young men left for New England with their merchandise. Their procedure, after they arrived in a town, was to go to a music shop, say, or a hardware store, and get the proprietor to let them set up a temporary rug department in return for a ten-per-cent commission on sales. The tour was a triumph. In the communities A.E. and his companion visited there appeared to be a hunger for rugs which they had arrived in the nick of time to satisfy.

The first thing A.E. did after he sold a rug to a lady for a thousand dollars in Concord, New Hampshire, was to send a money order for fifty dollars to his father in Turkey. The sensation caused by its arrival was recounted to him years later, when he returned to Cesaria a rich man. A.E.'s father looked at the money order with skepticism, and he was assured by his neighbors that he could not get cash for it at the post office. At the post office he asked for the money in small silver coins, then brought it home and poured it on the kitchen table. The neighbors crowded in to look. The elder Kazan pointed with pride. 'Didn't I tell you my son is a genius?' he said. 'Look, we are rich!'

Women were as helpful in furthering A.E.'s career during the New England tour as they were later, with the assistance of overhead, in helping to undo him. In Bridgeport, an elderly lady came in and examined rugs for two hours. A.E.'s patience long outlasted that of his partner, who was always irritated by interminable shoppers. Finally the lady bought a rug for thirty-five dollars. She asked A.E. to deliver it to her house. The partner sneered, but A.E. stuck to business. He delivered the rug at dinnertime and was invited to dine. 'After dinner,' he recalls, 'as I sat on my hostess's lap, she got on the telephone and began making calls all over Bridgeport.' She sold $14,000 worth of rugs for him to her friends. 'American women of that era,' says A.E., 'were very sympathetic if you came from Constantinople and were poor.' From this one contact, A.E. got a fine dinner and $3,000 in commissions. He promptly returned to New York and quit his job. He approached a Fifth Avenue dealer with a proposal that they sell rugs at auction, so that they could influence the prices by bidding against each other when necessary. The merger was a great success. A.E. recalls vividly a pair of silk rugs of a crème-de-menthe color (he dwells lovingly on these two rugs, after a lapse of nearly half a century) which were bid up to seven hundred and fifty dollars, though they had cost him and his partner only sixty-two dollars. Those were wonderful years: America was a new and hospitable and rug-hungry land; there was youth and a growing intimation of genius in finance; there were women of all ages, sympathetic to a good-looking boy from Constantinople; and, above all, there was no overhead.

A.E. was soon averaging five hundred dollars a week, but he continued to live in the boarding house near Wanamaker's. Boarding houses, he says, were a symbol of respectability. It helped establish credit to live in a boarding house; it was an index of honesty and industry. During the panic of 1907, A.E. was occupying a large room for which he had paid a year's rent in advance. When Wanamaker's began discharging salesgirls, many of them came to A.E. for help, and he helped. One of the more idyllic of his memories is of this period. The girls used to come to his room in the evening and talk and sing to him while he repaired his rugs. He tolerated no indiscretion; it did not go with the boarding-house façade; he was a Platonic pasha.

A.E.'s career, from this point, followed swiftly the pattern set by many immigrants of those days. He was in a world in which you outsmarted everyone you could, in which you vowed revenge when you were outsmarted, even though you could not help having a certain admiration for the outsmarter. One example, taken from *Kazanova*, will serve as an illustration of this phase of his life:

Bob: At the age of 23, a poor boy, I sold at auction to a lady one silk carpet for $1,700 costing me $550. This was a profit of $1,150. An artificial gentleman dealer saw this lady and spoiled the sale of the silk carpet, and the lady returned it. This was a big loss for a poor man. I registered this evil act of the so-called gentleman in my mind. Fifteen years later I was sitting in a fashionable café. This same dealer came in and sat with me at a table. I bought him a drink. He bought me three drinks and then he went out and bought me a cigar which cost fifteen cents and one for himself which cost sixty cents. Now what is the catch? He asked me to lend him $25,000. 'Yes, if you send all your rugs (worth about $120,000) to my store I will lend you the $25,000 and charge you $12,000 commission whether all the rugs are sold or not.' I started working on the proposition and in a month I sold $37,000 worth and thereby collected my $25,000 and $12,000 commission. I sent the dealer back the balance of the rugs. He cost me $1,150 fifteen years ago but I got back from him $12,000 in one month. Bob, here is the benefit of not calling a fool a damn fool to his face. Bob, if you are willing to give a cigar to another friend, give same cigar that you smoke, not a fifteen cent cigar to him and a sixty cent one for you.

There began the period of A.E.'s life that he describes in *Kazanova* as 'Genius in Business and Technique'. In this period he acquired more partners and he acquired overhead. His success was great, and he began to make quantities of money. His years of wealth, characterized by him in a subtitle as 'High Living Days: Genius and Amoeba,' lasted until the liquidation of his fortune of several million dollars in the crash of 1929. The first big step toward success came when Orlando Jones, a bookmaker, introduced him to another bookmaker, who wanted to buy some rugs. A.E. took the prospect to the largest rug dealer in New York. One of the salesmen there offered A.E. a thousand-dollar commission on the transaction, which came to $5,000, but A.E., remembering the dropped coin in Constantinople, refused, and asked only the customary ten per cent. The news of this startling heresy reached the boss, who, overcome by A.E.'s spectacular honesty, gave him a job at $4,000 a year, plus commissions. After four years of this, during which, A.E. recalls, the boss 'liked him every day', he was given an account of $300,000 and sent to Constantinople on a buying trip. He bought too freely and when the home office heard about it he was discharged by cable. He promptly formed a partnership in Constantinople with a local banker named Castelli. In the next few years A.E. was involved, first in Constantinople and then back in New York, in a series of dissolving partnerships. One of them had an almost immediate but charming dénouement. A jovial partner, whom A.E. greatly liked, was caught cheating after one week. A.E. reproached him. 'I have been a crook for forty years,' said the candid culprit. 'You can't expect me to be honest in one week.' In spite of the sweet reasonableness of this argument, A.E., dissolved the partnership.

From this period, too, comes an interesting account of the pastime of 'rug-walking', taken from *Kazanova*:

Uncle, they tell me you used to chase customers from your store. Is this true?

Answer: Yes but only those rich customers who were egotists or better traders than myself. . . . For one of my best customers and friends I spread a large rug on the floor and he asked me what is the price. I said $800. He says, 'I'll take it.' (Being a bargain for him.) We were walking on the rug and I spoke to him in jokes—stories to keep him walking to the good end of the rug but he walked to the opposite end of the rug and then he said, 'No, I do not want it.' I asked him what's the matter with the rug. He said, 'The rug is worn out.' 'How do you know?' I said. 'You haven't touched it.' He said, 'I felt with my feet that it is worn out.' I said, 'Here's a cigar—but we won't do business with anyone who knows that a rug is worn out by touching it with his feet.' But we wined and dined many times after that.

In 1912, A.E. felt himself strong enough to do without partnerships and founded his own firm, the Kazan Carpet Company. The firm had a rating of AAA in Dun & Bradstreet's, and he had so much money that it was not necessary for him to be respectable. The boarding-house era was over. He moved into progressively finer apartment houses and eventually took an apartment at the Ritz Tower and had it furnished at a cost of $75,000. The 'High Living Days' period swung into its halcyon rhythm. It was then that he had his sofa made, and when he went to Paris he took it with him. (Can it be possible that this is the first record of a man taking a bed to Paris?) One evening there, he went to dine at the home of a count who was also fond of good living. On the third floor of the count's mansion was a bathroom which aroused A.E.'s envy; it had walls of exquisite mosaic and a bathtub big enough for two. A.E. couldn't get the magnificence of this bathroom out of his mind. He was like an art lover who has looked at a tantalizing picture and cannot rest until it hangs on his own wall. The next day he called the manager of Claridge's, where he was stopping, and had him, with the count's permission, visit the bathroom. A copy of it was installed in his suite at Claridge's. He kept this apartment, as well as the one in New York, all through the High Living Days.

A typical high-living day is described in Episodes 621 and 622:

In the morning my customary coffee served in my room, Masseur, osteopath or Turkish bath, alternately; besides my own gymnasium in my apartment. Every morning the barber comes at the same hour to shave me. Even if it is only to talk, the manicurist comes now and then. No worry for expenses (keep the change). A tailor comes once a month with samples and I buy a suit of clothes or an overcoat whether I need it or not.

Good organization at the store. Customers buying my rugs at any price,

as I am almost a monopoly. I look at the newspapers—stocks go up.
At one o'clock before I go to lunch I stop in at the stockbroker and buy
1000 shares of some stock on which I already have a tip. (To be sold at
1¼ point profit if it goes up. This profit will pay for my luxurious expenses.) And they go up. Arrive at 61st Street restaurant. Plenty of
beautiful girls. Of course I am welcome to these girls because some of
checks go on my account (and their sweeties are working at the time).
I go with some of the girls back to the apartment, either to play bridge
or dance or drink (Prohibition). Some of them jump on my electric horse
and camel. Bob, I was very generous with my girls. If they went out
dining and wining with a nicer looking man than myself, I forgave them.
Otherwise, elimination.

This life of easy gymnastics occasionally has a more astringent note.
As in Episode 638, on 'The Influence of Heredity':

Bob, here's an example of how a person can inherit certain habits from
his parents. When I was in Constantinople, I used to visit my father every
Monday in the suburbs where he lived. In his bathroom I saw a cake
of soap which had been made from little scraps of left-over soap. That
was economy! And I, the damned fool, had lost $5,000 the night before
playing poker. Did I learn anything? We shall see. In New York, I lived
at a Tower Hotel. I was wealthy and lived very expensively. Yet I also
had a cake of soap made from little scraps of left-over soap. Even today
I do the same thing. These are the little things that you inherit from
your parents. And here's how it benefited me. A girl once came to ask
me for $125 for a Chinese dog that she wanted to buy. When she happened
to go into the bathroom and saw my cake of soap which had been made
from little scraps of left-over soap—she left the room without carfare.

It is doubtful whether any man has ever been franker than A.E.
in disclosing his failures with women. He seldom recalls an amorous
episode that did not have some economic aspect. This is very hard
to understand, because A.E. is a handsome, imposing man even today.
Possibly, if he had remained poor, women would have been touched
by his need for love, as they were in his non-overhead days, but it
is hard to be sorry for a very rich man. If there is one idyl in the
life of A.E., it is his nostalgic worship of the lady whose identity is
veiled in his lavish numerology as Sweetheart No. 5. (He is inclined
to say less about Nos. 1 through 4.) He loved and wanted to marry
this girl and yet, even in this case, his nostalgia is soured a bit by
the fact that, although he spent a fortune on her and wanted to send
her to school and to educate her, she left him, when he began to

lose his money, to marry a man who had had the good sense to remain a millionaire. He still thinks with tenderness of Sweetheart No. 5 and writes to her now and then, but she does not answer his letters.

Some of Kazan's innumerable trans-atlantic crossings during the high-living days were dictated by romance. Sensitive to the merest inflection of infidelity, he once quickly abandoned a Paris sweetheart because, in an absent-minded moment, she called him by the wrong name. To salve his wounded *amour-propre*, he sailed at once for New York, only to have his New York sweetheart make a similar unfortunate slip of the tongue. One incident in *Kazanova* is reminiscent of a painful episode in *Of Human Bondage*—when Philip gives his friend the money to go away with Mildred—and is none the less poignant for being told so pitilessly:

> I made arrangements with a new manager to take care of my business as I was sailing for Europe on the Majestic. When I arrived on the ship I received from a real friend the following telegram (4 words): 'You are a donkey—Bill.' But after I got on the boat I changed my mind—I wanted to get off—but the first whistle for leaving had blown. The second steward, who knew me well, said, 'The only way you can get out of here is to get sick'—and I got sick plenty. They had to lower the plank and I got off. This cost me $100. Now what was my idea? First, I was not doing justice to my business. Second, I wanted to go and watch my exclusive sweetheart, for her I bought a small house in the suburbs, and to see if she was in love with someone else. On two occasions I went around her house but did not have the courage to go in and see for myself if... I never justified my suspicions because I never found out. Damn fool—but this is love.

Kazan attributes his failure in business and his present impecuniosity to his gambling and extravagance and what might be called the 'flat tire' quality in his character, but not for a moment does he regret his romantic expenditures, financial and emotional. He indulges in no sentimental what-might-have-beens even about the practical Sweetheart No. 5. And toward all women he still retains an attitude of incorrigible gallantry. If his life has been an unending immolation of the altar of Eros, he feels no remorse. In this sense he is a true Casanova, the perennial Don Juan, a perfectionist in amour. It is perhaps A.E.'s most striking and ingratiating quality that he is detached and unregenerate. He looks upon his own failings, as he does upon honor in others, with equanimity, as eccentricities of character to be observed and catalogued and appraised for their instructive value. He is constantly contrasting his brother, who is the father of Elia Kazan, the stage and screen director, with himself. This brother has been successful in the rug business, but not so spectacularly as A.E. He is respected in his business circle in New York and in New Rochelle, where he and his family live. In *Kazanova*, A.E. refers to him as 'my noble brother'. He applies this epithet not with irony but with real reverence. 'He is a good man,' A.E. will say. 'Never did anything dishonorable. A good man, a thousand times better than I.' But he says it in a tone of casual inventory, as if he were estimating the value of a rug or a diamond. He does not envy virtue. For the good brother's son, his nephew Elia, he has an admiring affection. He repeats with relish conversational tilts he has had with Elia.

'Once,' he says, 'I asked him for five hundred dollars.'

'You are always telling me,' Elia answered, 'to save my money. How can I give you five hundred dollars and still save my money?'

'Because,' A.E. said, 'when you give you get back more.'

A.E. won the argument and the five hundred dollars.

His nephew's increasing fame and success have not been an unmixed blessing for A.E. 'Formerly, friends sometimes helped me,' he says. 'Now they say, "Why should we help you? You have a millionaire nephew. Why don't you go to him?"' (In A.E.'s circle you can't be merely affluent; you are a millionaire or nothing.) There is a story that Oscar Wilde, when he was living in poverty in Paris, wrote the synopsis of a play called *Mrs Daventry* and one day sold it to a producer, promising to write the play. He didn't write it, but he kept the advance. He repeated the process several times with other impresarios, always using the same synopsis. Finally, one of these men got someone else to write the play around Wilde's synopsis and put it into rehearsal. When Wilde heard of the impending production, he wrote an indignant letter to this producer. 'By producing this play,' he said, 'you rob me of a certain source of income!' A.E. feels somewhat this way about his nephew's success.

The small hotel room on West Fifty-eighth Street in which A.E. has lived for nine years seems even smaller than it is because most of it is occupied by the much-travelled sofa. The sofa is the worse for wear, and its generous proportions make living in the room somewhat of a maneuver. Pressed against it on one side is a bridge table, on which A.E. does his writing. The table is covered with manuscripts. Next to the sofa, on the other side, is a huge wardrobe trunk plastered with labels: 'Berengaria 1926;' 'Paris 1927 to Hold on Arrival.' Into the trunk, A.E. recalls, he once threw $1,500 after an alcoholic card game and didn't answer it till five years later, when he was rummaging for a collar button. The sofa, bridge table, and trunk form a small triangle. In this little triangle, most of A.E.'s existence is now confined.

Kazan's sofa was made to order by the Tiffany Studios in 1921. 'I paid seven hundred and fifty dollars for it, but now I couldn't get ten dollars,' he says, not ruefully but as a comment on worldly mutation. No other man has ever been so faithful to an article of furniture. Even when he lived in his apartment at the Ritz Tower, which had a magnificent bed, he slept on the sofa. Whenever he was ready to go to Paris, he would simply order his chauffeur to ship the sofa ahead. When he arrived in his apartment at Claridge's, it would be there. Now it is his workbench as well as his bed. He lies on it, collecting his thoughts, and when he is ready to set them down, there is the bridge table. The sofa, A.E. says, is his pal. It is a relationship analagous to the one between Elwood P. Dowd and Harvey.

A.E.'s degeneration into a writer took place in this way. In 1941, yielding to one of his rare bouts with apathy, he didn't go out of his room for three days. On the fourth day, the maid who does his room prodded him, 'You haven't been outside the room for three days,' she said. 'What's the matter with you? You must be a writer!' The writing germ, a non-filterable virus, entered A.E. at that moment. By the end of a week, A.E., now dedicated, was at work on his first manuscript. His new avocation, he feels, has lifted him above the ordinary, material plane on which he had always lived. On the floor of his room are three worn rugs; he estimates their total value at ninety cents. On Christmas Day of 1944, A.E. was alone in his room with his work. He looked down at the rugs and found himself remembering that once he had had in his store two thousand rugs, each worth between five hundred and $2,000. He laughed. He went out to the Automat for his Christmas dinner, and while sitting there, drinking a glass of milk, he laughed again. It is his conversion to art, A.E. feels, that gave him the power to laugh on that Christmas Day.

A.E. takes a certain pride in the magnitude of his downfall. In 1929, he went bankrupt for a million dollars, and he still carries, and likes to display, a newspaper clipping recording this handsome débacle. Since 1929, he has done no formal work. He is an authority on the late sport of horse racing. He had elaborate formulas for betting, the most incomprehensible of which he called the 'unit system'. Once he evolved an intricate scheme for a betting pool with a capital of a million dollars. He perfected the plan with patient lucubration and then offered it as a sort of gesture to the Greek community in New York. It was turned down. He was rather hurt by this, because he was prepared, he says, to devote all his time to it. For a while, after the crash, he lived in the Hotel St Moritz, and he still goes there almost every afternoon and sits on a yellow-leather chair at his regular table in the Café de la Paix. He loves the Café de la Paix. The proprietor of the hotel, a Greek by the name of Taylor, is an old friend. The waiters and clientele also know him. When he tips the waiters, they good-humoredly refuse the tips. They don't want to be tipped by their friend, they say. When A.E. arrives at the Café de la Paix, he sits down at his *Stammtisch* in one corner. He talks to his regular waiter in French. He has known this waiter for thirty years, since the days of the old Café Martin. They inevitably recall the night Stanford White was shot there. They were at the Café Martin when it happened. A.E. puts on a pair of horn-rimmed glasses, takes some long sheets of yellow foolscap from his pocket, and asks the waiter to read to him from his work in progress, *My Life at the Café Martin*. 'The proprietor, Martin, was like my brother,' says A.E. 'What a man I was!'

Back in his room, A.E. puts in an hour before dinner at his writing. The pockets of his double-breasted black overcoat and of his jackets are stuffed with foolscap covered with writing—newly remembered stories of his past, amplifications of stories he had already told. Afflicted with graphomania, he keeps adding and adding to his reminiscences and speculations. If you visit him in his room, he insists upon your reading his works aloud to him. He will reach into a pocket and pull out a sheet of paper. 'Read this,' he will say, in the voice of one long accustomed to obedience. 'Aloud!' When you start reading, A.E. tilts his head back and a little to one side. A faint smile curves his lips and the expression on his distinguished, strongly modelled face softens to benignity. As the sentences set in motion the stream of memory—of opulence, of power, of defeat, of voluptuousness—the benign look deepens, and it is plain that the voices he hears are mellifluous. At last the passage is finished. There is a silence. The sun lights up a column of motes rising from A.E.'s sofa to the window. He gets up and adjusts his boxlike jacket against the back of his collar. 'Damn fool,' he mutters. 'Damn fool.'

'What would you still like to accomplish in life?' his visitor asks, to snap him from his past to the future.

'You will find the answer,' he says brusquely, 'in the blue—797A.'

It is there, on the last page, just before the addendum, which is a little manual on horse racing. It reads:

> Bob asked his uncle: 'Why did you start writing this book?'
>
> Answer: 'It is a good hobby, if you are lonesome, and an education. You will become a better person reading your own memoirs and experiences, and I am tired of stretching a dollar as far as it will go. I am also trying hard to make this book more successful so I will be able to reciprocate favors which I receive from my family and my friends, and will be able to establish a small orphanage and live with the children and see them happy. When they come and jump on my lap and kiss me, that is the only genuine kiss in the world with no hidden personal interest, except, of course, mothers'.'

Ecce iterum the irrepressible BOY JONES! Prison evidently had no terrors for him; for, no sooner was he liberated from Tothill Fields, on 2 Mar., than he, almost immediately, set to work to repeat his former escapades. On the day previous to his liberation, he was visited by Mr Hall, a magistrate, who tried to persuade him to go to sea; but Jones made certain conditions which could not be acceded to, and he did not go. This gave an opportunity for the *Satirist* to come out with the following appropriate lines:

> The impudent urchin, whom sure the devil owns,
>   And Government wants to send into the Navy;
> Will not go to sea—and 'tis cunning of Jones,
>   Who, thus, may avoid his relation, Old Davey.

He was then delivered into the care of his parents, with strict injunctions to them to watch his actions; and, for some days, his conduct was unexceptionable; he frequently attended a Methodist chapel, and expressed his intention of joining a teetotal society. But the charms of notoriety were too strong for him; and, again, he was drawn, as it were by a magnet, to Buckingham Palace. Indeed, it possessed such attractions for him, that, when required to pledge himself, before leaving prison, not to visit the Palace again, he said he would not promise, as his curiosity was so great.

On 15 March, shortly after 1 a.m., the sergeant of police on duty at the Palace imagined, as he was going along the Grand Hall, that he saw someone peeping through the glass door, and this turned out to be the case; for, on his approach, Jones ran up against him, and was, of course, immediately secured. In consequence of his previous visits, two extra policeman had been appointed, whose duty it was, on alternate nights, to watch all the staircases and interior of the building, and it was owing to this arrangement that Master Jones was stopped early in his career, on this last occasion.

Like most boys, Jones had a keen appreciation of a feast, all the more enjoyable because irregularly come by; and, when he was arrested, he was found to have been sitting at his ease in one of the royal apartments, regaling himself with some cold meat and potatoes, which he had conveyed upstairs in his handkerchief. On being questioned how he obtained an entrance, his reply was, 'the same way as before'; and he boasted, moreover, that he could, at any time he pleased, get into the palace; but he was extremely taciturn, and refused to satisfy curiosity, more particularly on this point.

What he confessed at his examination by the Privy Council is not known, as the proceedings were in private, reporters being excluded, and the public were left in possession of only the above bare facts. He persisted that the only motive for his intrusion was to hear the conversation at Court, and to write an account of it; but this plea of simplicity did not save him from a repetition of his old sentence of three months' imprisonment in the House of Correction, with the uncomfortable addition, this time, of hard labour. Perhaps the best punishment for this juvenile addition of Paul Pry would have been that suggested by the *Satirist*, in the following paragraph: 'As the urchin Jones, in a letter to his father, stated that his reason for entering the Queen's house was to "seek for noose, in order to rite a book", it is a matter of general regret that, instead of magnifying the affair into Home Office importance, the young rogue was not accommodated with a rope's end.' His visit, however, necessitated the appointment of three additional sentries at the palace.

What became of him afterwards, nobody knows and nobody cares, but, one thing is certain; he was *persuaded* to go to sea.

—John Ashton, *Gossip*

S. BARING-GOULD

The Alphington Ponies

During the forties of the last century, every visitor to Torquay noticed two young ladies of very singular appearance. Their residence was in one of the two thatched cottages on the left of Tor Abbey Avenue, looking seaward, very near the Torgate of the avenue. Their chief places of promenade were the Strand and Victoria Parade, but they were often seen in other parts of the town. Bad weather was the only thing that kept them from frequenting their usual beat. They were the two Misses Durnford, and their costume was peculiar. The style varied only in tone and colour. Their shoes were generally green, but sometimes red. They were by no means bad-looking girls when young, but they were so berouged as to present the appearance of painted dolls. Their brown hair worn in curls was fastened with blue ribbon, and they wore felt or straw hats, usually tall in the crown and curled up at the sides. About their throats they had very broad frilled or lace collars that fell down over their backs and breasts a long way. But in summer their necks were bare, and adorned with chains of coral or bead. Their gowns were short, so short indeed as to display about the ankles a good deal more than was necessary of certain heavily-frilled cotton investitures of their lower limbs. In winter over their gowns were worn check jackets of a 'loud' pattern reaching to their knees, and of a different colour from their gowns, and with lace cuffs. They were never seen, winter or summer, without their sun-shades. The only variation to the jacket was a gay-coloured shawl crossed over the bosom and tied behind at the waist.

The sisters dressed exactly alike, and were so much alike in face as to appear to be twins. They were remarkably good walkers, kept perfectly in step, were always arm in arm, and spoke to no one but each other.

They lived with their mother, and kept no servant. All the work of the house was done by the three, so that in the morning they made no appearance in the town; only in the afternoon had they assumed their war-paint, when, about 3 p.m., they sallied forth; but, however highly they rouged and powdered, and however strange was their dress, they carried back home no captured hearts. Indeed, the visitors to Torquay looked upon them with some contempt as not being in society and not dressing in the fashion; only some of the residents felt for them in their solitude some compassion. They were the daughters of a Colonel Durnford, and had lived at Alphington. The mother was of an inferior social rank. They had a brother, a major in the Army, 10th Regiment, who was much annoyed at their singularity of costume, and offered to increase their allowance if they would discontinue it; but this they refused to do.

When first they came to Torquay, they drove a pair of pretty ponies they had brought with them from Alphington; but their allowance being reduced, and being in straitened circumstances, they had to dispose of ponies and carriage. By an easy transfer the name of Alphington Ponies passed on from the beasts to their former owners.

As they were not well off, they occasionally got into debt, and were summoned before the Court of Requests; and could be impertinent even to the judge. On one occasion, when he had made an order for payment, one of them said, 'Oh, Mr Praed, we cannot pay now; but my sister is about to be married to the Duke of Wellington, and then we shall be in funds and be able to pay for all we have had and are likely to want!' Once the two visited a shop and gave an order, but, instead of paying, flourished what appeared to be the half of a £5 note, saying, that when they had received the other half, they would be pleased to call and discharge the debt. But the tradesman was not to be taken in, and declined to execute the order. Indeed, the Torquay shopkeepers were very shy of them, and insisted on the money being handed over the counter before they would serve the ladies with the goods that they required.

They made no acquaintances in Torquay or in the neighbourhood, nor did any friends come from a distance to stay with them. They would now and then take a book out of the circulating library, but seemed to have no literary tastes, and no special pursuits. There was a look of intelligence, however, in their eyes, and the expression of their faces was decidedly amiable and pleasing.

They received very few letters; those that did arrive probably contained remittances of money, and were eagerly taken in at the door, but there was sometimes a difficulty about finding the money to pay for the postage. It is to be feared that the butcher was obdurate, and that often they had to go without meat. Fish, however, was cheap.

A gentleman writes: 'Mr Garrow's house, The Braddons, was on my father's hands to let. One day the gardener, Tosse, came in hot haste to father and complained that the Alphington Ponies kept coming into the grounds and picking the flowers, that when remonstrated with they declared that they were related to the owner, and had permission. "Well," said father, "the next time you see them entering the gate run down and tell me." In a few days Tosse hastened to say that the ladies were again there. Father hurried up to the grounds, where he found them flower-picking. Without the least ceremony he insisted on their leaving the grounds at once. They began the same story to him of their relationship to the owner, adding thereto, that they were cousins of the Duke of Wellington. "Come," said father, "I can believe *one* person can go mad to any extent in any direction whatever, but the improbability of *two* persons going mad in identically the same direction and manner at the same time is a little too much for my credulity. Ladies, I beg you to proceed." And proceed they did.'

After some years they moved to Exeter, and took lodgings in St Sidwell's parish. For a while they continued to dress in the same strange fashion; but they came into some money, and then were able to indulge in trinkets, to which they had always a liking, but which previously they could not afford to purchase. At a large fancy ball, given in Exeter, two young Oxonians dressed up to represent these ladies; they entered the ballroom solemnly, arm in arm, with their parasols spread, paced round the room, and finished their perambulation with a waltz together. This caused much amusement; but several ladies felt that it was not in good taste, and might wound the poor crazy Misses Durnford. This, however, was not the case. So far from being offended at being caricatured, they were vastly pleased, accepting this as the highest flattery. Were not princesses and queens also represented at the ball? Why, then, not they?

One public ball they did attend together, at which, amongst others, were Lady Rolle and Mr Palk, son of the then Sir Lawrence Palk. Owing to their conspicuous attire, they drew on them the attention of Lady Rolle, who challenged Mr Palk to ask one of the sisters for a dance, and offered him a set of gold and diamond shirt studs if he could prevail on either of them to be his partner. Mr Palk accepted the challenge, but on asking for a dance was met in each case by the reply, 'I never dance except my sister be also dancing.' Mr Palk then gallantly offered to dance with both sisters at once, or in succession. He won and wore the studs.

A gentleman writes: 'In their early days they made themselves conspicuous by introducing the bloomer arrangement in the nether latitude. This, as you may well suppose, was regarded as a scandal; but these ladies, who were never known to speak to any one, or to each other out of doors, went on their way quite unruffled. Years and years after this, you may imagine my surprise at meeting them in Exeter, old and grey, but the same singular silent pair. Then, after an interval of a year or two, only one appeared. I assure you, it gave me pain to look at that poor lonely, very lonely soul; but it was not for long. Kind Heaven took her also, and so a tiny ripple was made, and there was an end of the Alphington Ponies.'

SOURCES AND ACKNOWLEDGEMENTS

'The Boy Jones' by John Ashton, from *Gossip in the First Decade of Victoria's Reign* (London: Hurst and Blackett Ltd, 1903).

'The Alphington Ponies' by S. Baring-Gould, from *Devonshire Characters and Strange Events* (London: The Bodley Head Ltd, 1908).

'The Snail Telegraph' by S. Baring-Gould, from *Historic Oddities and Strange Events* (London: Methuen and Co., 1891).

'Dr Achmet Borumborad' by Sir Jonah Barrington, from *Personal Sketches of His Own Times*, Vol. 1 (London: Henry Colburn, 1827).

'The Red and the Blue' by S. N. Behrman, from *The Suspended Drawing Room* (London: Hamish Hamilton Ltd, 1966), reprinted by permission of the author.

'Cagliostro (and Seraphina)' by William Bolitho, from *Twelve Against the Gods* (London: Jonathan Cape Ltd, 1929).

'Mr Smyllie, Sir' by Patrick Campbell, from *35 Years on the Job* (London: Blond and Briggs Ltd, 1973), reprinted by permission of Muller, Blond and White Ltd.

'Dan Graham' by Harold Dearden, from *Queer People* (London: Hutchinson and Co., n.d.).

'The Female Infidel' by Thomas De Quincey, from *Autobiographic Sketches* (*London Magazine*, 1821).

'The Author of "Sandford and Merton"' by John Fyvie, from *The Independent Review*, 1898.

'The Duke of Wellington's Miss J.' by Derek Hudson, from *The Forgotten King and Other Essays* (London: Constable and Co. Ltd, 1960), reprinted by permission of the publisher.

'The Private Enterprise of Anne Hicks' by Stanley Hyland, from *Curiosities from Parliament* (London: Allan Wingate (Publishers) Ltd, 1955), reprinted by permission of the Hamlyn Publishing Group Ltd.

'The Converted Murderer' by Charles Kingston, from *Rogues and Adventuresses* (London: John Lane Bodley Head Ltd, 1928), reprinted by permission of the Bodley Head Ltd.

'The Man Who Tried to Convert the Pope' by Ronald Knox, from *Literary Distractions* (London: Sheed and Ward Ltd, 1958), reprinted by permission of the Earl of Oxford and Asquith.

'Indecent Assault by a Colonel' by Giles Playfair, from *Six Studies in Hypocrisy* (London: Secker and Warburg Ltd, 1969), reprinted by permission of the author.

'Robert de Montesquiou The Magnificent Dandy' by Cornelia Otis Skinner, from *Elegant Wits and Grand Horizontals* (Boston: Houghton Mifflin Co., 1962), reprinted by permission of International Creative Management, Inc. Copyright © 1962 by Cornelia Otis Skinner.

'Muggleton' by Lytton Strachey, from *Portraits in Miniature and Other Essays* (London: Chatto and Windus, 1931).

'Florence Nightingale' by Lytton Strachey, from *Eminent Victorians* (London: Chatto and Windus, 1918).

'Behind the Tablet' by Christopher Sykes, from *Four Studies in Loyalty* (London: Collins Publishers, 1946), reprinted by permission of the author and his agents, Hughes Massie Ltd.